BEHIND THE EMBASSY DOOR

Canada, Clinton and Quebec

James J. Blanchard

SLEEPING
BEAR

PRESS

Sleeping Bear Press
121 South Main
P.O. Box 20
Chelsea, MI 48118
www.sleepingbearpress.com

Published in Canada by McClelland & Stewart Inc.

Printed and bound in Canada

10 9 8 7 6 5 4 3 2 1

Cataloguing-in-Publication Data on file.
ISBN 1–886947–59–7

CONTENTS

To my wonderful wife, Janet,
my Ambassadrina

PROLOGUE

U.S. Ambassador's residence, Ottawa, 8:15 p.m., October 30, 1995.

The polls have closed in Quebec. The TV commentators are saying what everybody knows: the referendum vote is going to be very close. Every ballot counts, and since every ballot is going to be counted by hand, it's going to be a long night. Janet and I have just finished dinner by the crackling fire. I found it hard to swallow, much less digest, my food, waiting for the numbers to start coming in. Now I'm feeling almost sick. Time seems to be standing still. It's like one of my own elections, especially the difficult night when I was defeated in Michigan in 1990 by the narrowest of margins. But this is worse, because the survival of a nation that we've come to know and love is at stake.

I'm thinking of the tens of thousands of Canadians who rallied to save their country in Montreal last week.

I'm thinking of all the friendly, understated, cheerful, earnest, naive, sincere, frugal, sensitive, nitpicky, hearty, wholesome, interesting, party-loving, and above all honorable people we've met across this beautiful country during the two years since our first marathon journey from Newfoundland to British Columbia in 1993. And I'm thinking of the hundreds of good friends we've made here, who welcomed us into their homes and made us part of the family. If I'm feeling the way I do at this moment, I can't imagine what they must be feeling, as their magnificent country stands at the precipice of destruction. My heart is with my old pal David Peterson, who first suggested I take this job, his wife, Shelley, and their kids; with Eddie Goldenberg and John Rae, who have fought the good fight on this and so many other battles; with Jean and Aline Chrétien, who have given so much of themselves out of their love of Canada.

In a couple of hours I'm going to have to go on "Nightline" to try to explain to my fellow Americans what's been going on up here. I'll need two scripts in my head, one for success, one for failure. How can I ever explain to them why Janet and I have come to feel so much affection for this crazy place? That would take a book. Maybe, if Canada and I survive tonight's vote, I will sit down some day, pull these journals together, and write one.

— *I* —

THE PRESIDENT CALLS

The call came around ten o'clock at night on Monday, December 21, 1992, long after I had given up expecting it ever would.

"Jim," said Warren Christopher, co-director of Bill Clinton's transition team and soon to be his secretary of state, "I'm calling on behalf of President-elect Clinton."

I was stunned. "Really?"

"We want to begin processing you to be secretary of Transportation. I know it's late and you're just returned to Michigan, and we don't want to interrupt your Christmas holidays, but we need to begin to vet you. I'm afraid that's going to require you to go back to Washington right away."

"That's great, Warren," I said, though I remained a bit suspicious. I had been hearing that they were thinking of several names for the post. "But, look, if you're asking me to go through this to make me feel good, then I'm not interested.

3

I've just got home to celebrate the holidays, I have my son here, my wife's about to fly in from Washington, and we're going to go out and buy a Christmas tree."

"No, no," he insisted. "You're it. Subject to the final, final decision by the president-elect, you're it. You're the only one we're looking at."

"When are you planning to make the announcement?" I asked.

"Wednesday, Thursday at the latest," Christopher said. "But it's a complicated business. We're going to need your tax returns, financial statements, all that stuff. One of our people, Jim Hamilton, will phone and put you in touch with Charles Ruff, who'll process you in Washington."

I hung up and told my son, Jay, the news. As it sunk in, we both became really excited, and I couldn't wait for my wife, Janet, to get home so we could share the excitement with her. Though I had been a congressman for eight years and governor of Michigan for eight years, being a member of the cabinet in charge of a major federal department was going to be a new challenge as well as a great honor. In fact, because of my interest in the automobile and aviation industries, Transportation was almost the only post that really attracted me and one of the few for which I felt truly qualified. Now, suddenly, it had been given to me, and I felt like a kid who had just received the most wonderful Christmas surprise ever.

The origins of that telephone call went back a decade, to late November 1982, when I first met Bill Clinton at an evening get-together held by Averell and Pamela Harriman in Washington, D.C. They were legendary figures. He was a former governor of New York, a distinguished ambassador to many posts, and Wise Man to several presidents; she was a glamorous hostess, active Democrat, and former daughter-in-law of Winston Churchill. So I was delighted when, shortly after being elected governor of Michigan for the first time, I was invited to meet some of the people who supported "Democrats for the 80s," the political action committee Pamela had founded.

Though Harriman himself was there, confined to a wheelchair, the reception was really Pamela's, and she was the one I came to know best in the years ahead. She liked people in power, she was interested in foreign policy, she later became an excellent diplomat as U.S. ambassador to France, but I felt that she was first and foremost a damn good politician. Because she was so beautiful and fit, even into her seventies, many people missed how bright and serious she was about ideas. And because she was so wealthy, with elegant homes in Virginia, Sun Valley, and Barbados, many people assumed that her main contribution to the Democratic Party was money. In fact, she relished politics, and her decades of knowledge and experience near the center of power in both England and the United States gave her a measured judgment about the ways of the world. To me, too, she was always loyal, generous, and never dull.

Among the other new governors present were Bob Kerrey of Nebraska and Bill Clinton of Arkansas. Pamela asked each of us to talk a little about how we got elected and what we hoped to do. And I remember thinking to myself at the time, boy, this guy Clinton is really charming. We took an immediate liking to each other.

Bill had been governor of Arkansas from 1979 to 1981 before being rudely defeated, and he had just staged a comeback for another two-year term. He was obviously ecstatic. Those two years out of office were so awful, he said, he had felt like walking around the state with a bag over his head. Instead, he had gone about begging forgiveness for having been too ambitious, too aggressive, too big for his breeches during his first term. He listened to the people's message and learned some humility, and I could see in his eyes that he was determined to govern with more care this time round.

I had been elected to one of Michigan's nineteen seats in the House of Representatives in November 1974, the same election in which Clinton lost his only run for Congress, but I never thought of him as younger or less experienced. On the contrary, I viewed him as a real political pro and looked to him for advice, precisely because he had known defeat and fought his way back from the wilderness. I was impressed, too, that he was the only Yale graduate and Rhodes Scholar I ever met who didn't somehow work into the first conversation that he was a Yale graduate and Rhodes Scholar. I assumed by his folksy manner and southern slang that he was just a good old boy from Arkansas.

I soon realized, of course, how intelligent, well-educated, and well-read Bill Clinton really was. And he may be the best American politician in modern times. People I know who worked with John Kennedy say that Clinton is even better on the hustings. In private, too, I found him warm, engaging, and fun. After that first encounter at Pamela's, Bill and I naturally gravitated toward each other at party events and governors' conferences. When the meetings, receptions, and dinners were over, we would invariably end up in the bar of some hotel, by ourselves or with a few others, having a nightcap, smoking cigars, and talking politics.

At one point I said to him, in private, that I thought he would make a great candidate for president someday. I could do no wrong after that, it seemed, and he began to confide in me from time to time. As host of the 1987 Governors' Conference in Traverse City, Michigan, I worked to promote him. It was there, I believe, that he gave his first public performance as a saxophonist.

If the presidency was Bill Clinton's ultimate ambition, it wasn't mine. I might have harbored that fantasy when I was eighteen, but my more realistic goal was to become a United States congressman. I achieved it at the age of thirty-two, and I didn't think that anything could ever match the thrill of being elected that first time. I went on to serve four two-year terms in Congress. By 1981 I was still a young man, riding high on having authored in the House the package that saved the Chrysler Corporation from bankruptcy. But Ronald Reagan was ruling the roost in Washington by that time, and the next few years didn't look like much fun for a Democratic congressman. If I were ever going to achieve something more in politics, it was the moment to go home and run for governor.

Michigan was flat on its back in those days. It had more unemployed people than the entire population of some states, it was tied with Puerto Rico for the lowest credit rating in the United States, and it was going through the toughest economic troubles since the Great Depression. After twenty years of Republican governors, I figured it was time for a Democrat with a whole new deal, based on the kind of coalition between business and labor I had helped forge during the Chrysler rescue effort. To make a long story short, I was elected governor in 1982 and again in 1986, with the largest plurality in the history of the state – and then lost by 16,000 votes on my third try in 1990.

This is not the place to fight old campaigns, so I'll just say that everything that could go wrong in that campaign did go wrong. My party was divided, and my opponent benefited from the abnormally low voter turnout. The fact that I should have run a better campaign bothered me more than losing it. I couldn't be governor of Michigan forever, after all, and it was easier on my psyche to know that I had lost by a hair and was leaving the governor's mansion having presided over the creation of 650,000 net new jobs and seen the state's credit rating raised to AA. So I quickly adjusted to the defeat and decided to get on with my life as a lawyer in Michigan and Washington.

One of the first calls I got was from Bill Clinton, who had just won his fifth term as governor of Arkansas. He sounded genuinely upset. "Let me tell you something," he said. "You've got to orchestrate your exit as carefully as possible, because, you never know, you might want to run again. Say a nice goodbye to everybody, be very careful, and whatever I can do, let me know."

A few months later, in February 1991, the Oakland County Democrats held a dinner in my honor, and they invited Governor Clinton to be the guest speaker. I urged him to accept: if he ever decided to be a candidate for president, Oakland County, in suburban Detroit, would be important. It is the second-largest county in Michigan and one of the most affluent in America. So he came, and at some point during that visit I offered to help him if and when he decided to run.

We bounced the idea back and forth all that spring and into the summer. In August he called to say he was close to a decision. His dilemma was whether to finish his term as governor (as he had declared he would) or run now and make use of the support system that came with being governor. "What do you think, Jim?"

"Number one," I said, "nobody ever talks anybody into – or out of – running for president. Number two, I've already said I'll help you in any way you want, though I can't do it full-time because I have to work for a living. Number three, these other guys like Gephardt, Rockefeller, and Bradley are thinking about not running because they think George Bush is invincible. Well, he may look invincible now, but I believe you're such a good candidate, you'll make such a positive impression on so many Democrats with your charm and capability, that you'll be poised for a bright future even if you don't win. You're from a small state, not many people know you, and I think you'll really stand out."

The next thing I knew, I was invited to a meeting of the Clinton Exploratory Committee on September 13th in Washington. It was a group of about twenty of Clinton's oldest, most intimate advisers, people like Sandy Berger, Vernon Jordan, Dick Riley, Harold Ickes, and Hillary Clinton. The subject was Bill's campaign. After a couple of hours of talk, I was bothered that no one had mentioned the one reservation I had been hearing over and over from party activists whenever Bill Clinton's name came up: the rumors of his womanizing. Not that I myself believed them. I had traveled throughout the country with Clinton in 1988, attending seminars and conferences as Democratic platform chairman, and I had never seen him with another woman in all that time. But I thought he needed to deal with the whispering campaign against him and have a short, honest answer that didn't invite further questions. So I raised the question.

You could have heard a pin drop. Then everybody said, yeah, yeah, he's right. "The answer," Bill finally said, "is that Hillary and I have had our ups and downs like every married couple, but we love each other and we've stayed together."

"That's a great answer," we all said. Hillary may have been annoyed with me for having raised the subject. I've never discussed it with her. But the truth is, I brought up the issue as an act of friendship. And since someone was bound to ask the question at some point, the meeting decided to defuse the issue by having the Clintons give that answer at a press breakfast a few weeks later. The strategy worked perfectly, at least until Gennifer Flowers showed up in the media the following January, claiming to have had an affair with Bill.

If charm had been my first impression of Bill, ambition was my first impression of Hillary. She seemed much more serious, disciplined, and focused than Bill, who's more the huggy, fuzzy extrovert. In that respect, they complement each other. And living with Bill Clinton can never have been easy. I often had the feeling she was working hard to keep him in politics and pay the bills. People admired her professional success, and they respected her for the sacrifices she had to make to help him.

Clinton decided to run for president, of course, and on October 3, 1991, I took a quick trip to Little Rock to watch him announce his candidacy. I brought with me a list of governors I had recruited on his behalf. Though I couldn't work flat out on the campaign, because my new law practice demanded a lot of time and attention, I was happy to help by writing strategic memos and putting together his team in Michigan. Meanwhile, my wife set up his Washington office with Gloria Cabe, Clinton's long-time staff member from Little Rock, and soon rose to a paid position as head of volunteers. After the Gennifer Flowers bombshell dropped during the New Hampshire primary, we both went into the state with three other Democratic governors to knock on doors, give speeches and press conferences, and generally "validate his character," as our task was called. Bill Clinton had been a good friend to me, and I wanted to be with him in victory or defeat.

"He seems like a decent enough guy," we heard wherever we went. "But how well do you really know him? And what's all this stuff about women?"

Janet and I both replied, "We think he'll make a great president." But, I admit, we had no idea how resilient he would prove to be.

As it turned out, Bill exceeded all expectations in that primary by coming in second and so made his reputation as "The Comeback Kid." Then he went on to win Georgia, (a campaign skilfully managed by my successor in Ottawa, Gordon Giffin) followed by eight primary victories on Super Tuesday. But the big question was whether he could win in the north. The pundits assumed he would take Illinois, but they didn't think he could carry Michigan because of his support for the North American Free Trade Agreement (NAFTA) with Canada and Mexico in the face of labor opposition. In fact, he won it two to one. That victory made it almost certain that Bill was going to be the Democratic nominee.

A few months later, in July, at the Democratic National Convention in New York City, I announced Michigan's vote for Governor Bill Clinton in Madison Square Garden, and that night Janet and I celebrated his nomination with his family and top staff in his hospitality suite at the Intercontinental Hotel. From then until election day in November, I worked almost full-time as co-chair of the Michigan campaign and Janet organized "Women for Clinton/Gore" there. Ultimately Bill Clinton carried our state, the first time a Democratic presidential candidate had won Michigan since 1968.

A week before the vote, I accompanied Bill to a rally in Saginaw. When we were alone in the car, I said, "It's all over. You're going to win, but it's kind of sad."

He looked at me as if I were crazy. "What do you mean?"

"Well," I said, "you're still a young man. But once you're president, you're never going to be young again."

The night before the election, at the end of one last swing through Michigan, I rode with him to the Detroit Metro

Airport. Just before he stepped into the plane, I said to him, "The next time I see you, Bill, you're going to be the president of the United States, and you're going to be a great president."

"You've been like a brother to me, Jim. You've been with me from way back."

"Yeah, and you would have won if you had run four years ago, but you weren't ready for the job. Now you are."

Along with other key supporters, Janet and I were invited to fly down to Little Rock for election night, but we wanted to celebrate with the magnificent team in Michigan. So the next time I saw Bill, now President-elect Clinton, was at a small victory party at Pamela Harriman's a few weeks later. "I want you to come down to Little Rock and talk to me," he said.

In all our discussions during the campaign, I had never spoken to Clinton about a job, should he win. Now I thought about it, and when asked by Clinton insiders, I let it be known I had some interest in Commerce or Transportation. Commerce went early to Ron Brown, chairman of the Democratic National Committee. As the weeks dragged on without any word from anyone, as key appointments were announced and rumors swirled about the others, I convinced myself that nothing was going to happen. Soon it was time to fly home to spend the Christmas holidays with Janet and Jay in our new home in suburban Detroit. And then the phone rang.

The morning after Warren Christopher's call, as requested, I returned to Washington to meet with Charles Ruff at his law firm. He already had a huge file on me – every job I had ever held, every political accusation ever leveled against me, all the tax returns my accountant had faxed him. After a couple of hours he said, "Everything seems to be in order. I've just got a few more things to check, and I want to call a few of your old friends and associates. Then I'll report back to Christopher that it looks fine. If I were you, I'd go home, book your tickets to Little Rock, sit tight, and wait for the final call."

So that's exactly what I did. I flew back to Michigan, made plane reservations from Detroit to Little Rock for late Wednesday afternoon, and took Janet and Jay out to dinner for a private celebration. Even though we had been sworn to secrecy, I started getting congratulatory calls from friends who had somehow heard the news. On Wednesday morning Charles Ruff phoned to say he had submitted his final report. "Everything's a go," he said. "You'll be hearing from him in an hour or two, so I hope you have your tickets."

Time passed slowly. Then I heard on CNN that Clinton was going to delay announcing five cabinet posts, including Transportation, until after the holidays. I thought that looked kind of sloppy, but it probably explained why I hadn't heard anything more. Around three o'clock Jim Hamilton, from the vetting team, phoned to say that Warren Christopher was meeting with Clinton at the governor's mansion. "I think there's a holdup," he said, "but it doesn't involve you." Nevertheless, given the CNN report and the late hour, I decided to postpone my flight to Little Rock until I got a definite go. I've often wondered how different my life would have been if Janet, Jay, and I had simply jumped on that plane and walked into that madhouse (which one participant likened to a chaotic game of musical chairs) and said, "Hi! We're here! When's the press conference?"

Later that night, around nine o'clock, I was on the phone with former Virginia Governor Jerry Baliles when Janet walked into the room and said there was a CNN report they'd picked Federico Peña for secretary of Transportation. Sure enough, CNN confirmed it half an hour later. I was flabbergasted! I mean, there I was with my wife and son, with not a Christmas tree or decoration up, and all I could get was Warren Christopher's voice mail.

Christopher called back the next morning. "Jim, I suppose you've heard the news. I'm really sorry. The president would have called you himself, but he had to do some last-minute Christmas shopping with Chelsea. The fact is, he wanted to name you, but the president felt very strongly that we needed two Hispanics in the cabinet. He was planning to name Bill Richardson as secretary of the Interior, but the environmental groups raised strong objections, so we're going with Bruce Babbitt for Interior and Federico Peña for Transportation. However, I am authorized to offer you deputy secretary of Transportation."

"No, you don't want to be offering me that," I said, trying to keep my feelings under control. "I'm not going to say anything, I'm not going to complain, I'm a team player, but I want to talk to Bill Clinton."

"Well, I'm sure he'll be happy to talk to you after the holidays."

I thanked him, but I was thoroughly disgusted by the whole process.

Whenever people ask me about Bill Clinton, I always say that it's easy to get to know him, but very hard to get to know him well. I thought I knew him really well up until this moment. Then I decided I didn't know him at all. When I hung up the phone, I remember wondering, how's my friend Bill going to explain treating a buddy this way? "He won't, he can't," a member of his staff told me later. "You'll never hear from him about it, he'll put it out of his mind, because he is unable to bring himself to deal with bad news."

I was reminded of that later, when I became ambassador to Canada and Clinton was in Ottawa on his first official visit. We were going over the final draft of his speech to the

House of Commons and he asked me what I thought they were hoping for. "They're hoping you're not going to speak as long as you did at this year's State of the Union address," I said jokingly. He gave me a hurt, bewildered look, as though nobody had told him that his eighty-five-minute speech had been the longest State of the Union address in American history. And that's when I knew for certain, however much I admired him, I could never have served on his staff.

Soon after all this, in fact, "Mack" McLarty, Clinton's childhood friend who was now his chief of staff, called to ask if I would become assistant to the president for personnel, but I said no. Janet did go into the White House, however, as office manager to the director of personnel during the transition and after the inauguration as associate director for presidential personnel for boards and commissions. After several similar offers, I even flew to Little Rock on January 14, 1993, to explain in person to McLarty why I didn't want to work in the White House. As I was leaving, he said that the president was waiting to meet with me. But, knowing that Clinton was going to try to talk me into taking a White House staff job I didn't want, I said I had to dash to a meeting I had scheduled in Chicago. Instead, I asked McLarty to give Clinton a note, which basically said that he needn't worry about Jim Blanchard, I was on his team, and I would always be his friend.

McLarty couldn't believe that I wouldn't meet with the president. "You mean to say, you flew all the way down here to tell me no and hand me this letter to pass on?"

"That's right," I said, and I left for Chicago.

And that was that, until I was invited to a small luncheon in the Library of Congress for governors, former governors, and their wives at the time of the inauguration. We were all standing around talking, maybe forty people in all, when

Clinton came in and started making the rounds. When he got to me, he gave me a huge bear hug and thanked me for my note. It was the closest he ever came to saying sorry for interrupting my Christmas holidays.

In retrospect, it was easy to forgive him. If I had been made secretary of Transportation, the department would have missed the valuable service of Federico Peña and I would have lost the opportunity to become ambassador to Canada – and the exciting life that unfolded for Janet and me in the invisible world next door.

⚊ ⚊

Early one December morning, between the election and the inauguration, while I was working out on my treadmill in our apartment in Virginia, I got a call from my good friend David Peterson. Currently a lawyer and businessman in Toronto, he had been premier of Ontario when I was governor of Michigan. In those days, whenever I was asked about the young leaders of the future, I used to say that the two sharpest people I'd met, with the greatest promise, were Bill Clinton of Arkansas and David Peterson of Ontario. My line, after David's defeat in September 1990, was that one of them went on to bigger, better things and the other became president of the United States. His response, after my own defeat two months later, was that we had much in common: we were born a year apart just two and a half hours from each other, he went into the provincial legislature the same year I was elected to Congress, he became premier shortly after I became governor, we shared the same political philosophy, and we both left office for reasons of health: the people were sick of us.

"So what's going on down there?" David asked. "Are you going to be in the government or what?"

"I don't think so," I said. "It looks like I'm condemned to making money."

"What about ambassador to Canada?" asked David. "You'd be perfect. For once we'd have somebody who knows something about Canada, and the American ambassador is a pretty important guy up here."

I had always dreamed of being an ambassador someday, but viewed it as something I would do later in life, perhaps to cap off a political career, and that's what I told David. He had planted a seed in my mind, however.

About three months later, on February 24th, on my first trip to the White House after the inauguration, I dropped in on my friend Bruce Lindsey, who was then serving as Clinton's director of personnel. "I wish you had taken this crazy job," he said. The White House was already suffering from disorganization and ineptitude.

"It wasn't something I wanted to do," I replied. "But, speaking of crazy, do you know how bizarre that whole business about my being secretary of Transportation was?"

Bruce kind of nodded and said, "Is there something else we can give you?"

"No, not really. The only thing, you know, is that at some point in the second term I'd like to be considered for ambassador to Canada or maybe Germany."

"At the rate we're going, there won't be a second term," he said. "Why not now?"

"No way," I said. "I've worked my whole life in politics and I've finally got a close friend in the Oval Office, so why would I want to leave town, let alone the country, just now?"

"Canada's not exactly Timbuktu," he answered. "But, look, while you're here, the president wants to say hi."

Bruce walked me into the little office that adjoins the Oval Office, and there was President Clinton all by himself. After a warm greeting, he gestured toward the shelves and said, "This is my presidential library, I've got all my books about American presidents here." Then he opened a closet door. Inside was a rack of golf putters. "You like golf," he said. "Here, take this. Bush left it behind." And he handed me a putter.

While we were chatting, Sandy Berger, Clinton's deputy national security adviser, came rushing in. "Excuse me, Jim," he said, "but, Mr. President, you need to call Brian Mulroney. He's just announced he's going to step down as prime minister of Canada."

Canada must have been in my stars because from that day on, I started hearing from my wife that there was regular talk at the White House personnel meetings about getting Jim Blanchard to go to Ottawa. "A lot of people want it," she said, "but I think they're holding it for you." Partly, I suspected, because they felt guilty that I had been left out of the cabinet. Partly, I was told, because they wanted somebody with my qualifications in that job. One day I got a call from Pamela Harriman, who had already been designated for France, and she told me that the State Department also thought that I'd be the ideal choice. "It's a great place," she said. "You'd be crazy not to take it."

Everything seemed to conspire to get me to accept. On April 2nd Janet and I went to Long Boat Key, Florida, for a vacation. Just as we arrived, I turned on the TV and saw Bill Clinton and Boris Yeltsin at their first summit meeting, hosted by Brian Mulroney, in Vancouver, British Columbia. Hey, that looks exciting, I thought. Just then I got a call from Tom Weston, a college friend who had just been made deputy assistant secretary of state for European and Canadian affairs in the State Department.

"I don't know if you're aware of this," he said, "but we're sitting over here at the State Department with your name penciled in for Canada or Germany. Either one is probably yours if you want it. I hope you realize that very few people ever get an opportunity like this. I'd advise you to do Canada. It's perfect for you. It's a better fit and you don't speak German. Besides, being ambassador to Canada is the next best thing to being a member of the cabinet. You get to deal with every issue, you get to deal with every department, you coordinate the whole thing, and Ottawa is an extremely beautiful city with a wonderful house and a beautiful office on Parliament Hill. It is a good use of your experience and it would prepare you to serve in almost any department in our government afterwards. I think you should grab it."

At that moment something clicked. What Janet had been telling me, what I saw from Vancouver on TV, and my respect for Tom's opinion as a career foreign service officer all propelled me to call Bruce Lindsey to check if Canada were still open. "So you're finally getting interested," he said. "Yes, we've been holding it for you, but we can't hold it much longer. If you want it, it's probably doable, but we need to know fairly soon."

That afternoon Janet and I did a little research. We went into a bookstore in Long Boat Key on the slight chance that it had a book or two about Canada. Instead, we found walls of Canadian books and all the major newspapers from Montreal and Toronto! In fact, once we started paying attention, it seemed as though half the town was made up of Canadian tourists or winter residents. It looks like I'm destined for Canada, I said, laughing. By the time I got back to Washington, I had a lot more material about Canada, the Embassy, and the issues, and I was ready and eager to serve.

Almost all I knew of Canada up to that point was southwestern Ontario and Toronto. As a very young child growing up in the Detroit suburb of Ferndale, Michigan, about ten miles – north! – from the border, I remember being driven through the tunnel under the Detroit River to Windsor, Ontario, and realizing for the first time that Canada was a foreign country right next door to the United States. It even struck me as foreign, with its own kind of signs and money. I thought the border guards somewhat cold and formal. I was interested to see that there were more fireworks for sale than were available at home. And I noticed that the Ford cars had different names and grillwork. But I also learned right off the bat that Americans and Canadians had much in common. Windsor, after all, being so close to Detroit and so tied to the automotive economy, was seen almost as another Michigan suburb, and masses of people traveled back and forth across the border every day without a passport or hassle.

In those days the Detroit area got an extra television station, in addition to ABC, NBC, and CBS, for we picked up the Canadian Broadcasting Corporation through CKLW in Windsor. As a result, I was exposed at an early age to more things Canadian, including Canadian politics and Canadian football, than most Americans. I remember, for example, following the 1957 election in which John Diefenbaker first became prime minister. And when my mother and I took the shortcut from Detroit to Boston by driving through Ontario to Niagara Falls, I remember how excited I was as a thirteen-year-old boy to pass by the stadium in which the Hamilton Tiger-Cats played.

In 1959, my sister Suzanne married Bob Brook, a Canadian-born naturalized citizen she had met at Michigan State University, and in 1970 they moved to London, Ontario. I visited them regularly for more than a decade. In June 1985, two years after becoming governor of Michigan, I was at the wedding of their son Jeff in London when I first heard about David Peterson. Himself a native of London, David had just become the Liberal premier of Ontario after forty-two years of Conservative rule. "I've only been in your country less than twenty-four hours," I joked with the Canadians at the reception, "and I've already toppled a Tory government!" As the Democratic governor from a neighboring state, I thought I should get to know him, so I phoned him a few days later. We began working together, and we've been working together ever since. He's still my best friend in Canada, and his family is like my own.

I often say, when talking about American-Canadian relations, that the true cradle of cooperation is Michigan and Ontario. The two-way trade between them is larger than the trade between most nations and far exceeds the trade between Canada and any other country. Of the $365 billion of trade between the United States and Canada in 1997, it was estimated that $100 billion of it moved across Ambassador Bridge between Detroit and Windsor. The Auto Pact of 1965, so pivotal to the integrated economies of Michigan and Ontario, was the forerunner of the Free Trade Agreement of 1989 and NAFTA in 1993. And the International Joint Commission, whose most important responsibility these days is to monitor the water quality of the Great Lakes, was created in 1909 by the first environmental treaty between our two countries with the mandate to manage the health of our boundary waters. During my time as governor of Michigan, I was continually involved in economic, environmental, and tourism discussions with Ontario officials.

I was really pleased, therefore, when President Clinton called me on May 10, 1993, and said, "Jim, I want you to be my ambassador to Canada."

"Great," I said.

"I want to put people who are close to me in key ambassadorial posts," he explained, "so that the countries will know they're important to the United States."

To gauge how important Canada was in his eyes, I asked how often he had been there. Several times, it turned out: to Montreal, to Ottawa, to Vancouver and Victoria – and he had loved it. Hillary had even driven the Trans-Canada Highway in her youth. "They're good people there," the president said. As a matter of fact, he added, he had made up his mind to run for the presidency while he and Hillary were on a short vacation in Victoria in the summer of 1991. That kind of positive exposure, which is rarer for a Southerner than for someone from New York or Michigan, would make my new job easier, I thought to myself. And I thanked my lucky stars that I didn't have to lobby and then wait end-lessly, like some ambassadors do, to be given such a wonder-ful appointment.

According to diplomatic protocol, the White House wouldn't announce my appointment until Canada had approved it by what's termed an *agrément*, which eventually came through on May 21st. Until the president's announce-ment on May 27th, however, I was pledged to secrecy, which proved a farce in a leaky town like Washington. When I showed up at Pamela Harriman's swearing-in as ambassador to France on May 21st, about half the State Department people in the room seemed to have heard the news, perhaps because it had been reported in that day's *Toronto Star*. I even got a hug from the wife of the British ambassador. Meanwhile, I had already been receiving calls from friends in Washington and Lansing who had been contacted by security agents asking provocative questions.

The worst part of the entire job turned out to be the mountain of paperwork I was given to complete at that stage, though mine was smaller than most because I had just been vetted for a cabinet post and had been a public official for almost two decades. I didn't have any unexpected personal secrets to reveal or complicated financial arrangements to disclose. Even so, it took me weeks to complete the dozens of documents, questionnaires, and forms. By the time I got through all the details about every place I had ever lived and every neighbor I had ever had, I declared that nothing could ever be more tedious, arduous, or time-consuming. "The long nightmare is over!" I shouted to my secretary. "Praise the Lord!"

Once that was done, preparing to go to Canada became enormously interesting and enjoyable. Because we still had an apartment in Washington, I could immerse myself in preparing for the job. I ceased to practice law full-time. I consulted as many cabinet members, senators, Canada-watchers, and former ambassadors to Canada as would see me. And I started meeting three or four times a week with the seven State Department experts at the Canada Desk (actually a suite of offices on the fifth floor, which for historic reasons was included in the European bureau) and getting briefed by every other relevant section at State. The Canadian agenda, I discovered, was huge: there were files on some seventy-five different issues, from beer to cruise missiles to acid rain, not to mention NAFTA, NATO, NORAD, and the independence of Quebec, each with a short summary of its history and the U.S. position. At least half of the items were trade issues, which was perhaps predictable given the size of our trading relationship.

The modern State Department had been set up by General George C. Marshall, the former head of the Joint Chiefs of Staff during World War II who later became Secretary of State, and it retained the air of a military organization, replete with a military-style command system and military-style secrecy. Indeed, the State Department is the largest intelligence-gathering operation in the world – far bigger than the Central Intelligence Agency, the National Security Agency, or the Federal Bureau of Investigation – though its information doesn't come from covert or clandestine sources. It has diplomats and sources in virtually every country in the world sending back cables and reports that are read, filed, and passed along. Between two-thirds and three-quarters of the president's national security briefing each morning comes from State Department sources.

One day Janet and I were invited to the Office of Foreign Buildings, where we saw photographs of each room in the ambassadorial residence in Ottawa. We were allowed to make color changes ("No, leave it as it is," we said, but when we got there we found they had painted every wall beige!). We were told how many personal belongings we could ship at government expense. We were shown samples of the china and crystal and a computerized inventory of every spoon and cup for which we would be personally accountable.

Then we were enrolled in the series of ambassadorial seminars known affectionately as "Charm School." (When I asked Pamela Harriman about it, she said, "I didn't go. I've had my own tutors.") They lasted about two weeks and included everything a new ambassador, especially a political appointee with no experience in diplomacy, might need to know, from the essential to the mundane: how the department works, how an embassy functions, what an ambassador does, how to behave in certain situations, how to write a diplomatic cable, how to do a TV interview. We were briefed, for example, about the Arts in the Embassy program, which had been created in 1974 to promote American artists abroad. It turned out to have different security classifications, from safe embassies to high-risk, in order to protect the borrowed works. I could get just about anything I wanted for Ottawa, but when one of my colleagues said he was bound for Chad, he was told, "You, sir, will get a John Lennon poster!"

Later we traveled to Fort Bragg to learn how to cope with a terrorist attack. We heard from the assistant secretary for economic affairs, the assistant secretary for narcotics, and others. Ultimately we met with the deputy secretary and the secretary of state themselves. There were about a dozen in our "class," destined for Taiwan, Uruguay, Croatia, or the European Union, and they were a mixture of career officers and neophytes. Most countries, including Canada, select their ambassadors from a highly skilled, somewhat esoteric corps of foreign-service professionals. The United States has always been different. By law our ambassadors aren't simply representatives of the country; they're appointed by the president, with the advice and consent of the Senate, to be his *personal* representative abroad. He can appoint whomever he wants, therefore, and that has often meant that the most prestigious appointments go to close friends or strong supporters.

In earlier years there had been complaints about the number of big-money socialites being given plum posts, so the White House agreed to a formula in which seventy percent of our ambassadors would be career foreign service officers and thirty percent non-career. Presidents have been more or less bound to it. And though there have been traditions about which countries are career, and which are non-career or political, there are no hard-and-fast rules. Canada, like Japan, Mexico, or Germany, has usually had a mixture of career and political as U.S. ambassadors.

It's to Clinton's credit, I believe, that a high percentage of his non-career ambassadors were, in fact, career public servants, such as Walter Mondale, Admiral William Crowe, Congressman Jim Jones, Stuart Eizenstat, and myself, all of whom had been involved in government issues and foreign policy for many years. Sometimes, in fact, ambassadorial appointments are easier for people like us than for State Department lifers who have become accustomed to low-level management and keeping their heads down. They're not always used to leading or being in charge; they're not often comfortable with media attention or high-powered politicians; and it can be quite an adjustment. In fact, I probably had a broader hands-on experience with public policy as a congressman and governor than many foreign-service officers in the State Department. And an ambassadorship can also be a real adjustment for some business people or others who have had no experience in public life. They often start with an anti-government bias that sees the State Department types as un-American know-nothings or officious bureaucrats who've never had to meet a payroll. Again, those of us with a public-service record tend to have a more positive attitude.

Going in, I expected to encounter some resentment by the foreign service of my political background. I found, on the contrary, that the majority saw my previous experience as an asset and bent over backwards to make me feel welcome. More than most citizens, members of the foreign service and career government officials are much more likely to view government as an important force for good, which puts them closer to the Democrats than the Republicans. That's not to say I haven't met plenty of Republicans in the foreign service, but the majority would probably lean toward the internationalist, free trade, pro-defense wing of the Democratic Party.

All through June and into July I continued to bone up on Canadian history and politics, attend State Department briefings, and extricate myself from my law practice. I was repeatedly cautioned not to say anything or meet with anybody that appeared to presume my Senate confirmation as the ambassador to Canada. It's never a done deal until you are confirmed by the Senate, and nothing angers senators more than having their approval taken for granted. Thus, when Prime Minister Mulroney came to Washington on his farewell tour of major world capitals and expressed an interest in a brief, informal get-together, I had to risk insulting him by declining. Nor was I allowed to have any business meetings with the Canadian ambassador, John de Chastelain, though Janet and I did sneak over to his residence one Sunday afternoon for a cocktail party.

Conditional on my confirmation, I interviewed people for the two embassy positions I was allowed to fill among the huge staff I would inherit. I was extremely fortunate to find Joanne Holliday to be my secretary in Ottawa and Jim Walsh, a highly regarded career foreign-service officer who was just returning from a post in Argentina, to be my deputy chief of mission.

The final and most important hurdle was my confirmation hearing before the Senate's Foreign Relations Subcommittee on Western Hemisphere Affairs. It was held on the morning of July 20th, along with those of Jeffrey Davidow and Thomas Dodd Jr., bound for Venezuela and Uruguay respectively. Such hearings can be a nerve-racking experience – the State Department even prepares its nominees for any tough questions by putting them through a mock hearing known ominously as the "murder board," but I didn't feel particularly nervous about it. I had served in Congress; I had testified before Congress many times as governor; I had made myself available to talk to any senator who was interested in Canada; and there were no controversial issues involving me.

After my brief opening statement, Senator Chris Dodd (D-Connecticut), the chairman of the panel and an old friend of mine, asked me what the United States might do if Quebec separated from Canada. I was ready for that, of course, and refused to speculate, though I did say that we have always enjoyed an excellent relationship with a strong and united Canada. Senator Richard Lugar (R-Indiana) asked if I intended to remain involved in Michigan politics, and I replied that I had no plans to do so. When Jesse Helms (R-North Carolina) stated that we seemed like well-qualified nominees, I knew that the rest of the hearing would be routine. The whole thing lasted about an hour and concluded without a hitch. Ten days later, July 30th, the final senate confirmation came by unanimous consent.

Finally, just three months after the president's call (a record time), at 11:30 on the morning of August 10th, under a beautiful blue sky, I was sworn in at an outdoor ceremony on the front lawn of the White House. Most ambassadors are sworn in either at a small, private ceremony in the State Department or at a large and fairly formal event, usually in its Benjamin Franklin Room, with several hundred friends, guests, and family members. Sometimes, for prominent ambassadors, the vice-president will issue the oath. By law the president can't. In my case, because I knew both the president and vice-president personally, and because I wanted to use the occasion to convey Canada's importance to the United States, I had asked if it were possible for me to be sworn in at the White House with the president presiding. He agreed.

It had to be a small ceremony, held on short notice to fit his schedule. President Clinton gave a short speech, Vice-President Al Gore administered the oath, and Janet held the Bible. Those present included my mother, Rosalie, and her husband, Baxter Webb; my son, Jay; my sister and brother-in-law; a couple of dozen friends, law partners, and staff members; Ambassador de Chastelain and representatives of the Canadian media. After I gave a few remarks, I officially became the eighteenth Ambassador Extraordinary and Plenipotentiary of the United States of America to Canada.

"When I nominated Jim Blanchard for this post," the president said in his brief but generous remarks, "it was a sign of the importance I place on our relations with Canada. For our relationship with Canada is unquestionably one of our most important in the world."

~ 2 ~

THE INVISIBLE WORLD

NEXT DOOR

Janet and I were eager to go to Ottawa and see our new home. We also needed to figure out what to bring, and I wanted to see my office. So, on August 3rd, one week before my swearing-in and two weeks before our official arrival, we slipped quietly into Ottawa for a half-day visit. We had to fly from Baltimore, because there was no direct Washington-Ottawa flight linking our two capitals. I found that hard to believe, but it was the result of an outdated aviation agreement that I had already learned was one of our most difficult and long-standing issues with Canada. This first, frustrating experience reinforced my vow to get it resolved.

I had been to Canada's capital once before, on a cold and rainy day in March 1988. Prime Minister Brian Mulroney had invited me, along with several other Great Lakes governors, to visit with him to discuss the Free Trade Agreement that was then being negotiated between our two countries. After a brief meeting in his office, we had lunch at our ambassador's residence and flew out again. Both Ottawa and the ambassador's residence were only dim memories, marred by the gray weather.

This time, however, things were entirely different. Ottawa was enjoying a gorgeous summer day, and both Janet and I were dazzled by the beauty of the Ottawa Valley from the air, its old villages, its tidy farms, its rolling hills, and the magnificent river flowing between Ontario and Quebec from the northern woodlands down to Montreal. It was a wondrous sight to behold, and it increased our excitement about the new life that was about to unfold. We were also struck by how quiet and orderly the airport seemed, compared to almost any airport in the United States. (As we would eventually discover, the whole country is quieter and more orderly.) We were met by Vaughn Cameron, a Canadian army veteran from Nova Scotia who had been chauffeuring our ambassadors for twenty years in what looked to have been the same old, oversized Cadillac with flags flapping pretentiously on the front fender. I made it a priority to get a newer, less ostentatious car. It took a month to locate and ship a Lincoln Town Car from a State Department warehouse in Maryland, but at least I was able to get rid of the flags at once.

As we drove into town, alongside the meandering Rideau Canal, which had been built in the early nineteenth century to link the Ottawa River with Lake Ontario (and which is now used as the world's longest skating rink in winter), the sky and water were intensely blue, the grass and trees were a surreal green, the streets and houses were spick-and-span. There were no billboards. Instead of shopping centers and

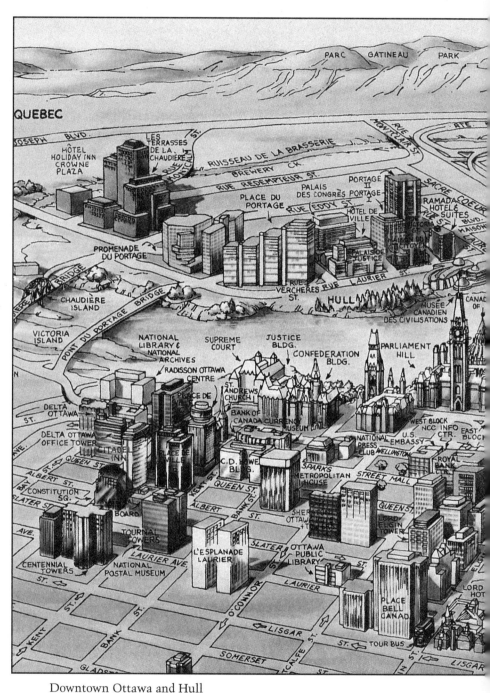

Downtown Ottawa and Hull
© 1998/89/86 Unique Media Inc., Toronto

strip malls, there seemed only to be bright flowers and tall evergreens in scores of parks. The neo-Gothic Parliament Building with its tall bell tower and ornate facade looked like a piece of Victorian London dropped into the wilds of North America. The place was so picturesque, it seemed like a storybook illustration of the capital of a gentle kingdom, and much more European than I had expected. "This is going to be even better than I thought," I said, and I was pleased to see how happy Janet looked.

We drove by the Chateau Laurier, the grand old hotel that looks like a huge castle with its turrets and arches, and along Sussex Drive, which boasts the new National Gallery, a cliff-top view of the Ottawa River, the stately residences of the British and French ambassadors, Canada's foreign ministry, the City Hall, and the elegant home of the prime minister. Passing Rideau Hall, the park-like estate of the governor general, we entered Rockcliffe, Ottawa's most exclusive residential quarter, a quiet, wooded village in which a host of cabinet ministers, senior civil servants, diplomats, and high-tech millionaires reside. And, among its grand houses, none is grander than "Lornado," the American ambassador's residence since 1935, a thirty-two-room, three-story limestone mansion built by a railway tycoon in 1908 and set at the top of a long, winding drive in twelve acres of gardens and pine trees. When an old friend of ours from Flint, Michigan, a mortician by trade, came to visit, he said, "Hey! This place would make a great funeral home." But we never found anything eerie about it, except perhaps for the rabid raccoon that once evaded all our traps on the eve of a big lawn party.

The house is perched on the highest point of land in the region, which means that it offers panoramic views down to where the Gatineau River meets the Ottawa River and across to the Gatineau Hills in Quebec – refreshing blues and greens in summer, phantasmagoric colors in autumn, blinding white in winter. It is an enthralling site from which to watch thunderstorms and blizzards, gentle sunrises and flaming sunsets. Indeed, the sentimental old song "Canadian Sunset" became an anthem for us because we spent so many delightful evenings watching the sun go down from the picture window in the living room, the glassed-in porch, or the stone patio. I came to call that living-room window my "window on the world," and I never got tired of its vista. In fact, for all the size and grandeur of the house, it had a remarkable intimacy and comfort, certainly compared to the more formal and high-maintenance palace Pamela Harriman had in Paris. "Lornado" could accommodate all the overnight guests and diplomatic functions we had, without losing the sense that people were coming into our home, replete with cozy chairs, four fireplaces, and a blissful tranquillity. It felt like a true home to us because we ended up living there together longer than anywhere else to date.

The first thing I did, in fact, was carry Janet over the threshold, just like I had at the governor's residence in Michigan the day we married in 1989 and again the day we left it for private life. The seven members of the household staff, who were all lined up in the foyer, looked at us as though we were a bit wacky. They soon got used to our funny ways, of course, and we soon became familiar with theirs too. I sometimes felt as though we were living in the famous TV series, "Upstairs, Downstairs," about the interwoven lives of a family and their servants in aristocratic England. We got to know all about their disputes and their dreams, their foibles and their attributes, their crises and their successes, and they became like kin to us.

Unlike many American embassies around the world, the residence (which is technically the embassy) and the executive offices (called the Chancery) are separated in Ottawa by a ten-minute drive. So, after lunch, we went downtown to see where I was going to work. The Chancery was still located in its home since 1932, an imposing and very distinguished neo-Renaissance building directly across Wellington Street from the lawns of Parliament Hill, though plans had been under way to construct a larger, more contemporary building on Sussex Drive between the Chateau Laurier and the National Gallery. My office turned out to be a palatial room – much nicer than I had had as either a congressman or governor – with North Carolina pine paneling, a Vermont marble fireplace, an oriental rug, glass chandeliers, and ceiling-to-floor windows and French doors that opened up to a superb view of the Parliament Buildings. I was told that former prime minister Pierre Elliott Trudeau had thought it should be the prime minister's office, because of its location and grandeur, and once the Canadian government takes over the building in 1999, it may become exactly that.

About eighty people worked in this building on everything from agricultural issues to trade disputes to law enforcement to foreign policy. Another two hundred or so military, commercial, cultural, customs, and immigration personnel were scattered next door and in various buildings around town, and several hundred others were sprinkled across the country in our six consulates in Halifax, Quebec City, Montreal, Toronto, Calgary, and Vancouver. Because of their size, range of activity, charming facilities, and proximity to the United States, the consulates themselves are among the most highly sought-after posts by foreign-service officers in the State Department, and I made it a point to visit them as often as possible.

Janet and I were thrilled by everything we had seen, and we couldn't wait till we would be coming back to Canada to get to work.

— —

Two weeks later, on August 17th, we returned to Ottawa for my official arrival. This time we were greeted by our top embassy staff, all lined up in a row headed by Jim Walsh, as well as a Canadian protocol officer. "Have you ever been to Ottawa before?" he asked.

"Yes," I said. "It's very beautiful."

"Borrrrr-ing!" he corrected. I realized I had met my first, classic, self-effacing Canadian. "The best thing about Ottawa is that it's only two hours from Montreal," he added. I heard that line a lot in the next three years. But Ottawa was far from boring. That very day, for example, I found myself enjoying a previously scheduled luncheon at the residence for seventy-five senior judges (including U.S. Supreme Court Justice Anthony Kennedy), who were attending a convention. It was great fun and very interesting. Though I couldn't officially preside at it, since I hadn't yet presented my credentials to the Canadian government, Jim Walsh joked to the learned judges that I was their host *de facto* if not *de jure*.

Two days later I performed my first official ambassadorial duty by presenting my credentials to the governor general, Ray Hnatyshyn, a former Conservative cabinet minister from Saskatchewan who had become the Queen's representative in Canada in 1990. Some of our friends who came up from Michigan and Washington for the ceremony had a hard time understanding his role. I tried to explain, usually without much success, that the governor general was appointed by the Queen of England, but selected by the prime minister of Canada for a five-year term; that he was the head of state, but not the head of government; that he was commander-in-chief, but never made military decisions; and that he signed the laws, but did not make them.

For Americans, of course, the president is the embodiment of both the state and the government. He presides over the ceremonial duties in addition to governing. (And since he derives a certain amount of political popularity from doing the ceremonial, he's not likely to give it up to someone else.) Even though we are fundamentally an anti-government nation that regularly beats the daylights out of our politicians in the press, we often elevate our presidents into quasi-deities. Canadians, on the other hand, seem averse to allowing their prime minister to claim the flag, so to speak. They don't want to put their politicians on that pedestal. Countless Canadians told me that Brian Mulroney's most unforgivable mistake was to try to make the prime minister-ship presidential, to the point of upstaging his own governor general during a visit by President Reagan to Quebec City in March 1985.

Shortly after eleven o'clock on the morning of August 19th – the birthday, I noted in my journal, of both Bill Clinton and Al Gore's wife, Tipper – all decked out in a fitted morning coat and striped trousers, I was driven a few blocks from our new home to the front gates of Rideau Hall, where I had to climb into a horse-drawn landau along with Larry Lederman, Canada's chief of protocol, and an aide-de-camp. We clip-clopped up the long drive, escorted by scarlet-uniformed Mounties on each side and followed by soldiers in tall bearskin hats, until we reached the enormous house. Larry gave a special knock upon the door, some kind of traditional code to allow entry, and we entered the front hall for a procession into the ballroom, where the invited guests and the governor general were waiting.

The rest, which I will paraphrase from the official "Order of Ceremony for Letters of Credence", can best be imagined as a slow-motion pantomime. The ambassador (that's me) and the protocol officer entered the ballroom and proceeded to the center, where they bowed to the governor general. The protocol officer presented the ambassador to the governor general. The ambassador addressed a short speech to the governor general, stepped forward, handed his Letters of Credence to His Excellency, and returned to his place. The governor general handed the Letters of Credence to the government representative, who handed them to the secretary. After a few words from the governor general, the ambassador stepped forward and shook hands with His Excellency. The governor general then presented the government representative to the ambassador. The ambassador, moving to the right-hand side of the ballroom, presented his spouse to His Excellency and, moving to the left-hand side, presented the members of the embassy delegation. Following which, the governor general, the ambassador (on his right), and the government representative (behind) left the ballroom and proceeded to His Excellency's study where they conversed for about ten minutes. Refreshments were served. In the meantime, the ambassador's spouse, the embassy delegation and the members of the household proceeded to the Long Gallery, where refreshments were also served and the secretary proposed a toast to the ambassador's spouse. Once the "tête-à-tête" between the governor general and the ambassador was finished (along with the ceremonial glass of champagne), they were escorted to the Petit Salon, where two photographs were taken: one of the governor general and the ambassador together and one of them with the government representative. Then the ambassador took leave of His Excellency and was escorted to the Long Gallery – whereupon he grabbed his wife and skedaddled home as quickly as possible for the happy celebration, with hundreds of dignitaries, family members, American visitors, and embassy personnel, on the sun-drenched patio overlooking the river and the hills.

It was my first experience of how seriously Canadians take their protocol. It must have stemmed, I suppose, from the British and French connections. It certainly wasn't like anything I was used to seeing in the United States. I never even had a chief of protocol in Michigan, yet I was constantly greeted by one wherever I went in Canada, whether Saskatchewan, Newfoundland, or Quebec. The length of Vice-President Gore's official visit to Ottawa in July 1994 was unfortunately cut in half because Canadian protocol officers thought it would be improper for the prime minister to go to dinner with a mere vice-president at our residence.

This obsession with proper behavior manifests itself in Canadians in various ways. They are sticklers about punctuality and keeping their word, and they may be the most honorable and polite people in the world. They were certainly the most dependable people I've ever lived or worked among. If you agree to meet someone at six in the morning at the corner of Sussex Drive and Wellington Street, and it's thirty below in a blizzard, most Americans won't show up and some won't even call. They'll assume you know the weather is bad and there's no sense in going out. But the Canadians would be there – probably early.

I didn't know it at the time, but one small item almost destroyed this heavenly day. Even before my arrival I had been under pressure to show up at an Ottawa Rough Riders football game scheduled for that evening. "It's practically a tradition for the new American ambassador to go and throw the football before the game," my new commercial counselor informed me. "Besides, the owner's a guy from Michigan – he's been giving us free tickets, so you really should."

"Politicians who go to sporting events in the United States get booed," I said.

"You'll never get booed in Canada. You're the American ambassador."

"Maybe," I argued, "but I don't think it's in good taste that the first thing I do in Canada is throw a ball at a football game. Tell him I'll come and sit in his box for a little while, that's all."

When I happened to mention it to Vaughn Cameron as he was driving me around town, he only frowned. "Oh, I'd stay away from that, sir. The guy's fallen into real disfavor here. Everybody was all excited when he bought the team, but things haven't turned out too well. He's quarreling with the city about some subsidy he says he was promised, and the team's losing bad."

"Well, I did say I wouldn't throw the ball."

"No way you want to do that, sir," he said. "You don't want to be seen as some pushy American throwing the ball around. Still, I wouldn't trust those people. You get over there, he'll start yelling your name over the loudspeaker, and then, bang, before you know it he's put a ball in your hand. It's pretty risky, sir."

"So you think I've been ill-advised by my staff?"

"Between you and me, sir, let's just say they don't know what's happening on the ground," Vaughn confided. "And they're getting free tickets, after all."

"My instincts are with you on this one, Vaughn. I think we'd better tell the Ottawa Rough Riders that something's come up, I've got to get back to Michigan, I'm leaving tonight."

The next morning, after a wonderful dinner at home with our out-of-town visitors, Vaughn handed me the newspapers just as Janet and I got in the car for the airport. And there was a big story about what had happened at the game. The owner had had a tantrum, stormed on to the field, harassed a player, and threatened to fire his coach.

"Vaughn," I laughed, "you're my new top political adviser." And, from that point on, whenever I had a tough problem, I'd always ask him what he thought my predecessors would have done.

— —

Now formally installed in the job, I went home to Michigan with Janet to pack our boxes and say goodbye to friends, then drove back to Canada on August 28th to begin work. Just fifteen miles from our home, we came through the tunnel to Windsor, Ontario. There we were stopped for a routine check at the border by a Canadian immigration officer. "What's the purpose of your visit?" he asked.

"We're moving to Canada," I said. "I'm the new American ambassador."

"Are you landed?" he asked.

He must have thought I meant I was a landed immigrant.

"No, I'm an American."

Then he asked if my working papers were in order. Thinking back to all the forms I had filled out for the State Department and the Senate, I answered yes, and he waved us through.

It's a five hundred-mile drive from Detroit to Ottawa, which can take ten or twelve hours if there isn't a blizzard or traffic jam. On this trip, however, we stopped overnight at David and Shelley Peterson's farm in London, Ontario. My job began then and there, for David's friend Tom Hockin, Canada's minister for international trade in Prime Minister Kim Campbell's government, and Shelley's father, Don Matthews, a businessman and Conservative Party activist, came by and wanted to talk politics over dinner. "If we lived in the United States," Hockin surprised me by saying, "Kim Campbell and I would be Democrats." The next day, within hours of arriving at our new home in Ottawa, I was invited to a luncheon for NATO ambassadors with Perrin Beatty, the Canadian foreign affairs minister. The day after that, I got a call from Bob Rae, the premier of Ontario, whose leftist New Democratic Party had defeated David Peterson's Liberals in 1990, inviting Janet and me to dinner at his summer cottage on Big Rideau Lake, about fifty miles south of Ottawa.

When we got there, we had to take a boat across to a small island, where we were greeted by Bob and his wife, Arlene. Bob had just been swimming and he soon gave us a demonstration of his loon calls. Because he had defeated my friend Peterson, I was inclined not to like him, but a lot of people told me he was a pretty good guy personally, even when they viewed him as a socialist who had stumbled into office, was piling up enormous deficits in the province, and opposed NAFTA. Our visit was a social one, but we talked politics into the night. He had a serenity about him, which impressed me, given how unpopular his party was at the time. He admitted that his chances of re-election weren't great. "I'm just trying to do what's right," he shrugged, "and hope it works out."

Then, on September 2nd, I was invited to meet with Prime Minister Kim Campbell in her office on Parliament Hill. Bright, blonde, vivacious, and young, she had succeeded Brian Mulroney the previous June as leader of the Progressive Conservative Party and prime minister of Canada. Mulroney was a likeable guy – everybody down in Washington liked him – but it was understood in the State Department and in our Ottawa embassy that he had fallen into disfavor with

Canadians. In part this was because he had been nine years in power, in part because he had been seen as too cozy with us, and he wisely left office while he was still on top. Campbell was seen (to use a football metaphor) as a last-ditch, Hail Mary pass to save the Conservatives. Though she had served as minister of justice and national defense, she came across in the media as quick-witted and fresh-sounding. So far, according to the summer polls, the strategy appeared to be working: her popularity had soared to a record level, though my staff in Ottawa was still predicting that the Liberal Party under Jean Chrétien was going to defeat her.

Unlike an American president, the prime minister is free to call an election at any time during a five-year term, but the Conservatives' five years were nearly up. What I was hearing was that Canadians were uncertain, at a time of deep recession and high unemployment, whether the Free Trade Agreement (FTA) of 1989 had been such a good deal. As a result, any one of a number of trade disputes, from beer to lumber to sugar to wheat, could erupt into a campaign issue, and though NAFTA had been negotiated by the Conservative government and passed by the House of Commons, it hadn't yet been officially proclaimed into law.

As part of my indoctrination, I had received a long and interesting memo from Dell Pendergrast, my public affairs officer at our embassy, outlining the situation. "The arrival of a new ambassador in Ottawa occurs in a public affairs climate where Canadian attitudes toward the U.S. are dominated by certain basic features," he wrote. "Widespread public belief that Canada-U.S. free trade is a mistake that hurt Canada and deepened the recession. The belief that the FTA crippled Canadian manufacturing through a massive job exodus to the U.S. is now a political correctness in Canada, which also colors the attitudes toward NAFTA.... The Mulroney/

Reagan/Bush era was widely viewed as Canadian subordination and obsequiousness. Canadians ultimately want the benefits of close relations with the U.S. while retaining a strong sense of national identity and independence."

"You're coming at a really difficult time," David Peterson confirmed. "Everybody's been mad at Mulroney for being so friendly to the United States. Whether Campbell or Chrétien wins, they're going to have to work overtime to keep some distance from you. You're going to have to deal with a lot of anti-American sentiment. It's a good thing you've got political skills."

"Why didn't you tell me that when you were urging me to take the job?" I shot back. Later I decided that, being from London and living in Toronto, he was oversensitive to the anti-American strain that is mostly limited to the anglophile traditionalists and NDP leftists of Ontario.

In early July, Prime Minister Campbell had met with President Clinton during the summit of the Group of Seven (G7) industrial nations in Tokyo. As I heard it, she went on and on to him about the importance of protecting Canada's cultural industries from American domination and how Canada needed a contact point in the White House to handle hot disputes. Clinton agreed to the second point.

"You did *what*?" Warren Christopher reportedly asked in disbelief afterwards. "But that's what the State Department is supposed to do. That's why we have ambassadors." And Mickey Kantor chimed in, "Yeah, and I'm in charge of the trade issues."

"Well, ah, you know," Clinton stammered, "she was really eloquent about it, and I didn't want to hurt her feelings."

The reaction around the Canada Desk was that caving in to Campbell's sob story had been a dumb thing to do, but in light of the president's promise and the lack of an American ambassador at the time, there was no choice but to go along. As a result, when Jim Walsh and I walked across the street and strolled the short distance to the Parliament Buildings for our forty-five-minute meeting with her, I handed her a letter in which Clinton designated Bowman Cutter and Sandy Berger as contacts in the White House. I didn't mind the idea. In fact, it suited me to have friends and allies who could help over there, should a real problem flare up. My job, as I saw it, was to make sure that none did.

Indeed, my foremost objective upon arriving in Canada was to keep the United States out of the election as an issue. That meant keeping our various departments in Washington from inadvertently making a statement or filing a lawsuit or convening a hearing that would push either Kim Campbell or Jean Chrétien into taking a hard-line position with which they would be stuck as prime minister. And that meant getting my embassy staff to closely monitor the hundreds of files affecting trade, immigration, commerce, agriculture, defense, and so forth. Whenever I got wind of a problem, as happened when Agriculture Minister Charles Mayer phoned me in the middle of the campaign to ask if the rumors were true that we were intending to file a complaint on wheat under NAFTA, I'd call down and ask our people to back off until after election day – which they were happy to do.

It was to the political advantage of both Campbell and Chrétien, I understood, to put some distance between themselves and Brian Mulroney's "love affair" with the United States. Campbell admitted as much during our meeting by denying it too vehemently. "I know that you people are worried that I'm going to go in the opposite direction to Brian," she said, "but I want you to know that I haven't got an ounce of anti-Americanism in my body. I love America.

I think your president is great. You don't have to worry about me. I'll never get into Yankee-bashing."

"Oh, oh," I thought, "we're in big trouble. The lady doth protest too much." But I merely said that she and Clinton had a lot in common.

"Yeah," she said, "including this." And she pointed to her full-figured derrière.

As I was getting ready to leave the meeting, after a useful discussion about Bosnia, Canadian culture, and other topics, I looked out the window and saw our embassy across the lawn. "If I wave some time, will you wave back?" I asked.

"I'll do better than that," she said. "I'll talk to you and you can pick it up with your parabolic microphones."

We all had a good laugh. There was a common belief in Ottawa, spread by the tabloids, that the antennas on the roof of our building were really listening devices to eavesdrop on cabinet meetings and government activities. The CIA always instructed me not to comment on security matters, while I always tried to convince them that "no comment" was a confession of guilt. The truth is, we don't spy on good friends like Canada and we never have in modern history.

— —

Two days later our real fun and education began. After months of reading about Canada, hearing about Canada, thinking about Canada, dreaming about Canada, Janet and I were off to see Canada at last. At noon on September 4th, we departed from Toronto's Union Station on the start of a month-long odyssey across Canada by train, plane, boat, helicopter, and automobile. I had undertaken a similar survey, a six-and-a-half-day tour of the entire 3,300 miles of Michigan shoreline by boat and helicopter, when I was governor. It was a great experience, not least because it gave me a physical feel for our state, our water, our shoreline, our harbors, and our towns and people.

In the case of Canada, with its ten different provinces and regionalized economies, I thought it would be a good idea to see it all at once, before getting caught up in the time-consuming routines and high-level atmospherics of Ottawa. It would also be a way to introduce myself to Canadians as the new American ambassador. In fact, one of President Clinton's direct instructions when he asked me to take the post was not to ignore the provincial premiers. He had met a few when I invited them to discuss trade issues with us during the National Governors Conference in Traverse City in July 1987. "Canada's a very decentralized country," he remembered, "so keep in touch with all of them."

Our embassy people were taken aback at first by how much organization the trip would involve, but they soon came to embrace the idea. And luckily, because the ambassadorship had been vacant since January, there was enough money in the travel budget to support the trip. "We're going to be into an election any day now," they said, "so there's no reason for you to be sitting in Ottawa. All the players and all the action are going to be out there anyway." As well, it would give me a chance to meet our consulate staff across the country. I even invited each of the U.S. consuls, one by one, to join us as we passed through their territory. Thus we were waved away by George Kennedy, our consul general in Toronto, and escorted westwards by Bill Witting, our consul general in Calgary.

We traveled all day and all through the night in two adjoining compartments, viewing the spectacular scenery from our easy chairs and being briefed by Witting. When we awoke the next morning, we still had not left Ontario! In fact, it took us twenty-nine hours to go from Toronto to Winnipeg, Manitoba, through the northern mining city of

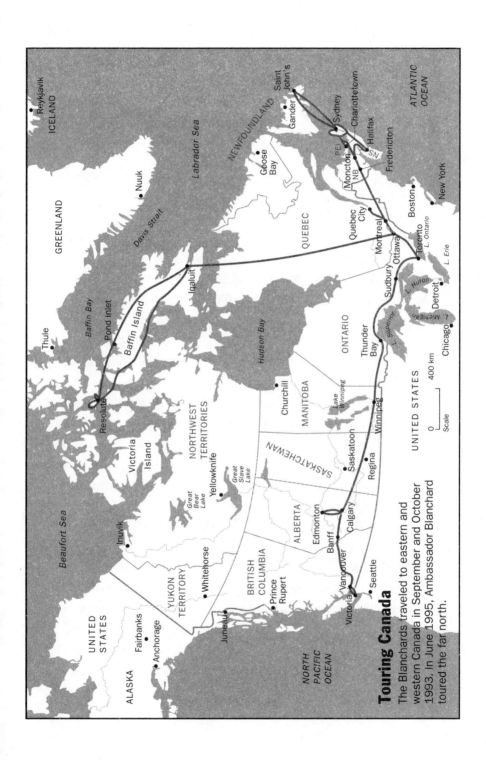

Touring Canada

The Blanchards traveled to eastern and western Canada in September and October 1993. In June 1995, Ambassador Blanchard toured the far north.

Sudbury, over the top of Lake Superior and past Sioux Look-out, with hour after hour of wilderness, lakes, rocks, and pine trees scarcely interrupted by a town, a cottage, a native reserve, or a trace of civilization. It reminded me of Michi-gan's Upper Peninsula, but a whole lot bigger and with many fewer people. For hours at a time, on both sides of the train, there seemed to be nothing but water connected by bits of forest, rocks, and marsh. "It would be easy for the Canadian government to get rid of its deficit," Janet remarked at one point, looking out the window. "All it's got to do is sell everyone a lake and pocket the money."

It was a highly appropriate introduction to Canada for us, because the whole idea of the Great White North, the True North Strong and Free, of pristine nature and infinite space, of aboriginal people and bountiful wildlife, of summer cot-tages and canoe trips, remains at the core of the Canadian psyche and Canada culture – in books, in films, in paintings – despite the fact that most of the population lives in cities, many of the native reserves suffer from squalor and alco-holism, and much of the national economy depends on cut-ting down forests, digging up minerals, and hauling in fish.

If Northern Ontario reminded me of parts of Michigan, the people and landscape of Manitoba reminded me of Minnesota, where I had gone to law school. In Winnipeg we took a tour of the city with the president of the university, had lunch with Premier Gary Filmon and some of his key cabinet ministers, dropped in on the lieutenant governor (the provincial equiva-lent of the governor general) and the leader of the opposition, met the editorial board of the *Winnipeg Free Press*, played golf with the ceo of Cargill in Canada, visited the Boeing plant, and had breakfast with Lloyd Axworthy, the Liberal member of Parliament who was destined to be an important player in Jean Chrétien's cabinet. Everywhere I went, I asked everyone to show me what they were most proud of, because I think that always reveals a great deal about a people and a country. Of course, I wanted to hear their election predictions too.

"We're expecting the election call at any moment," said Axworthy, who had gone to Princeton in the 1960s and been a big Bobby Kennedy fan. Though the early polls were now predicting a tight race, he was confident of a Liberal victory and outlined on a piece of paper how the strength of the Reform Party in the West and the Bloc Québécois in Quebec would undercut the Conservatives. It required some mental adjustment on my part to go from the two U.S. parties I had been dealing with all my political life to four national parties and one very powerful regional one. As a rule of thumb, I interpreted the Liberals as centrist Democrats, the Conservatives as moderate Republicans, the New Democrats as left-of-center Democrats, the Reform as right-wing Republicans and Perot-style populists, and the separatist Bloc Québécois as something unimaginable in the United States.

"There's a real horse race in the election," I jotted in my notes. "It will be jobs versus the deficit. The old pro versus the modern woman who represents change. A long-time politician versus nine years of Tory rule."

One evening in Winnipeg, out for a stroll near our hotel I came across a good cigar store. I was in the midst of savoring the scent of a Monte Christo No. 4 when the manager surprised me by saying, "Hey, aren't you the new American ambassador?" He had seen me doing my rounds of pre-trip media interviews on CTV's breakfast show with Valerie Pringle. Someone had told her I was fond of cigars, so she mischievously asked me if I'd be enjoying any Cuban cigars while in Canada. "When I heard that," the manager said, "I wondered to myself if you'd ever come into my store and buy some from me. Welcome to Canada!"

He wasn't the only person to recognize me as I crossed the country. One of the American super-stations that was beamed into Atlantic Canada, the prairies, and the Far North carried the NBC, ABC, CBS, and PBS affiliates from Detroit, where I had been on TV almost every day for eight years as governor. I was stopped in some of the remotest corners of Canada by people who knew my face, if not my name, including an elevator operator in Saskatchewan, a protocol officer in Newfoundland, and a local official in the Northwest Territories. One night in Jasper, Alberta, I was amazed to turn on the TV and see my friend Dennis Archer, who was running for mayor of Detroit, conducting a press conference! The downside was that many Canadians were really turned off by all the crime and violence on the Detroit local news, to the point where there were frequent petitions to have it removed from the air. But when I passed along their complaints about how bloodthirsty the coverage seemed, the Detroit TV executives reacted as though I were attacking freedom of the press. They were just giving Detroiters, they argued, what they want.

Canada has far less crime and violence than the United States. By history and temperament, Canadians are more peaceful and law-abiding than Americans – except, possibly, on the hockey rink. Their founders were proudly loyal and respectful toward the British authorities, not revolutionaries like John Hancock and Thomas Jefferson. Nor was the right to bear arms ever a guiding principle or necessity for them, because the early Canadians tended to see the government as a protector rather than an oppressor.

I sometimes say to the Americans, "You know, we pride ourselves on being the freest people in the world. We invented freedom, or at least we think we did. In most respects, that's true. But, in one major respect, we're not as free as Canadians." You can hear a pin drop at that point and see a look of great offense on people's faces. "For example, Janet and I can walk in almost any city or street anywhere in Canada and never have to worry about being mugged or robbed. We don't have to worry about avoiding parking garages. We don't have to walk quickly from our cars into the safety of a shop or restaurant."

"What do you mean?" they say. "We read about this big murder in Toronto when we were up there."

"Yeah," I answer, "but that's just the Canadian media imitating us. Canadians think they have a lot of crime, they think it's on the increase, they worry about it, and if you watch their news, you might get the impression that it's a big deal. But, unless you really go out of your way to find a rough neighborhood and make yourself a target, you're not likely to experience violent crime. And that means you're free."

The crime statistics demonstrated the difference between our two nations. During our first year in Canada, I read that there were eighty-three handgun murders. In the United States, the figure was over 13,000. To be comparable, Canada would have had to have had 1,300 murders. Furthermore, most of the killings in Canada involved people who knew each other. There were few of the random shootings that plague the United States. And when they do happen, Canadians are often grief-stricken.

During our time in Ottawa, for example, a young Englishman named Nicholas Battersby, who worked for Bell-Northern Research, was shot dead while walking along a downtown street. Three teenagers, it turned out, had been shooting a gun from a car window. Drive-by shootings are not uncommon in the major cities of America, but this was a huge shock in Ottawa. Though Nicholas Battersby had been in Canada only a few months and knew about a dozen people, his memorial service attracted 2,000 mourners. They filled the church and poured onto the street. His family was really moved by the community's reaction, and so were Janet and I.

Such a thing can still happen in a small town in the United States, but I'm not so sure about our cities. Even in Toronto, a much bigger city with a lot more crime, hundreds of strangers brought flowers to the site where a young woman was killed during a hold-up in a downtown café and 3,500 people showed up at her funeral. "You ought to thank the Lord for that kind of attitude," I told my Canadian friends. "You ought to get down on the ground and kiss the earth and thank God you live in a town like that, because many Americans can't say that." And that's a fact.

A part of the difference, I perceived on my travels, is due to the fact that Canada doesn't have the same percentage of urban poor. A part comes from being a smaller society, where criminals are easier to track down and catch. And a part of it stems from the totally different attitude toward the widespread ownership of handguns. Though hunting is popular in Canada and unrestricted gun ownership finds political support in rural areas and throughout the west, Canadians were constantly asking us why Americans tolerated so many lethal weapons in our cities. Our cabin master on the train from Toronto to Winnipeg had stood out for his loud opposition to the gun-control legislation being talked about in Ottawa, but later I found out that he was a gun dealer on the side.

After Winnipeg, we flew over a vast flatland of golden wheat to Regina, the capital of Saskatchewan, for another round of visits with politicians, business leaders, and the media. As with Ottawa and Winnipeg, I was staggered by how beautiful the city was, full of parks and flowers, and its legislative buildings were equally impressive. In fact, one of the things I noticed wherever I went in Canada was how well-maintained the public buildings and public spaces are. There seemed to be a greater investment and pride in keeping them clean and proper than in the United States.

Premier Roy Romanow seemed particularly interested in Bill Clinton – What's he like in person? How's he doing? Is he going to get his health-care plan? – but he also wanted to talk about NAFTA and gun control. Though he was the leader of the provincial New Democratic Party, he sounded to me like a moderate Democrat. I was amazed, in fact, how popular Clinton was with his generation of Canadian politicians, regardless of whether they were Liberal, Conservative, or NDP.

Then it was on to Calgary, Canada's oil-and-gas capital, and since Canada provides the United States with more energy than any other country in the world, a city of real importance to Americans. The farther west we went, the more the people sounded like Ross Perot voters. Calgary certainly didn't seem conservative in the moderate, pragmatic tradition of Brian Mulroney and Kim Campbell: it came across as a town of Western populists, a combination of Denver and Houston with a dash of San Diego. "Calgary is just like Texas," a friend once told me, "only less anti-American." And Alberta as a whole, with its cattle ranches and oil wells, is the most Americanized province in Canada. Everyone to whom Janet and I spoke, from the oil executives at the Petroleum Club to our own consulate staff, predicted that the Reform Party under Preston Manning, a Christian evangelical who was the son of a former premier of Alberta, was going to do really well in the west at the expense of the Conservatives.

The day before, in fact, Kim Campbell had "dropped the writ" triggering the national election and immediately stumbled by predicting that unemployment would remain high until the year 2000. Even if it were accurate, it was a politically naive thing to say. "She's just lost the election," I said to Bill Witting on the plane from Regina to Calgary. "Even if she doesn't believe that government can help create new jobs, a politician has to offer people hope. That's what Clinton did, and that's what Chrétien's doing."

"Maybe," said Bill, "but Canadians are different. They care more about the deficit than about jobs."

I wasn't convinced. "That may be the way things look in Calgary, where people are doing well. But, barring some crazy development, this election is over, done, finis." The only outstanding question in my mind was whether Chrétien would get a majority of the seats in the House of Commons or would have to govern Parliament with the support of some third-party votes.

"Liberals have grabbed the job issue, Campbell has stumbled," I wrote in my notes, and I saw an interesting parallel between U.S. and Canadian politics, with Kim Campbell as George Bush, Jean Chrétien as Bill Clinton, and Preston Manning as Ross Perot. "Liberals' rhetoric is similar to Clinton's on the economy. Tories' is more like Republicans'. But a lot of interest everywhere in reinventing government, NAFTA, health care, guns, violence in Florida. Jobs and the deficit seem to be the issues, not NAFTA, not the Free Trade Agreement. The press is more negative in its questions and comments than the people I meet are. Each region identifies with the U.S., not Ottawa or Ontario. This seems to be a country of city-states."

While in Calgary, I had the first of many happy and instructive encounters with Peter Lougheed, a leading businessman and statesman who had been premier of Alberta from 1971 to 1985. He gave me some sound advice that

I heeded throughout my term in Canada. "In one sense this is a very small country," he warned. "Don't joke around with the Canada-U.S. relationship. At the leadership level, unlike in the States, everybody knows everybody, even if they're in different parties with different philosophies in different parts of the country. You can have lunch with somebody in Toronto and make some stupid remark, and I promise you it'll be in Vancouver by suppertime. Treat every province as unique, but treat everyone you talk to as if you're talking to the whole country."

We flew up to Edmonton to attend a luncheon Premier Ralph Klein held in our honor, then back to Calgary for the international horse show at Spruce Meadows. (It was September 11th, and it snowed!) The event turned out to be a good opportunity to meet some important Albertans and other dignitaries, including a host of American participants, because Canadian high society is more of a horsey set than its American counterpart. Spruce Meadows itself was all about show-jumping and dressage, not calf-roping and racing, and there were more Europeans than cowboys in the crowd. Later, in Toronto, we saw the same phenomenon at the Royal Winter Fair, where the social and corporate élites show up every year in formal wear and fancy gowns to watch horse competitions in a huge barn-like coliseum smelling of hay and manure, along with thousands of farmers in blue jeans and hockey jackets. "Mink and manure" it's called with a touch of pride. I had never seen such a thing in the United States.

From Calgary we drove the tourist route to Banff, Lake Louise, and Jasper through some of the most spectacular mountain scenery in the world, past elk locking horns in the middle of the road, to idyllic lodges that seemed from another age of romance and comfort. I was astounded on a morning walk to see dozens of elk and deer and hundreds of ducks and geese all over a golf course. At Jasper Bill Witting handed us over to Mike Gallagher, our consul general for British Columbia and the Yukon territory, and we hopped the overnight train to Vancouver.

With its backdrop of snow-capped mountains, its beaches and forests, its harbor full of gleaming sailboats and pontoon planes, its ocean air and modern buildings, Vancouver is an urban paradise. I consider it the most beautiful of Canada's many beautiful cities and perhaps the most beautiful in North America. (It's a game I liked to play on my travels and, for what it's worth, I kept a list. The most interesting city: Montreal. The quaintest: Quebec City. The most dynamic: Toronto. The most American: Calgary. The friendliest: St. John's. The most forsaken: Iqaluit. The best-kept secret: Ottawa.) But all of Canada's major cities, strung from sea to sea along the U.S. border like jewels around the neck of North America, and containing a large majority of the population, are remarkable for their cleanliness, their well-preserved cores, their safe neighborhoods, and their efficient governments, not to mention the vast and ubiquitous networks of underground malls that connect the downtown office towers to each other and protect pedestrians from the winter cold. Many Americans enjoy vacationing in Canada as much for the liveliness and character of its cities as for the beauty and wildness of its nature.

Though I later attended meetings with civic and environmental leaders in British Columbia's capital, Victoria, which appeared to me as though a chunk of Bermuda had been dropped onto the Upper Peninsula of Michigan, I actually met Premier Mike Harcourt in his Vancouver office with its distracting view of the water and the mountains. Another New Democrat like Bob Rae and Roy Romanow, he seemed very calm for someone who was then in political trouble, and full of curiosity about Clinton and Gore.

One of the things I did wherever I went was to ask Canadians who their heroes were. By their own admission, heroism is something they're reluctant to acknowledge. Often I'd get a really long pause or some kind of cautious answer (like the janitor at the local school who saved a kid from drowning), as though nobody wanted to get tricked into admitting that there were any big shots in Canada. Churchill, Roosevelt, and Kennedy were popular Canadian responses, along with Sir John A. Macdonald and Pierre Trudeau. Harcourt's heroes were Franklin Roosevelt and Tommy Douglas, the socialist premier of Saskatchewan in the 1940s who is considered the father of medicare in North America. Even though Canada's national health-insurance system has come under increasing criticism and cost problems in recent years, most Americans would be surprised to learn how popular it has been among Canadians.

Harcourt and I also talked about gun control and the environment, which was of special concern in British Columbia because of its great natural beauty, its economic dependence on forestry and fishing, and the strength of its ecological lobby. The Greenpeace movement had been founded there, and the provincial government seemed perpetually caught in a fierce, highly publicized struggle between the "tree-huggers" from around the world and the "clear-cutters" among the lumber companies and their unions. For all the reasonable business arguments, I couldn't help but be shocked by the bare, scarred mountainsides we helicoptered over on our way to see the glaciers near Whistler or saw from 35,000 feet on our way back east. I found it hard to believe that the environmentally conscious Canadians would have allowed such detrimental practices to have gone on for so long – long after they had been stopped in the United States – just as I was surprised to hear the good people of Victoria defend the dumping of their raw sewage into the Strait of Juan de Fuca because, if I heard them correctly, they weren't going to be bullied into spending a lot of money on waste treatment by a bunch of pushy Americans in Washington State!

I had barely arrived in British Columbia when I started being told, by corporate executives and university professors and talk-show hosts, that I was in another world. This wasn't eastern Canada; it wasn't even Alberta, though it shared Alberta's wariness, indifference, or downright hostility toward Ottawa and Toronto. Some called it "British California" or "Hongcouver"; some considered it a part of "Cascadia" along with Washington State and Oregon. Whatever the name, it was booming, bustling, and uniquely beautiful. "Put the rest of the country out of your mind," the movers and shakers said. "We don't need it, we don't want it, we're totally different."

I had heard that everywhere, in fact. Manitoba is different from Ontario; Saskatchewan is different from Manitoba; Alberta is different from Saskatchewan. I had even heard that Edmonton is different from Calgary. "They're Texan cowboys down there," said the Edmontonians, "whereas we're urbane, sophisticated, intellectual, compassionate Canadians." Then the Calgarians would say the same about Edmonton. The only thing they admitted to having in common was an enemy: the eastern power-brokers.

As David Peterson had joked over a beer one night, "The thing that keeps this country together is that everyone hates Ontario. And the thing that keeps Ontario together is that everyone hates Toronto. And the thing that keeps Toronto together is that everyone hates the money guys on Bay

Street. And the thing that keeps Bay Street together is that everyone hates lawyers. If you understand that, Jimmy, you'll understand Canada."

I did encounter a lot of anti-Ottawa feeling as well. Many Americans like to rant and rave against Washington, of course, but we still take our children to see its great monuments and they cry in front of the Lincoln Memorial. Canadians don't do that sort of thing. I was surprised by how few Canadians have ever been to Ottawa. Except perhaps for the politicians, Canadians seem to travel south rather than east or west. That said, I also found Canadians much more political than Americans, which is perhaps a sign of a healthier democracy. Their voting rate is higher, and they seem more interested in talking about politics. Not just their own, either. While it's true that I was usually dealing with the leadership class, whether government leaders, business CEOs, or opinion-makers, wherever I went I met a friendly curiosity about Clinton and Gore. I met very little anti-Americanism, far less than I had been warned to expect.

On September 16th Janet and I flew back to Ottawa for a few days to do some office work and drop off the laundry, went on to Washington to attend a couple of farewell dinners, then returned to resume the second part of our trans-Canada journey, through the four Atlantic provinces and into Quebec. Again we were greeted by each of their premiers – Clyde Wells in Newfoundland, John Savage in Nova Scotia, Catherine Callbeck in Prince Edward Island, Frank McKenna in New Brunswick, and Robert Bourassa in Quebec – as well as business people, community activists, the media, and our local consul general, in this case Roger Meece in Halifax. And again we were impressed by the diversity of the people, the towns, and the landscape as we hopped from place to place.

Newfoundland looked like Ireland and, I was told, is closer by air to Dublin than to Toronto. Even its inhabitants seemed more Irish than Canadian, and they glowed with the Irish love for sea chanties, tall tales, and warm hospitality – particularly, it seemed, toward Americans. In part this may have been because of the large number of Newfoundland women who married U.S. soldiers posted to the military bases there. It's so friendly, the police don't carry guns. In St. John's we saw the superb natural harbor, where Sir Humphrey Gilbert had landed to claim the "new found land" in 1583 as the first English possession in North America; Signal Hill, where Marconi received the first wireless message across the Atlantic; and Gibbet Hill, where convicts were hanged, shoved into a barrel, and tossed into Deadman's Pond. And though we saw the poverty of the old fishing outports along the coast, we also saw the hope for future prosperity in the gigantic Hibernia oil platform, still under construction in a dammed-up cove, looking like a high-tech missile installation for a James Bond film and swarming with thousands of workers.

While in Newfoundland I encountered some concern about the closing of the United States military base at Argentia. Our government had already worked out a severance package for several hundred workers, but the unions and their political allies were agitating to renegotiate it to their further advantage. Among those allies was John Crosbie, the powerful ex-minister in Brian Mulroney's government. "You've got to do more for those people," he told me when we met. I promised to look into it. A couple of hours later when I got back to the lieutenant governor's residence where Janet and I had been invited to stay, I discovered Crosbie on TV urging people to picket me. Within minutes, it seemed, there were protesters outside the gates. I had to laugh. "Here I am," I said to myself, "on my first visit to what's supposedly the friendliest province in all of Canada, and I'm being picketed!"

Back on the mainland, we were met by Vaughn Cameron, who drove us from the coal-mining city of Sydney in northern Nova Scotia through the breathtaking highland wilderness of the Cabot Trail on Cape Breton Island, where we saw colorful Acadian villages, the home of Alexander Graham Bell, and plenty of moose, before heading south to Halifax. It seemed more like a small New England city, with its historic citadel and brick homes overlooking the harbor. In fact, because of its close connection to Boston and what some Nova Scotians still call "the Boston states," Halifax was the site of the first U.S. consulate (established 1827) in the loyal British colonies of North America. Haligonians are extremely hospitable people, even to the extent that they have a tradition whereby cars will stop to give pedestrians the right-of-way to cross the road, no matter what color the light or how broad the thoroughfare. It also seemed obvious from the election posters alone that the Liberals were going to do well.

As British as Nova Scotia felt, New Brunswick felt more so, and it was the first place I really started to hear a lot of talk about the United Empire Loyalists who had fled the American Revolution in order to remain under the authority and protection of the British Crown. Most of the anti-Americanism that exists in Canada can be traced back to the fact that the majority of the early European settlers in Ontario and the Maritimes were loyal to England, loyal to the King, and wanted nothing to do with the American Revolutionary War. They thought of us as treasonous rogues and they left the Thirteen Colonies during or shortly after the war. In other words, English-speaking Canada was founded by people who were more obedient, more authority-prone, more law-abiding, more pro-government than the Americans. They even called themselves the Loyalists with pride, and many of their descendants still think of themselves in that way. It's a crucial difference.

Even though the Loyalists had moved into the other northern colonies by the tens of thousands, they are a particularly vital presence in Fredericton, New Brunswick's capital, which still prides itself on its Anglican cathedral, its garrison history, and its Loyalist cemetery. In a typically Canadian contradiction, however, the province's eastern shore is the homeland of the French-speaking Acadians, whose communities and traditions have survived since the earliest days of New France. Indeed, New Brunswick is Canada's only officially bilingual province, and I was amused to meet the attorney general, whose name was Eddie Blanchard. Though my Blanchard ancestors were French-speaking Swiss Catholics and the other side of my family was Scottish, I liked to boast that my full name – James Johnston Blanchard – qualified me, by itself, to be an ambassador to Canada.

After a short ferry ride and a wonderful day on Prince Edward Island, the small province of pastoral farms and red beaches that was then in the throes of debating the impact of the new bridge to the mainland and the hordes of summer tourists (not least all the Japanese who were coming to worship at the home of Anne of Green Gables), we returned to New Brunswick to catch the overnight train from Moncton to Montreal – which, as yet another testament to the world's longest undefended border, actually traveled across the top of Maine.

I had been to Montreal once before, but had missed seeing it in its heyday before the threat of Quebec independence chased away so many businesses, investment dollars, and anglophones. Now my first impression was that it needed some tender loving care. Its buildings cried out for renovation; its roads begged for repairs; its parks looked shabbier than those in the other major Canadian cities I had seen; and there was more trash on the sidewalks. "You should have seen it in the old days," I was always being told. "It was a really great place." But it still struck me as a great place: scenic, interesting, stylish, and vibrant. It combined European flair with North American can-doism, and for a supposedly dead city, its streets were animated until late into the night, its many bars and first-class restaurants were packed, and its people were full of spirit and kindness, except when behind the wheel of a car. I firmly believe that whenever the constitutional conflicts get resolved in favor of a unified Canada, and all the talent, energy, and resources available in Montreal get mobilized for more productive purposes, it will undergo a dazzling renaissance.

Everybody, it seemed, was obsessed by the pros and cons of Quebec independence. French-speaking Quebeckers had certainly come a long way from their old second-class political status in Canada and their second-class economic status within their own province. Every Quebec government since 1960 had moved to make the political, economic, bureaucratic, educational, and linguistic reforms necessary to lift francophones to the commanding heights of business and society. Pierre Trudeau and Brian Mulroney, both fluently bilingual Quebeckers and staunch federalists, had dedicated themselves to making French Canadians fully active players in Ottawa. But all this progress did not satisfy those hardline nationalists who wanted a country of their own in the United Nations or those softer ones who wanted some undefined, fifty-fifty partnership with the rest of Canada. Two compromise solutions, known as the Meech Lake Accord and the Charlottetown Accord, had failed under Mulroney, in good measure because they were seen as too much by English Canada and not enough by French Quebec. And, in the wake of those failures, the separatist movement began to regain the momentum it lost after the 1980 referendum, when sixty percent of Quebeckers voted no to an ambiguously worded question to negotiate, not separation, but "sovereignty-association" with Canada.

While in Montreal, I had a meeting with Premier Robert Bourassa, the leader of the Quebec Liberal Party, who kept an office there as well as in the capital. Bourassa had first been elected premier in 1970, mere months before a gang of Marxist terrorists kidnapped the British trade commissioner and murdered one of Bourassa's cabinet colleagues in the name of the liberation of Quebec. Six years later Bourassa was defeated by René Lévesque, the charismatic ex-journalist who founded the separatist Parti Québécois in 1968 and led it to power on a platform of good government. Then, after the PQ's referendum defeat and Lévesque's retirement from politics, Bourassa was able to lead the Liberals back to power in 1985, and it was he who tried to orchestrate the two failed accords. When I saw him, he had just announced his own retirement, not least because he was undergoing treatment for the skin cancer that eventually killed him. At that point, however, he seemed healthy and at peace with himself, and we had a friendly conversation about the problems of national unity and the course of the federal election. Bourassa was famous for his coy, sly, exasperating evasiveness. It wasn't clear to me even after our talk whether he was supporting his political cousins, the federal Liberals, or, because he was closer personally to Mulroney, the Conservatives.

Immediately afterwards, at a reception organized by our consul general, Susan Wood, at her splendid residence overlooking the city on the slopes of Mount Royal, I had my first conversation with a committed separatist, Bernard Landry, a leading member of the Parti Québécois in the Quebec National Assembly.

Then and later, the separatists always told me the same thing right off the bat. "We're pro-American, we're pro-free trade, don't be afraid of us. All the anti-American rhetoric comes out of Ottawa or Toronto. And, sure, we'd like a little help from the United States, but we don't mind your present position, which is that it's up to Canadians to work out their future by themselves."

I found that our reluctance to comment on Canada's domestic affairs was being used by the separatists as a sign of support, sympathy, or indifference to the idea of Canada's break-up. They pounced on the words of every minor intellectual or low-level official who ever claimed that the independence of Quebec was either desirable or inevitable or of no account. I myself had met one or two policy-makers of that sort in Washington. "The hard-liners will never be happy until they have a separate country," went their argument. "Ottawa has already given up the ghost. The decentralization of powers and tough language laws have been allowed to go too far. Quebec and Canada have already drifted irreparably apart. So why fight it? Either it will all work out okay or we'll go in and pick up the pieces."

But that seemed to me a totally false analysis. It is more likely, barring some terrible slip of history, that Canadians will go on talking about the problem for hundreds of years rather than ever reaching a final parting of the ways. And the vast majority of Americans, inside and outside the government, have absolutely no sympathy or patience for the notion of secession. That's rooted, reasonably or not, in our own Civil War and a warm, fuzzy feeling toward Canada, as well as in international law and the terms of our bilateral agreements. Most of us believe that the independence of Quebec would be a tragic event for everybody – not just for Canadians, but for Americans, Quebeckers, and the world.

— —

By the time we returned to Ottawa on October 2nd, after twenty-nine stops and more than a hundred events all across Canada, I realized how privileged I had been to have crossed the country before being weighed down by my duties in the capital. I was even luckier in the months and years ahead to be able to see many of the other parts of Canada I had missed on that first trip, including the coves and towns along the Atlantic coast south of Halifax, the enormous hydro-electric facilities at James Bay in northern Quebec, the site of the pre-historic native buffalo run at Head-Smashed-In-Buffalo Jump south of Calgary, a string of Inuit communities in the Arctic and a high-tech mining camp near the magnetic north pole. Most American tourists, perhaps even most Canadian citizens, only ever get to see bits of Canada, but I now knew that my perception of its people and politics would have been grievously distorted if I had confined myself to the Ottawa-Montreal-Toronto triangle. My experience of Canada was all the more powerful because I had seen so much of it all at once. That enabled me to appreciate how diverse the Canadian provinces are from each other – much more diverse than the American states. Each province is socially, culturally, and politically distinct, and each has a mighty array of constitutional powers to defend and extend its distinctiveness.

In that sense, Canada is much more of a true confederation with a very strong states-rights sentiment than the United States. Canadian provinces have far more power than the American states, and Ottawa has far less than Washington, even though the founding fathers in each country intended the precise opposite. The United States actually tried a loose-knit confederation before it failed and gave way to the present constitution, while the makers of the Canadian union dreamed of a strong central government in 1867 and ended up, because of court decisions, federal-provincial politics, and other factors, with what is today the most decentralized federation in the world.

As well, Canada has had a more sympathetic policy toward ethnic diversity, probably because of the presence of a large and historic minority of French-speaking Roman Catholics from its very start as a nation in 1867. Canadians prefer to describe themselves as a mosaic of people, rather than a melting pot in the American sense, and though neither is entirely true, the generalization is close enough in relation to official government policy. Certainly Canada was working on issues of ethnic identity and ethnic pride long before the United States. It was even a national policy by the Liberal Party to encourage immigration, which undoubtedly explains why most New Canadians vote Liberal. While there were political battles over the numbers of Irish, Ukrainians, Italians, and Chinese allowed in, there wasn't the same pervasiveness of quotas and restrictions that American governments introduced early on.

Before the 1970s, the rule of the day for U.S. immigrants was to become an American as fast as you can. You shed your ethnic name; you spoke English; you sent your kids to public schools; you believed that George Washington never told a lie; and you pledged allegiance to the flag of the first and foremost free nation in the world. On graduation day at Henry Ford's trade school in Dearborn, Michigan, in the 1920s, all the kids from a multitude of ethnic backgrounds marched up a stairway, shed their native garb, and climbed into a gigantic pot. Then their classmates stirred the pot – the melting pot – to symbolize that out of many, came one: an American.

Whatever their social backgrounds and differences, Americans are bound by a single national story that goes something like this: Pilgrims came from England to escape religious persecution. Later they were joined by some great thinkers such as Jefferson and Madison, numerous entrepreneurs, and all kinds of fortune-seekers looking for new opportunities. They all decided they were being put upon by England, so they fought a great battle for independence and won. Then, inspired by God Himself, they wrote a constitution that was the best system ever devised by man. It triggered a movement for freedom and human rights around the world. But some selfish, greedy people down south tried to break it all up. We fought a terrible bloody war, the nation was preserved, and Lincoln freed the slaves. Then we brought forth unprecedented prosperity and became the world's greatest superpower. If I as governor had ever stood up and told people, "I'm a Michiganer first and an American second," they would have booed me off the stage. They'd think I was nuts.

Not only do Canadians not share our national story, they don't have one of their own. Rather, they have several. The Loyalists have one; the Québécois have another; the prairie settlers yet another; the native peoples yet another; the immigrant communities yet another; and so on. Not long ago, a Toronto cab driver offered me a simple solution to all Canada's woes. "The United States government should give every Canadian a million bucks. There only are thirty million of us, so you could afford it. We'd sell ourselves to you, we'd all be rich, and we wouldn't be anti-American anymore. For a million dollars, I think a lot of Canadians would be happy to become part of the United States. I would." In fact, when I pressed him, he said he'd settle for half a million!

But if Americans have a greater sense of nationhood – and they do – it was immediately clear to me that Canadians have a greater sense of community and security. They feel a greater need to look after everybody in society. The upside is that you'll hear even the super-rich worry about the poor, even if they share the universal dislike of paying taxes. The downside is Canadians need to talk things through, to consult with everybody, to seek a consensus, to find the right compromise, even if it takes years, before a decision is made. Issues and ideas take longer to play out, to the point where they become tedious. Commissions, committees, and government programs have to be established to make everyone feel included, understood, respected, loved, and fully compensated for all the wrongs done them. And the emphasis on community identity, while extremely tolerant of ethnic differences, has fostered a certain social conformity and class-consciousness that makes Canadians less tolerant of individual expression and unorthodox behavior than Americans.

You might get a similar sense of concern and sharing in Ferndale, Michigan, but you don't get it across the board in the United States. Americans are more individualistic and capitalistic, less apt to dwell on the need for inclusion and compassion. Many tend to feel that people less fortunate than they are don't work hard enough or have bad habits. And when we feel wronged, we don't negotiate, we sue. It doesn't matter what the cause, even an act of God, we're going to hold somebody responsible. We are incredibly litigious. On any given day, major automobile manufacturers face thousands of pending cases in products liability in the United States. In Canada the number is about a dozen.

We are truly different societies, in other words, each with something to learn from the other. Without giving up our pride in what we have accomplished, Americans should worry more about the violence and poverty in our midst. And, without slavishly imitating the United States, Canadians need to develop a stronger feeling for what a great country they have and how much it can offer the world. They should get past all the self-deprecating jokes, the media griping, and the regional squabbles that were playing themselves out in the election campaign I was witnessing. And they should celebrate Canada's incredible beauty, its cities that work, its diversity and peace. To my eyes, by the conclusion of our journey, it seemed unfathomable that anyone would want to tear apart such a vast and wonderful nation.

— 3 —

CAPITAL CONNECTIONS

On October 20, 1993, five days before the national election, Janet and I flew by propeller plane from Ottawa via Montreal for my first visit to Quebec City. No wonder Canadians have a unity problem, I thought, if they don't have a regular jet flight between the nation's capital and the capital of the province of Quebec – or a freeway from Ottawa to Toronto, for that matter. And I had more than national unity on my mind. I was on a secret mission to help save NAFTA.

We were met by our consul general, Marie Huhtala; a French-speaking policeman named Blanchard; and a metallic gold Mercedes stretch limo flying two American flags. I was appalled. "I don't want to hurt anyone's feelings," I said to Marie, "but we've got to get another car. The U.S. ambassador can't be seen riding around in a huge, gaudy thing like that without looking like the Ugly American. Worse, it's a

Mercedes. An American ambassador, let alone a former governor of Michigan, needs to ride in an American car. One of my jobs, after all, is to promote the sale of American goods and services. You don't do that by driving a German car."

We had no choice, however, but to take it into town. There were mobs of tourists on the narrow, cobbled streets of the walled city, many of them undoubtedly Americans, and it looked to me as though they all were pointing or staring as we rolled past. Janet and I tried to crouch below the windows, and I wanted to put a raincoat over our heads. I'm not sure that either Marie or the protocol officer, who had provided what he considered his best car, understood my skittishness, but from then on we went around in a Chevrolet Cavalier.

Marie hosted a luncheon in our honor at the U.S. consulate, where we were staying, a four-story townhouse with French doors and balconies overlooking the terrace that runs along the steep cliff above the St. Lawrence River. The grand Chateau Frontenac hotel was at one end of the boardwalk, the steps leading up to the old Citadel were at the other, and below was a scenic view of one of the most strategic positions in imperial military history, the "Gibraltar of North America." After lunch we were taken on a tour of the historic sites where the French had settled in 1608 and the British had conquered them in 1759. Like most American schoolchildren, I had learned about the Battle of the Plains of Abraham in history class, and I remembered the classic image of General Wolfe dying in the arms of his comrades at the moment of his victory. It thrilled me to think of the armies that had fought where we were walking and where the fate of the continent had been set.

According to our guide, the old French colony had been a happy place, with a thriving economy, no unemployment, and good social services. But then one night when the regular French troops were busy partying, leaving the town's defenses to the care of a motley crew of drunken guards, the perfidious British climbed up the cliff at night and sneaked up from behind like cowards. I recognized the story because the British had used the same tactic to seize Mackinac Island, Michigan, from the Americans during the War of 1812. "Oh, the old sneak-up-from-behind-in-the-dark trick," I said to the guide, but she didn't laugh. This was serious business to her, for it meant the end of the happy times: after the conquest came British imperialism and the English language.

Being an American means subscribing to a set of ideas and principles, not membership in a particular ethnic group, but we do insist upon a common language – and that, of course, is English. Even where we've had bilingual programs, designed to promote the transition from another language to English, their existence has been hotly debated even by liberals. Americans are not about to allow the United States to become a bilingual country. As a result, many Americans believe that English-speaking Canadians only caused trouble by letting the French-speaking Canadians get more and more militant about their language. They would argue it was probably a mistake two hundred years ago to encourage the French colonists to stick to their language in North America after the British Conquest. It created a division that probably needn't have occurred. I think, however, that it is not worth debating now. Indeed, Canadians have made the best of the situation by turning their two official languages into a national and international asset. And I get impatient with Americans who project our society onto Canada's.

Official policies aside, I regretted that I didn't speak French myself. I had signed up in May for the free lessons offered by the Foreign Service Institute, but they couldn't find an instructor until early July, by which time I had only a few weeks to pick up a few phrases. I found, however, that if I told French-speaking Quebeckers that I was an American, they didn't view my ignorance of their language as a sign of disrespect. Many American tourists are actually afraid to visit Quebec. All they've heard is about terrorist bombs and language tensions. I always told them, particularly those going to Quebec City or the rural areas, first of all, you'll be well-treated, and secondly, mention that you're an American as quickly as possible. You'll be treated more warmly than if they think you're from Ontario. Montreal is even less of a problem. It's a very friendly, mostly federalist city, and it's more accustomed to hearing English. My only trouble was, I got so proficient at saying, *"Excusez-moi, je suis americain,"* that people assumed I was bilingual and shot back their response in rapid French.

On our second day in Quebec City, we had a private lunch with Jacques Parizeau and his wife, Lisette Lapointe. At that time Parizeau was the leader of the Parti Québécois, the provincial separatist party that was then in opposition in Quebec's "National" Assembly to the governing Quebec Liberals. Both he and his wife were delightful people, very charming and fun to be with, though they were unequivocal separatists and true believers in the cause. Parizeau had studied at the London School of Economics, where, incongruously, he picked up the accent, dress, and mannerisms of a stuffy British gentleman. After a highly successful career as an economist for the Quebec government in the 1960s, he had moved into politics with René Lévesque's pro-independence party.

In his mind, Trudeau and Chrétien were the villains. They had pushed through the constitutional reforms and the Charter of Rights in 1982 over the objections of Quebec's National Assembly. They had fought the Meech Lake

Accord that proposed declaring Quebec a "distinct society" within Canada (though Parizeau himself had opposed it for not giving Quebec enough new powers). Quebeckers, he felt, now understood that even the feeblest of concessions would be rejected by English Canada. So they were more open than ever before – and the polls proved it – to the separatist option.

"We'll be an independent country with a seat in the United Nations, but we'll keep the Canadian currency and passport," he declared to me. "We'll have our own army, air force, and coast guard, but we'll remain good allies in NATO and NORAD. And, of course, we'll be part of NAFTA."

"The agreement doesn't say that, though," I countered. "There would have to be a formal accession, and that means you'd have to get the approval of Ottawa as well as Washington and Mexico City. You might get approval after a couple of years of wrangling, but in the meantime Quebec would be on its knees before Canada, begging for admission. I certainly can't imagine Washington saying yes if Ottawa doesn't want us to. In other words, you'll lose power, not gain it."

"No, no, no," Parizeau said, citing international treaties and the common law about successor rights to bolster his wishful thinking. He had an answer for everything – a flimsy one in this case, I thought – and nothing would convince him otherwise. "Sooner or later, and probably sooner, we're going to get the votes for independence. And, unlike those anti-American guys in Ottawa, we're free-traders. That, by itself, should qualify us for NAFTA, whatever the law says."

Parizeau had his scenario all figured out. The Bloc Québécois, the new political party of Quebec separatists led by the popular Lucien Bouchard in the federal House of Commons, was going to pick up most of the Quebec seats in the upcoming national election. This would give the separatists a national platform on which to advance their cause. Then there would be a Quebec provincial election – September 1994 was Parizeau's guess – and the Parti Québécois would win it and he would become premier. Eight to ten months later the PQ government would call a referendum on the straightforward question "Shall Quebec become sovereign as of July 1, 1995?" And that, Parizeau thought, would be that.

I found his confidence both eye-opening and alarming. Besides the inbred hostility that most Americans feel toward the very notion of secession, business craves political stability. That's why the United States is such a magnet for money from all over the world, as is much of Europe. There's no doubt that Quebec, and to a lesser degree all of Canada, has been hurt economically by the threat of separation. Businesses have left; investors have shied away; the dollar has weakened; and there was a huge transfer of wealth and talent from Montreal to Toronto because so many anglophones and immigrants felt threatened by the ethnic militancy of the French-speaking nationalists. The future prosperity of Quebec depends on putting the uncertainty to rest, ideally with a clear decision by Quebeckers to remain part of Canada.

Even if the United States did decide to be reasonable and friendly toward an independent Quebec, it would probably demand its pound of flesh for re-entry into NAFTA – including, I would guess, the elimination of Quebec's protectionist dairy and poultry regulations and its laws protecting the French language. I can well imagine our trade people asking why American companies should be forced to label their soup tins in French or translate their movies. And I'm not sure Quebec nationalists understand the extent to which they have been able to protect their language and culture by being a part of Canada. In fact, I'm convinced that the price of independence would be a loss of the very things the separatists claim they want to enhance. Quebec would be a French-speaking minnow in the English-speaking sea of North America, and its fate would probably not be a happy one.

— —

Through all the weeks of the election campaign, I had been worried that NAFTA would explode into a hot and divisive issue. While the Conservatives and the Reform Party were in favor of it, the NDP was strongly opposed and the Liberals' support appeared to be conditional. They had vigorously fought against the Free Trade Agreement during the 1988 election, after all, and their much-touted policy platform, known as the Red Book, forthrightly declared that a Chrétien government would sign the deal only if significant improvements were made to the agreement regarding energy, culture, and the rules about subsidies and dumping. Since the Liberals were likely to win, and since any major modifications were virtually impossible, NAFTA was at risk.

Meanwhile, President Clinton was in the process of trying to push the agreement through Congress in the face of vehement opposition from union-supported Democrats and America-first Republicans. It was far from certain that he was going to get enough votes to pass it. The fear in the White House was that if the Liberals won on an anti-NAFTA platform, they would hand the president's congressional opponents the opportunity and excuse they were looking for to scrap the deal. "We're not even going to bring this to a vote if Canada wants to renegotiate," they would have said. "If Canada thinks it's a bum deal, that's good enough for us."

As the election wore on, however, I was encouraged by how restrained Chrétien sounded. He talked about jobs, health care, and social programs, but he didn't go to the barricades against NAFTA like the federal New Democrats were doing. He even invited an anti-NAFTA heckler in Vancouver to go vote for the NDP because the Liberals were free-traders. If he said that in public, I thought, it probably means he's on our side. And I came to realize that his position was really similar to Clinton's: pro-free trade, pro-NAFTA, but with some improvements. My read on Chrétien was that he was a good politician who needed to establish some independence from the United States – something many leaders around the world have to do. But Chrétien wasn't really playing the anti-American card in the election. Still, I had to make sure we didn't lose NAFTA at the last minute.

Shortly after I wrote a memo to the White House predicting a Liberal victory, I got a call from Bo Cutter, deputy director of the National Economic Council. "We accept your analysis that the Liberals are going to win, and we're worried there's going to be a problem with NAFTA. Is there any way we can get the Conservative government to proclaim NAFTA before election day?"

"No way," I said. "Technically they could do it, because it's already been passed by the House of Commons and the Senate. But if they tried, the result would be a political, legal, and constitutional nightmare. We can't ask them to do that."

"Well, then," Cutter said, "is there any way for you to secretly communicate with Chrétien or his people to see if they're truly supportive of NAFTA and whether they'll be sensitive to our struggle with Congress?"

"As a matter of fact, I'm scheduled to have a private meeting in Quebec City in a couple of days with Jean Pelletier, one of Chrétien's closest advisers. I should be able to convince him how delicate the situation is in Washington and that we need Chrétien's help."

Going to someone you think is going to be the head of government before he's even been elected was a rather unusual procedure. I was worried, if word got out, that it might look as though the United States were meddling in Canadian affairs by placing its bets on a Liberal victory. But it was worth the risk. Besides, what Chrétien said could easily influence American politics.

Marie Huhtala and I met with Pelletier in the living room of our consulate, overlooking the St. Lawrence. Pelletier was a former mayor of Quebec City and had been Chrétien's chief of staff in opposition. Distinguished in manner as well as reputation, he was running at the time as a Liberal candidate in the election. But everyone – including himself – expected him to lose to the Bloc Québécois candidate. Everyone also expected him to re-emerge as Chrétien's chief of staff if and when the Liberals won. (His educated guess at that point was 155 seats, eight more than needed for a parliamentary majority, and growing.)

"This is really sensitive, but I'll confide in you," I said to him. "Your new government will have the life-and-death power to kill NAFTA in an instant. And you can kill it without anyone ever knowing you killed it. You can kill NAFTA if, the day after the election, Jean Chrétien says that he's hoping to renegotiate it. If he says that, it's dead, because Congress will say they're not going to vote on it until they see the new deal and they'll walk away from it. If you want to kill NAFTA without leaving any fingerprints, I'm telling you now, as a fellow politician, you have a perfect way to do it. But I hope you won't."

"We don't want to kill NAFTA," Pelletier said. "We're a free-trade party. Jean Chrétien is a free-trader. We've got a few things we're concerned about, but we're for it."

"That's great," I said. "You know, Chrétien's campaign is very much like Clinton's. Clinton didn't campaign on trade. That was Bush and Perot. Clinton campaigned on jobs and people. And the president took a view similar to Chrétien's about NAFTA: it's fine, but it needs some additional things. And he got side agreements with respect to labor and the environment. You didn't have that when your party platform went to print."

Clinton's side agreements, I believed, paralleled what the Liberals were demanding in their policy Red Book, though they were also concerned about energy, water, culture, and the U.S. laws regarding subsidies and dumping. The first two were either non-issues or non-starters in the eyes of the American government, and the latter two were problematic, but I imagined we could figure out some way of handling them so that the Liberals could say they had got something from us, as they had promised to do. I understood that it would be politically tough for the new government simply to accept what Clinton got and no more.

Pelletier thought that some of Canada's concerns about subsidies and dumping could be resolved by the ongoing GATT negotiations. Was there any way the United States could delay the vote on NAFTA until they were concluded?

"No way, absolutely no way," I replied. "I wish we could. It would solve all of our problems. But we can't."

"So how can we rework and reword this agreement without putting it on hold?" he asked.

"Maybe through side letters," I suggested, "like the U.S. did on the labor and environmental standards. Chrétien could cite them as having been adopted after the Red Book went to press. Just tell us what you need to make NAFTA look more attractive to the new government and I'll let the White House know. But the important thing is that, no matter how many times you're asked, no matter how many different ways, on election night or in the days that follow, we would really appreciate that you not use the word 'renegotiate.' You can say you want to consult with us, you can say you have some concerns you want to discuss, but don't suggest renegotiating the agreement or it's finished."

Pelletier promised to look into the possibility of side letters with the senior bureaucrats. "Chrétien believes that the relationship between the United States and Canada can be friendly but business-like," he said. "We don't have to mix friendship with business. Friendship is friendship and business is business."

"But we need to set up good lines of communication," I said. "The president will want to call election night or the following morning to congratulate the prime minister. They can talk trade later. In addition, we've got to discuss when our two guys will get together. I understand that Chrétien isn't going to want to get on a plane to fly to Washington and Clinton isn't likely to fly to Ottawa immediately. We might think about getting them together at the APEC meeting in Seattle in November."

Pelletier and I made no promises, except to talk soon after the election, but I came away feeling very good about the meeting. "I'm confident they're for it," I reported back to Cutter and the Canada Desk. "We'll know soon enough. If Chrétien uses the word 'renegotiation,' he's pulled the trigger on NAFTA, and it won't be an accident. They've been warned."

To myself, I added, if he pulls the trigger, I'm going to be in for a rough ride as ambassador. Clinton's not going to want to work with Chrétien on anything ever again. It's going to be really bad.

Now there was nothing to do but wait and hope. We would have our answer soon.

The following day I resumed my other ambassadorial duties. I flew to Windsor for a meeting of the International Joint Commission, the panel of three Americans and three Canadians that oversees our boundary waters. I had been a strong advocate of U.S.-Canadian environmental cooperation as governor and remained interested in the issue as ambassador, but I didn't think that some of the clean-water activists helped their cause by dancing up and down the aisles during the commission's public session, ornately costumed as fish and birds. It hardly seemed a persuasive argument for the business leaders and academics present in the audience. While there, I couldn't help but notice once again that Windsor, itself an attractive town, has the world's best view of the Detroit skyline.

Both the similarities and differences between our two countries were brought home afterwards when Janet and I flew into Toronto to join Arlene and Bob Rae for dinner at Wayne Gretzky's restaurant and the last game of the World Series at the SkyDome. I was impressed by how respectful people were toward their premier, even though he wasn't very popular at the time, and how weirdly quiet the stadium felt at the beginning. "Don't be fooled," Rae told me. "Canadians are wound very tightly, so don't think they don't care about this game. There's a lot of tension here."

There I was, a proud American, torn between wanting the Philadelphia Phillies to win and the Blue Jay fans to be happy. I wanted Canadians in a good mood during my term in their country. In the ninth inning, the Blue Jays' Joe Carter hit his magical, game-winning home run and, sure enough, the crowd went completely insane. As we left the stadium, the streets were full of thousands of men and women running around, kissing each other, hugging strangers, high-fiving the police, no fights, no shootings, no vandalism, no arrests. "This kind of emotional outpouring couldn't happen in any U.S. city without incident," I thought. "It's amazing."

The next day, October 24th, I sat down with some Toronto pollsters and learned from their detailed numbers that the Liberals were on the verge of a massive victory, more massive than anyone had predicted at the start of the campaign. The big question was whether the Bloc Québécois or the Reform Party would finish second. The NDP was sinking in Ontario and the west, and the Conservatives might get as few as fifteen seats. To American friends who didn't understand how that could happen, I explained it this way: suppose in our last presidential election two powerful Democrats such as Jesse Jackson and Sam Nunn had decided to form their own political parties. Jackson would have argued that Clinton wasn't liberal enough and didn't care about the minorities; Nunn would have argued that Clinton wasn't conservative enough and didn't care about the south. And the possible result, if they had succeeded in getting their messages across, would have been Bush first and Clinton dead last. And that's what Kim Campbell faced.

On October 25th, just as predicted, the Liberals won the election, getting 177 out of 295 seats in the House of Commons with 41 percent of the vote and a respectable representation in every region. But the real political earthquake was the utter collapse of the Conservatives. They dropped from 152 seats to 2, even though they still took 16 percent of the popular vote, losing to Reform in the west, the Bloc Québécois in Quebec, and the Liberals in Ontario and Atlantic Canada. Stranger still, because the Bloc Québécois captured the lion's share of the Quebec seats, it placed second, two seats ahead of Reform, so that a rump of Quebec separatists under Lucien Bouchard became Her Majesty's Loyal Opposition. That's what you'd call a real opposition: they wanted to break up the country.

The strength of the separatists didn't seem to register in Washington, but the margin of Chrétien's victory and the decimation of Mulroney's party caused shock and alarm. While Bill Clinton was making his congratulatory call to Jean Chrétien, pandemonium reigned among the president's key advisers in the White House. A congressman had already claimed that the Canadian vote was an overwhelming repudiation of NAFTA, the jig was up, the game was over, the deal was dead. Every five minutes I'd get a call from someone screaming hysterically, "What's going on up there? What are we going to do?"

Meanwhile, Jean Pelletier had put me in touch with Chrétien's long-time political adviser Eddie Goldenberg, who would be handling the substance and details of the NAFTA issue in the Prime Minister's Office (PMO). I spoke to Eddie and reiterated what I had said to Pelletier. "If Chrétien's going to say anything, please ask him to choose his words carefully so that we can keep talking. I know he's going to be pressured to keep some distance from Clinton, but he should be continually reminded that Bill Clinton isn't Ronald Reagan or George Bush. Clinton is like him. He's a liberal, he's a political pro, and he's a great guy."

"Calm down," I told the top White House and United States Trade Representative (USTR) officials. "There's nothing to get worked up about. Chrétien's not going to do anything stupid. He's been around for thirty years or more. He ran on the same platform as Clinton. He took the same position on trade. He's a free-trader. Relax."

In fact, I myself was relieved a day later by Chrétien's response, at his first press conference, to the question of whether he intended to renegotiate NAFTA. "Look in the Red Book" was all he said. Some people thought it was a clumsy answer, but I assumed he was just trying to avoid the word "renegotiate." Meanwhile, the White House people, including some who were normally pretty cool characters, were still going crazy. On October 27th I was connected to the White House by speaker phone to what David Weiss later described as the worst meeting he had ever attended. While I was sitting quiet and alone in my Ottawa office, I had Sandy Berger, Bowman Cutter, Bill Daley, Rahm Emanuel, Bob Kyle, and David Weiss on the other end of the line sounding like they were in a state of panic. (It goes to show that if you get enough intelligent people at a meeting – anarchy prevails.) They didn't have the votes in Congress, yet they were angry at Canada.

"Can you give us any assurances?" they yelled. "Can you get Chrétien to say he didn't mean what he said in the Red Book?"

"That's not realistic," I said. "I don't think I can get the prime minister to stand up immediately after his election and repudiate his party's platform. But don't worry, we'll work this out."

"Can you guarantee that?"

"I can't guarantee anything. But if these guys had wanted to kill NAFTA, they would have done it by now. Chrétien didn't use the word 'renegotiate.' I told them, if you want to kill it, just use that word."

"You did *what*?"

"Look, I had to level with them. I trust these guys. They're political people. They're pros. Believe me, if they had wanted to kill it, it would be dead by now and we wouldn't be having this meeting."

The problem was that they were looking at Canada through the lens of the United States. They assumed, because Americans were debating NAFTA, Canadians must be debating NAFTA too. Ross Perot and Ralph Nader were citing Canada in their own protectionist arguments; Jesse Jackson was parading around Toronto with the NDP; and the Canadian party that had championed NAFTA had just been wiped out. The White House and USTR advisers never fully grasped that trade had not been a significant issue during the campaign.

Nor did they really understand the Canadian system. In Washington they were used to dealing with hundreds of people, all of whom had at least some ability to help or hurt them. Our Founding Fathers had deliberately built all kinds of checks and balances into the American constitution, while our political parties are really loose-knit coalitions of independent-minded, locally oriented free agents who come together primarily to help each other get elected. In Ottawa, however, all the power is concentrated in the House of Commons, and because there's formal party discipline, the majority party can do virtually anything it wants. It's as if the executive and legislative branches of the American system were merged into an all-powerful House of Representatives with the Speaker of the House, as leader of the majority party, becoming the president and with House members totally loyal on every vote.

The difference was brought home to me by the different reactions to the movie *The Madness of King George*. American friends who saw it said, "The king was nuts. No wonder we rebelled against those idiots." Canadian friends said, "See, the system worked beautifully. The government carried on very well without the king, thank you very much."

In other words, the Canadian parliamentary system was set up to be efficient government, to get things done, to carry on. The American system, with its three branches of government and two houses of one branch, was intended to thwart the consolidation of power. It was designed *not* to work, in the sense that no one was supposed to have king-like authority. "You guys have no excuse," I used to tell the Canadians whenever something got bogged down or ran off the rails. In practice, of course, Canada has developed its own checks and balances, from provincial rights to court rulings to regional sentiments, but Canada's checks and balances evolved almost by happenstance and hardly exist at the center. Ours were planned from the start and can still bring Washington to a state of paralysis.

The other important difference was that Canada has a cabinet made up of elected politicians drawn from the majority party in the House of Commons. Unlike American cabinet members, the Canadian ministers almost without exception have to run for office, they have to shake hands and be humble and give good speeches, they know what it is to win or lose. They all have active political antennae, which means they speak the same language and avoid the same mistakes. And they all share responsibility for the government's decisions in a collective way, rather than just running their departments as personal fiefdoms and gathering periodically for a fairly ceremonial meeting with the president, who has, as Lincoln once remarked, the only vote that counts in a cabinet meeting anyway.

In practice, almost everything in Ottawa is decided by the cabinet, which in turn is controlled by the prime minister. That means that when you're trying to manage issues with the Canadian government, you're really only dealing with fifteen or twenty key players in Parliament, the bureaucracy, and the Prime Minister's Office. If Chrétien wanted NAFTA, it would pass. If he didn't, it wouldn't.

The best I could do, therefore, was to arrange for our three top trade people – Mickey Kantor, Rufus Yerxa, and Ira Shapiro – to phone Eddie Goldenberg. Kantor called Eddie on

October 31st to see what concessions could be made to satisfy Chrétien without alienating Congress. Eddie called me the next morning. "I've told your people our concerns," he said. "We don't need a lot. What Clinton did with labor and environmental standards is a big help. But we do need some modifications. Mr. Chrétien would like to meet with you about this."

"Great," I said. "Anytime. When do you want to schedule it?"

"Well, actually," Eddie said, "we're sitting here right now in his office on Parliament Hill, if you can do it."

"You mean now! Sure, yeah, fine, I'll be right over." I was really impressed. In Washington it would take days, if not weeks, for an ambassador to get an appointment to see the president, and there would certainly be more involved than a walk across the street. Jim Walsh, my deputy, who happened to be out giving a tour of the Parliament Buildings to some relatives, was tracked down, and he joined me, slightly out of breath, while the meeting was already in progress.

Chrétien was still using his Opposition Leader's office, immediately below the prime minister's suite where I had been received by Kim Campbell. Though I hadn't met him since my arrival in Canada, I reminded him that we had met once before, in September 1991, at the Liberal International Convention in Lucerne, Switzerland. When I had arrived in Lucerne, I met two Canadian senators, Al Graham and Lorna Marsden, both devoted Liberals. "We've got our new leader, Jean Chrétien, here with his wife, Aline," they said. "He's a really great guy. So come and meet him at the reception we're having tomorrow."

I did. It was easy to see, from the crowd of delegates in the room, the respect with which the Liberal Party of Canada is held in international circles. It's the strongest Liberal party in the world. The very first thing I noticed about Chrétien was that he had an attractive and adorable wife. Aline bore an uncanny resemblance to Janet, in fact, and she shared Janet's friendly interest in what others were saying. Later, in Ottawa, they were occasionally mistaken for sisters. My second impression was how humble and unassuming Chrétien himself was, especially for a man who had first been elected to the House of Commons in 1963 at the age of twenty-nine, had held every major cabinet portfolio in the Canadian government, and came back from retirement to gain the leadership of his party. Rather than talk about his own achievements and problems, he wanted to get right into the upcoming presidential elections. And, third, he struck me as the consummate political junkie: Who was going to run for president? Who was I supporting? Why?

"Bill Clinton," I said.

"Who?"

"He's the governor of Arkansas, and he's really good."

"Tell him to do health care," Chrétien said. "It's the smartest thing we ever did."

It was a brief encounter on a whirlwind trip, but it proved serendipitous. A short while afterwards, when Clinton was getting ready to announce his candidacy for president, I said, "I really think you ought to throw in a phrase on health care. I was talking to this guy who's head of the Liberals in Canada, and he was convinced it's a winning item. And I know that people really worry about it in Michigan. You don't have to say what your plan will be. You don't have to say how you're going to do it or what the cost will be. Just say that you're going to present a national health-care plan to Congress within your first year in office. I think you should do that." There were many other people suggesting the same thing, no doubt, but I was able to add Chrétien's message as a reinforcement. And now, by another twist of fate, here we were sitting in his office on Parliament Hill, one the new prime minister of Canada, the other the new U.S. ambassador.

"We're at a sensitive moment," I explained, again. "We still don't have the votes to pass NAFTA. We'll get them, I believe, but it means we can't make any major changes."

He repeated his need for changes, but I got the sense that he wanted NAFTA to succeed. The real message, I felt, was his personal involvement with the issue. He wanted to move it along to a quick and painless conclusion. He slipped in, as an aside, that Ross Perot had called him to urge him to oppose NAFTA. If Chrétien were able to kill it, Perot promised to build a monument to him down in Texas. "But I don't want that," Chrétien told me.

I was worried, however, that he hadn't selected his cabinet yet. "What if we work all this out and your new trade minister wants further changes?" I asked.

"Then I'll have a new trade minister the next day," he replied.

Boy, I thought, would Bill Clinton ever love to have that kind of power, to make instant cabinet appointments without having to worry about Senate confirmation! I also wished that Clinton were as willing to fire people who were disloyal and get rid of people who weren't any good. In fact, all of Washington could use a dose of that kind of political accountability.

Since there was no Canadian trade minister yet, the task of working out a deal was passed to Al Kilpatrick, the department's senior bureaucrat, and his right-hand man, John Weekes. Now that they had the prime minister-elect's instructions, they started talking back and forth with our USTR people – though everyone was very careful not to describe the process as a negotiation. I left the technical

Top: Bill Clinton's saxophone debut in Traverse City, Michigan, July 1987, with Junior Walker, the Four Tops, Martha and the Vandellas, and Governor Blanchard.

JOHN ROCCO PHOTOGRAPHY

Above: Governors Clinton and Blanchard golfing in northern Michigan with Blanchard aides Greg Morris and Tom Scott, July 1987.

Top: Taking the oath of office, August 10, 1993.

Above: A conversation with President Clinton while Vice President Gore signs the oath. Jay and Janet Blanchard look on.

OFFICIAL WHITE HOUSE PHOTOGRAPH

Above: A very formal affair: the presentation of credentials to the Governor General at Rideau Hall, August 19, 1993.

Right: "All aboard the Canadian!" Janet and Jim on the train across Canada, September 1993.

Below: The residence staff poses with the First Lady.

Top: The first meeting between President Clinton and Prime Minister Chrétien in Seattle, November 19, 1993.
OFFICIAL WHITE HOUSE PHOTOGRAPH

Above: Meeting with Prime Minister Kim Campbell, September 2, 1993. Jim Blanchard (centre) with Jim Walsh.

Right: Virginia Kelley and Vaughn Cameron, October 1993.

Below: Out to dinner with former prime minister Pierre Trudeau in Montreal, January 1994.

Right: A relaxing moment for U.N. Ambassador Madeleine Albright at the ambassador's residence in Ottawa, spring 1994.

Below: Two well-known photographers, Yousuf Karsh and Tipper Gore, July 1994.

Above: Janet and Jim on the patio at the ambassador's residence, the view over the Ottawa River to Gatineau, Quebec behind them.

Left: With Jay.

Below: The ambassador's residence in summer.

Above: The view in winter.

Below: An early snowfall, November 1995.
GIANNI BERTAZZO

Above: The Fourth of July, 1994, on Parliament Hill, Ottawa. The U.S. Embassy is visible in the background.

Left: The Fourth of July celebration at the ambassador's residence is a major event in Ottawa. The scene before the throng arrives . . .

Below: . . . and later, the party in full swing.

details to them, who fortunately had worked with each other in the past, but I kept in constant communication with Pelletier and Goldenberg. They seemed pleased by how quickly Washington was ready to respond. I also kept in touch with our trade officials, who were relieved that NAFTA was back on track. Everyone was getting along just fine.

That probably would have happened eventually, but since time was of the essence, it was helpful to have had as ambassador a political person who knew the players and how to speed things along. I could understand what Pelletier and Goldenberg needed. Their challenge was to help the prime minister without derailing the legislation in Congress. "You're going to do really well here," Chrétien said during our first private dinner. "You're a politician. That's what we need in these jobs. These aren't academic or social jobs. They require political judgment and a sense of reality." It seemed the Clinton-Chrétien relationship was off to a good start.

The stickiest points remained culture, subsidies, and dumping. The Canadians wanted to be able to protect their cultural institutions from the overwhelming impact of American movies, television, radio, books, magazines, and music; the United States wanted the right to retaliate whenever Canada did that unfairly. The Americans wanted to be able to continue placing countervailing duties on imports that directly or indirectly benefited from an unfair government subsidy or were being dumped in the United States at an artificially low price in order to unload an oversupply or crack the market; Canada favored a system of appeal panels to limit the avalanche of legal actions they feared were pending under our trade remedy laws. Both sides advocated something less than pure free trade, everyone recognized, but both were considered legally and politically crucial to the national interest.

Within a couple of days, however, I was able to note in my journal, "We think we resolved the NAFTA problems. Our USTR people have been on the phone with the Canadians till 3 a.m. on the second and then again at 7:15 in the morning on the third." Basically, regarding culture, the United States would agree to the cultural "carve-out" Canada had secured under the original Free Trade Agreement, while we would retain our right to retaliate. Regarding subsidies and dumping, the United States would preserve its domestic trade remedy laws, while some working groups would be set up to review them. It was a good compromise and, best of all, it could be reached through side agreements without reopening NAFTA and going back to Congress.

The deal was virtually done, in fact, before the new trade minister, Roy MacLaren, was sworn in on November 4th, along with the prime minister and the rest of his cabinet. That ceremony was an eye-opener for an American. It was conducted by Governor General Hnatyshyn in the same ballroom in Rideau Hall where I had presented my credentials. Janet and I, watching it on TV, were shocked by how solemn and low-key the event was: more like a state funeral than an inauguration. In the United States, of course, such a historic moment would have been celebrated with cheering crowds, patriotic speeches, inaugural balls, once-in-a-lifetime souvenirs, and marching bands, but here there were only a few family members in the audience and the only hint of emotion came with the applause Jean Chrétien received. Why weren't all the members of Parliament, senators, and Supreme Court justices invited to attend? Why weren't the premiers brought from across the country to participate in this important occasion? Rather than finding the swearing-in of the new government a matter for national unity and pride, anybody who bothered to tune in was left to feel, ho-hum, here comes another bunch of boring politicians to screw things up.

I chuckled, however, when a reporter asked Chrétien afterwards why there weren't more people in the cabinet from Quebec. "The people have spoken," he answered. "They didn't elect enough Liberals to Parliament. And if they don't vote for us, they don't get into the cabinet, it's as simple as that." That sure was a contrast to Bill Clinton, who insisted on picking cabinet members from states that had never supported him, with the faint hope that they would support him in the future.

Roy MacLaren's appointment was well-received. He had a great reputation in our embassy as a businessman, a strong proponent of free trade with the United States, and a nice fellow. All I had been hearing since my arrival was "Let's hope Roy becomes trade minister. He's really studied this file for a long time. Not that there won't be differences, because Canada always has differences with us, but he'd go forward in the spirit of promoting trade and good relations." He certainly would do nothing to scuttle the compromise that the Prime Minister's Office and senior trade officials had patched together.

In Washington, all this while, the president and his people kept struggling to get the House to vote for NAFTA. And because there isn't the same serious discipline or party accountability that exists in Canada, that meant convincing, cajoling, and arm-twisting all 435 members, one by one, in the face of fierce opposition from the Ross Perots, the Pat Buchanans, the Ralph Naders, the Jesse Jacksons, and many unions. Even some prominent Democrats, including our majority leader and whip, were against NAFTA, and not all the Republicans in favor were keen to help Bill Clinton. In order to try to swing public opinion behind it, Vice-President

Gore even offered to debate Ross Perot on national television. Though I was happy to feed facts about Canada and NAFTA into Gore's briefing books, I thought it was the dumbest idea I had ever heard. It risked losing the agreement in a kind of game-show circus, and I discovered I wasn't the only one to think it was nuts. Most of the White House advisers and trade officials with whom I spoke put the responsibility for concocting it squarely on the shoulders of the president and vice-president. "See what happens when you politicians make decisions without your staff in the room!" Tom Nides, Mickey Kantor's chief of staff, joked to me.

"We were all wrong," I wrote in my journal on November 9th at the conclusion of the debate. Gore just wiped the floor with Perot and gave a much-needed boost to the pro-NAFTA side. Within a fortnight, in fact, late on November 17th, the House endorsed the agreement by a mere thirty-four votes. If only eighteen people had switched their vote, NAFTA would have been dead. The narrow margin of victory made me all the more certain that Chrétien could have killed it, deliberately or inadvertently, if our two governments hadn't reached a swift understanding.

The next day, November 18th, I flew to Washington in order to join the president on Air Force One for his trip to the Asia-Pacific Economic Cooperation (APEC) summit in Seattle. As I briefed him on Canada and Chrétien, I could see that he was dead tired from having been up half the night celebrating the NAFTA vote. His face was puffy, his eyes were red, and all he wanted to do by the time we arrived in the late afternoon was go straight to sleep. But first he had to give a pep talk to a huge rally of Boeing employees about airplane sales to China, and then he was supposed to meet Jean Chrétien.

This was the first get-together that I had been discussing with Pelletier and Goldenberg for almost a month. They felt, and I agreed, that the president should receive the prime minister on his first official visit to the United States before any of the other leaders who were pouring in from around the Pacific Rim. The meeting was set for 8:30 that evening. The Canadians wanted to follow it with a short, impromptu press conference (which they call a "scrum" and we call a "news-availability"), but that hadn't yet been confirmed by the White House, and the president was bone-weary.

While Clinton was speaking to the Boeing employees, I slipped over to the terminal where Chrétien's Challenger was due to arrive, and there I found his assistant Jean Carle pacing back and forth in a fury. "Who's in charge?" he fumed. "We've been asking for this press scrum for three weeks, but now I can't get through to anybody, nobody's being pleasant, I can't figure out what's going on."

"The White House is totally disorganized, that's what," I said. Keeping Chrétien's staff on side and happy was important to me, particularly until NAFTA was approved, and I even cashed a few IOUs to make sure that Eddie Goldenberg was included in the fancy dinner Clinton was going to host for the visiting heads of government. "The White House is full of policy makers trying to do logistics, who don't know enough to know how much they don't know. Dealing with them is like suggesting to a Rhodes Scholar that there may be something in the world he doesn't know. It's not your fault. I'll see what I can do."

Just then the Challenger landed – it was puny compared to Air Force One, but Chrétien had made an election issue out of getting rid of Mulroney's big Airbus – and I welcomed the prime minister and Aline to the United States. By the time I reached the hotel where the American delegation was staying, I found Jean Carle still ranting at a low-level White House official in the lobby about getting a "scrum."

I cornered Sandy Berger, the deputy national security adviser. "You know," I said, "this is really important. Chrétien did everything humanly possible to help us get NAFTA through Congress. It's his first official trip to the States. He will be the first leader the president sees. And we need to have it at least a photo op. This is a big deal in Canada, and the media need pictures."

"You're right," Berger said. "It's just that the president is really exhausted. Okay, we'll do it, but tell them to keep it brief. I'm afraid our guy might fall asleep on them."

The meeting had already been plotted in some detail. Originally we wanted to announce that we had a deal on NAFTA, but that would have made it look as though Chrétien had flown to the United States and immediately capitulated. Instead, the president would raise the subject, the prime minister would respond with his concerns, and they would agree to pass the file over to their trade officials. Then, if it all worked out according to plan, the Canadian cabinet would approve NAFTA in a few weeks and the government would proclaim it.

"Does your side intend to discuss any other issue?" Jean Pelletier had asked me.

"No, none, unless you have something. It's just to say hello, nothing substantive."

"We haven't anything either," he said. "We've briefed the prime minister that there's only going to be a short discussion about NAFTA, no other issues, then the whole thing will be delegated to our staffs."

The meeting finally took place at 8:30 p.m. As we walked to the meeting room in our hotel, I said to the president, "Remember, this guy's a veteran. Treat him like a pro."

"Yeah, okay," he said, looking and sounding really tired. "Does he play golf? Maybe I should invite him for a game."

"No, no, not now," I said. "He's just come off a campaign accusing Mulroney of being too close to the U.S. president. You don't want to do that to him."

Then Clinton turned to Sandy Berger and asked, "So what are we going to talk about?"

"It's just a get-acquainted," Berger replied. "You're going to thank him for his help with NAFTA, he's going to talk a bit about it, you're going to ask him what he needs, he's going to tell you a bunch of stuff. Don't worry, it's all pretty well worked out, but they don't want to announce it now. That's all they're expecting. It'll be brief. They're good people. You'll like them. Oh, and one other thing. Canadians love to be consulted. They love it when we ask them for advice. So why don't you ask Chrétien what you should do about Bosnia and Haiti? We might learn something, he'll be flattered, and that way he can do most of the talking."

I had a flash of anxiety about that, but I didn't think much more about it as we went into the meeting room. The setup wasn't conducive to a relaxed exchange of views. Clinton and Chrétien were seated beside each other at one end of the room. Fanning away from them were two rows of chairs, on which the half-dozen members of the American delegation sat facing their Canadian counterparts across an ever-widening gulf: Warren Christopher opposite André Ouellet, Mickey Kantor opposite Roy MacLaren, I was opposite John de Chastelain, and so on. After the opening formalities, someone mentioned trade, and Chrétien took off like a hyped-up boxer at the sound of the bell. Animated, hyper-nervous, talking a mile a minute in his convoluted English, he went on and on about energy policy and water rights and trade matters while Clinton looked dazed. The rest of the

Americans looked at me quizzically, as if to say, So this is the old pro you've been telling us about?

Eventually Chrétien slowed down and said what we were waiting to hear: Canada has a few concerns about NAFTA, he needs a little of this and a little of that, but everything's going to get worked out.

"Why don't we have our staffs do that?" the president suggested, right on cue.

"Yes, good, fine," the prime minister replied. I beamed across at Pelletier and Goldenberg, and they beamed back.

"Now then," the president said, "let me switch subjects. I'm really worried about this genocide in Bosnia. Thousands of people are being slaughtered, and things seem to be getting worse. What do you think the United States should do?"

Chrétien looked like he'd been hit with a sledgehammer. "Well, Mr. President," he said after a long and awkward pause. He looked to Ouellet, his foreign minister, who looked back without a clue. "Well, Mr. President," he tried again. He looked to Pelletier and Goldenberg, who looked as if they wanted to crawl under their chairs. "Well, Mr. President," he said, racking his brains, "that's a tough one. We've got to stop the killing, but we don't want to risk the lives of our soldiers over there. Yes, it's a tough one. I don't know."

"Well then, what about Haiti?" Clinton asked. "What should the United States do about restoring democracy in Haiti?"

Again a look of bewilderment crossed Chrétien's face. "Well, Mr. President," he began again. Again he looked to Ouellet for help. Again he shot a "what the hell's going on here, why didn't you guys brief me?" look at Pelletier and Goldenberg. All of us had tears in our eyes trying to stifle our amusement. "Well, Mr. President," he repeated, "that's another tough one." He paused. "I don't know."

"Well, I don't know either," Clinton said, and the whole room roared with laughter and relief. The two men seemed to bond at that moment, and they became the best of friends from that point forward. Although Clinton is more a policy wonk like Pierre Trudeau, and Chrétien is more a big-picture guy like Ronald Reagan, they turned out to share a passion for politics and golf. The next day I noticed that they lingered around each other at the APEC gatherings. I also noticed that, contrary to the Liberals' communications strategy, Chrétien didn't mind having his picture taken strolling, sitting, or joking beside the president of the United States. Indeed, he liked it. While some of his staff continued to manufacture spats and disputes for the press, in order to keep some political distance between the prime minister and the Americans, he himself never bothered to stoop that low.

"That went great," I said to Sandy Berger after we left the meeting and rode an elevator to the president's suite.

"He's a very unusual man" was all Berger said, but he had a funny look on his face.

As awkward as the meeting had been, I felt good about it. NAFTA, it told me, was a done deal. Ten days later, on November 28th, Eddie phoned to say that he hoped to have it approved by cabinet in a few days; on the twenty-ninth Roy MacLaren and Mickey Kantor met in Washington to finalize the wording; and on December 2nd the official announcement was made. "Press is negative on Chrétien," I wrote in my journal. "Generally very difficult on Canadian politicians. I called Eddie and offered my help." As it turned out, there was no reason to be so negative. In the first five years of NAFTA, trade between the U.S. and Canada increased by about 60 percent.

I summed up my feelings that day in my journal. "In three months of being here in Canada, so much has happened: the campaign, a new government, NAFTA resolved, transition between U.S. and Canadian government, ten-province tour, getting to know the Embassy and its people. And in three months I may have achieved as much as I could in several years. It is clear that this was the most important time for me to be here and for Bill Clinton to have me here. Why? Because we have a new government that needs to start out in a good relationship with our administration."

— 4 —

AT HOME IN CANADA

Virginia Kelley, President Clinton's mother, had accepted an invitation to address the Ontario Cancer Society in Ottawa on October 28, 1993 – three days after Chrétien's election. They had a fundraising event called Desserts and Coffee as part of their Breast Cancer Awareness program, and when they found out that Mrs. Kelley herself was undergoing treatment for breast cancer, they asked her to come and talk to them about her experience. It was one of her first public appearances since her son had become president and her first outside the United States.

I had met her once, just long enough to shake her hand, at the Democratic convention in New York the night Bill Clinton gave his acceptance speech. I wanted to make sure that she was properly looked after and entertained during her two-day stay. Through her secretary, Linda Beth Dixon, Janet and I invited her to stay with us at the ambassador's residence, and I made the services of the embassy available to her as well. We didn't know how much her health would allow her to do, but we were ready to give her a tour of the town.

On Wednesday, the twenty-seventh, I went out to greet Mrs. Kelley and Linda at the airport, along with some embassy staff and the ladies of the Ontario Cancer Society. And off the plane bounced a heavyset septuagenarian in a jumpsuit, with jet-black hair except for a single streak of white across the front, huge false eyelashes, and a ton of flashy jewelry.

"Welcome to Canada, Mrs. Kelley. How was your trip?" I said, knowing she had just been through a long and circuitous trip from Little Rock. "We're glad you're here. There's a greeting party waiting for you downstairs."

"That's great," she said, "but I need to sit down and rest for a few minutes."

I found her a side room. As soon as we got there, a frantic Linda lit up a cigarette and started inhaling deeply. It became clear that Mrs. Kelley wanted to rest only so that Linda could enjoy a bunch of cigarettes before facing the cancer awareness people – the irony of which I fully appreciated. Presently, we took the escalator down to the street level, where a couple of photographers were standing with several distinguished women, all wearing discreet pearls and fashionable hats.

One of them stepped forward. "Mrs. Kelley," she said in her most Upper Canadian manner to this feisty old Southerner in a jumpsuit, "on behalf of the Ontario Cancer Society and our Breast Cancer Awareness program, we want to bid you a formal welcome to Canada and to our capital, Ottawa."

"Thank you, thank you, thank you," said Virginia Kelley, sounding for all the world like Bill Clinton. She even had some of his personality and slang. "Good to be here."

"And we're so honored that you would come and address us on this important subject, breast cancer, and how it strikes families of all backgrounds and women of all ages, sizes, and shapes. Your coming here today will help us greatly in our cause."

"Thank you, thank you, thank you," Mrs. Kelley repeated. "You know, I champion only two issues, that's all. Breast cancer. . . and horse racing."

"Oh?" said the lady from the Ontario Cancer Society. She seemed to be uncertain if this was a joke. "Would you care for a refreshment?"

We then got in the car with Vaughn. On the way into town, Virginia Kelley asked me about the Canadian election, what the new prime minister was like and whether he would be nice to her Bill. I told her how everyone was looking forward to hearing her speech. "They're going to have a thousand people at this dinner for you. That may not sound like a lot, but, believe me, for Ottawa it's huge. In the States they'd charge $100 or $250 a head, but here it's only $25 because people aren't used to paying a lot of money. So they're absolutely thrilled."

"Are there things I should touch on," she asked, "besides my standard remarks about breast cancer?"

"Well, they'll want to hear about the president," I said, "you know, growing up with Bill and all that."

"Yeah, I assume that's why I got invited." She laughed.

"And you might want to talk about your experiences in Canada. Canadians are very sensitive about how much Americans know or don't know about them. If you've been here before, you'll want to talk about that. That would make them feel good. Have you been here before?"

"Yes," she said, pausing, "but only once. What's that city right next to Detroit?"

"Windsor?"

"Yes, that's it! The Windsor Harness Raceway!"

"On second thought," I said, "maybe you'd better leave that out."

At home we hosted a nice reception for her and Linda, and when our guests left, Janet and I enjoyed a quiet dinner with them. I kept thinking to myself, "If only people could see us now," as Linda dragged on a cigarette, Virginia knocked back the scotch, and I enjoyed a cigar. Mrs. Kelley was full of stories, and it was clear that she had had a hard life. William Jefferson Blythe III, her first husband and Bill's father, was killed in an auto accident before Bill was born. Her second husband, Roger Clinton, was an alcoholic and abused her. Bill's brother, Roger, had been into drugs, and she was still worried about him. Her third husband, Dick Kelley, was a great guy, however. I later met him golfing with Clinton and Chrétien in Washington, but he hadn't been able to come on this trip.

People think that Bill Clinton is from Hope, Arkansas. He is, but he spent most of his childhood in Hot Springs, the state's Las Vegas. And that's where Virginia Kelley's heart obviously was. Indeed, she and Linda were talking about visiting the real Las Vegas sometime soon. Mrs. Kelley had been there many times, including once to see Elvis Presley perform, and she told us that Bill used to do Elvis impersonations as a high-school kid to make her happy. It was obvious that, in her eyes, the president could do absolutely no wrong.

"I remember when he brought Hillary home for the first time," she said. "We were used to seeing beauty queens, but this one looked like she hadn't combed her hair in a week. Roger and I were sitting in the family room, and we looked at each other just aghast, because Bill had told us over the phone that he was going to be bringing home someone extra special. That's when I knew that this one was different. It was serious, and we must have looked surprised. When Hillary went into the bathroom, Bill pulled us aside and said, 'Listen to me, I'm tired of these sex goddesses. I want a woman I can talk to.'"

We put Mrs. Kelley in the large bedroom (one of eight in the residence) across the hall from ours. We couldn't help but hear that she had the TV on all night. "Did you fall asleep with it on?" Janet asked her at breakfast the next morning.

"Oh, no," she said. "I always leave it on twenty-four hours a day. On CNN. Because I want to see what they're doing to my boy. I want to hear what they're saying about him. I want to know where he is. I feel reassured just hearing that dear voice of his."

That day the governor general's wife, Gerda Hnatyshyn, held a luncheon in her honor at Rideau Hall; then our staff escorted her on a scenic tour of Ottawa. Though I noticed that Virginia had bruises on her arms from the cancer treatments, which Linda told me really wore her down, she looked well and had a great spirit, always ready to keep going. She even dropped in on the cancer clinic at the Civic Hospital on her way back to the airport. And she certainly gave a terrific speech. She had the dinner crowd at the Westin Hotel in the palm of her hand.

She talked about Bill, of course, but she had more to say about Roger. "He's pretty special, too, you know," she said, and the audience liked that. It was a very polished, almost political speech, with the right acknowledgments to the organizers and a moving account of her struggles with cancer. And at the end she said, "And I'll be back next year, if you'll have me, to see you all again." The crowd gave her a thunderous standing ovation.

We didn't know how sick she really was. She died two months later, on January 6th, the same day as my old friend, Tip O'Neill. Even before that, however, we had christened her bedroom the Kelley Room, and it stayed that way until the president and Hillary themselves used it, after which it became the President's Bedroom. We put a picture of her in it, and we sent the president an album of photographs, including one I took of his mother sitting beneath the portrait of Queen Elizabeth II in Rideau Hall. I inscribed it "Virginia, Queen of Canada."

There's more to an ambassador's life than greeting distinguished guests. If done well, the job is a lot of hard work, long hours, and countless days on the road. Socializing is important, but I actually had a busier social schedule as governor of Michigan than as ambassador to Canada. Politicians and businesspeople have inescapable social obligations, but there wasn't very much I had to do or attend as ambassador if I didn't want to. Early on, for instance, I decided to forgo the diplomatic tradition of visiting every other ambassador in order of protocol just to say hello. I had been warned that it wouldn't be the best use of my time, and I needed to plunge into the substantive issues, meet the key Canadian players, and get to know the country. Over the next few months I got to meet all my fellow diplomats anyway.

Nevertheless, dealing with the issues, handling the media, and managing the relationship between two countries does involve a significant amount of socializing. Diplomacy, like politics and business, is often a case of who you know, what you know, and getting to know everyone and everything better. In that respect, the residence, the staff, the dinner parties, and the travel are effective tools of the trade. If an ambassador is shy, or if he has a problem with liquor, he's going to have a hard time. There was a diplomatic party every night of the year in Ottawa, to celebrate a national day or welcome a distinguished visitor, and the American ambassador is invariably invited. So I had to be highly selective, depending on my schedule, Janet's plans, and the purpose to be served. I made sure, however, to accept invitations from small countries as well as the big ones, so that no one would be offended.

And then we were expected to do quite a bit of entertaining ourselves. The entertainment allowances U.S. ambassadors get are low given the demands of the job, and American ambassadors often end up spending their own money for official purposes. While Janet and I learned to make the State Department funds go a long way, I was always writing checks out of my personal account for social events. You don't have to be wealthy to serve as the American ambassador to most posts, but if you're a penny-pincher, don't bother to apply. The first thing I had to do after arriving in Ottawa, in fact, was write a personal check for $6,000 so that the chef could go out and buy the essentials: a pound of sugar, a pound of flour, a jar of mustard, a jar of peanut butter, and so on. It was like starting a restaurant from scratch. I also had to front-end all the initial expenditures for towels, salt shakers, and other household necessities. We even had to bring our own bed!

Even when there is money in the budget, not everything is reimbursed by the State Department. You can't get reimbursed unless you can demonstrate that the event is furthering U.S. interests. I obviously covered the costs of the family reunion surrounding my mother's eighty-fifth birthday in June 1995 and our annual weekend festivities for friends from Washington and Michigan. Less understandably, perhaps, you also can't get reimbursed for entertaining Executive Branch officials, because the budget-makers in Congress don't want ambassadors, cabinet members, and White House officials wining and dining each other at public expense. I personally paid for meals whenever a Washington cabinet member stayed over, therefore, and when the president and vice-president visited Ottawa, I provided the sandwiches, brownies, doughnuts, and coffee for the two dozen or so Secret Service agents who were all over the house and grounds for a couple of days. We were delighted to do it, but some career diplomats have been known to complain. Some have even sent bills to their guests!

In most cases I was reimbursed, but the system was so complicated that we needed a full-time bookkeeper to keep track of all the various accounts, to sort the official business from the personal expenses, and make sure there was still some money left. Our bookkeeper, Brenda Darrel, turned out to be the only American citizen on the household staff, and even that wasn't planned: her husband happened to be posted to Ottawa with the U.S. military. All the rest were Canadians, though of mixed backgrounds. The residence manager Roger Beauregard, was a French Canadian; the head butler, Gianni Bertazzo, was of Italian heritage; the chef, Cory Haskins, was from small-town Ontario; the sous-chef, Dino Ovcaric, was Yugoslavian; the two maids, Estelle Buenviaje and Nene Ting, were Filipinas; and our protocol directors, first Fiona McHugh and later Greta Poole, were both British-born with British accents. Whenever we had a party, they would all put on tuxedos or uniforms and help out. That way, I found, if you have staff buying the food prudently, and staff preparing the food, and staff serving the food, you can put on a pleasant party for a relatively small amount of money, especially if the wine and beer have been donated to promote American products.

At the office, too, while our career foreign-service officers must be Americans, limited to a three-year assignment, the rest of the personnel are largely Canadians. Known as foreign-service nationals, they include everyone from the medium-level managers to drivers. Many serve for years. They provide the infrastructure continuity, and by the time we arrived, some of them had been there for thirty-five years. We were horrified to discover, however, that most, including many of the long-timers, had never been invited to a meal at the ambassador's residence. So one of the first things we did was host a sit-down luncheon for forty-four of our foreign-service nationals, and from then on we invited them to our annual Christmas party as well.

I prided myself on treating the foreign-service nationals well. We were supposed to be diplomats, after all, as well as employers and human beings. All these employees went home to their relatives, their friends, their neighbors. If they felt good about the people they worked for, that would reflect well on the United States of America. If not, that would reflect badly. When the Republican-controlled Congress closed down the U.S. government in December 1995, our employees didn't get paid. ("These guys are acting like anarchists," I fumed in my journal.) Everyone was confused and shocked. I called a big meeting to explain our system to them and assure them that they would be paid eventually. In the meantime, we offered to help them with credits and loans. They were and are part of America's team, and every ambassador needs to demonstrate that.

Our Ottawa socializing was reduced by the time we spent traveling, whether around Canada or between Ottawa and Washington. I once estimated I was away from Ottawa about a third of the time, giving speeches and interviews, attending meetings, going to receptions, or dropping in on our consulates. In just one three-month period in 1995, for example, I went to Detroit, New York, Hamilton (Bermuda), Montreal, Toronto, Vancouver, Marquette, New York again, Hamilton (Ontario), New York again, Toronto again, Port Huron, Calgary, Winnipeg, Minneapolis, Oakville, Niagara-on-the-Lake, New York again, Windsor, and Halifax.

In a country as vast as Canada, I had to get away from Ottawa in order to be effective at my job and find out what was going on. And, as every politician and CEO will appreciate, it was remarkable how much business got done, how many opportunities unfolded, how much information got picked up, and how many connections were made by means of spontaneous, personal encounters. All at once there was a face to a name, a missing piece to the puzzle, an opened door. All these elements contribute to the building of the U.S.-Canada relationship. And that seemed particularly true in Canada, where the élites are so small in number and so interconnected.

I might get on a plane going between Quebec City and Ottawa and run into Saskatchewan Premier Roy Romanow, who would brief me about the national-unity issue. Or Janet and I might go down to the Shaw Festival in Niagara-on-the-Lake and end up spending the evening with John Turner, the Liberal leader before Jean Chrétien and briefly the prime minister of Canada in 1984, who would be full of opinionated, knowledgeable insights about Canadian-American relations. (Franklin Delano Roosevelt, he insisted, was actually born on Campobello Island in New Brunswick, but was whisked across the border by his mother and registered in Maine so that he could claim to have been born on American soil.) Or we might accept an invitation by my old friend Jacques Demers, the former coach of the Detroit Red Wings, then with the Montreal Canadiens, to see a hockey game at the Forum and encounter another former prime minister, Brian Mulroney, who between periods wanted to talk about NAFTA, the cruise missile, health care, and the political fortunes of Bill Clinton. The night before, by chance, we had had dinner with the Chrétiens at 24 Sussex, and the next night we went out with Pierre Trudeau, our friends Don and Heather Johnston, and Sue Wood to a restaurant in Montreal. So, within seventy-two hours, as I observed in my journal, I had spent time talking privately about Quebec, American politics, and international affairs with the three most important Canadian prime ministers of the past twenty years – all in the context of informal social encounters.

I had hardly arrived in Ottawa before I had an opportunity to meet five of Canada's six living prime ministers during a reception at the National Archives. In Washington, I observed, nothing short of a state funeral would get so many former presidents together in one room – there would be so much security that almost no one would get close to them. By way of contrast, one evening my press secretary went to a movie with his wife and ended up sitting a row away from the prime minister and Aline Chrétien, who slipped quietly into their seats with a bag of popcorn and no security agents. And it was not uncommon to go to a government reception or private dinner and find most of the major players from the cabinet, the Prime Minister's Office, and the civil service partying together.

For a quiet and sober people, Canadians love to party and drink. The Christmas season, in particular, which starts in early December and stretches well into January, is just one long floating drinkathon. At one memorable party in Hull Janet and I were about to leave around midnight, after four hours of wine and carols, when the jovial host nabbed us and led us into a room where tables were laden with virtually every variety of food known to man. When we finally headed for the door at 1:30, half waddling, half staggering, we were among the first to depart. "What's wrong?" the host called after us. "Didn't you have a good time? We'll probably carry on till four!" And then there was the Brazilian Ball in Toronto, one of the grandest charity fundraisers of the midwinter season. We were astonished. Here were the cream of the country's business élite in black tie and their very respectable wives dancing in conga lines with all but nude men and topless women brought in for the occasion from Rio. The puritan streak in the United States would never have permitted it, except perhaps in Las Vegas, yet the Presbyterian burghers of Toronto the Good were enjoying the time of their lives.

When Janet and I were in Ottawa, we probably averaged two or three events a week at the house. Quite often, to welcome a visiting dignitary to town, we would hold intimate lunches and dinners with a dozen guests or large cocktail parties for seventy-five to one hundred people – more when the weather was warmer and we could use the large patio – bringing together a diverse array of Canadian politicians, civil servants, journalists, academics, businesspeople, and artists. When high-ranking officials such as Defense Secretary William Perry, Labor Secretary Bob Reich, Attorney General Janet Reno, or FBI chief Louis Freeh were in town, we would invite everyone and anyone who might be helpful in their work or connected to their departments. Thus, we had environmental experts to meet the members of the International Joint Commission; we had cultural chiefs and university professors to meet Joe Duffy, the head of the United States Information Agency; we even had the entire U.S. Joint Chiefs of Staff to lunch with their Canadian counterparts.

Janet and I had to adjust quickly to the realization that

Canadians have their own sense of time. When you say you're going to have a reception from 6:00 to 7:30, most Americans come about 6:30, many come at 7:00, and lots stay until 8:30 if you let them. While business meetings in the United States generally start on the dot and political events kick off after about twenty minutes, if you don't arrive at a social event fashionably late, it's assumed that you have nothing better to do, which is not the message you want to convey. In Canada, however, 95 percent of your guests pull into the drive and line up at the door at 6 o'clock precisely. You open the door and they all march in. Then, about 7:15, everybody lines up to say goodbye and leaves.

It's almost a religion for Canadians to wait in line. Few Americans would tolerate going into a drugstore or license bureau and having one person behind the counter work slowly through a queue of twenty people. There would be a riot. We'd start shouting for the manager and throwing down our money, saying, "Here, keep the change. I'm out of here." Canadian salespeople and ticket-takers often look as though they're doing the customer a favor by engaging in grubby commerce, while Canadian customers just quietly, patiently, eternally wait. We could never figure out whether it had something to do with the deference to authority for which Canadians are renowned, their stoic politeness, their British heritage, or simply their relative lack of all-American, go-getting, consumer-driven, service economy.

Their concept of the weekend is different too. Canadians consider weekends a sacred time reserved for family activities, whether it's skating, skiing, reading, watching TV, or going to the cottage. I was surprised by how few events we were invited to on weekends, unless it was to be with someone's family. And virtually every major dinner I attended all across the country featured salmon. "No wonder you've got a salmon shortage," I told Canadians. "That's all you eat." In the United States, in contrast, the weekends are for getting babysitters, going out, and doing things. The big events for a Democratic politician in Michigan, say, are always on Friday, Saturday, or Sunday night, and the fare is inevitably steak or chicken. To make a very broad generalization, while the sense of family is still very strong in small-town America and among certain ethnic groups, its strength is much more evident everywhere in Canada.

That family feeling was contagious. Many, if not most, of the senior officials from Washington preferred to stay at our residence, rather than in a hotel, so we seemed always to have overnight guests. After the receptions and dinners were over, we would offer them a coffee or liqueur, and they were free to chat or watch the news or read a book by one of the three blazing fires on the main floor. That was always a special treat for Janet and me, a rare privilege we could never have had in Washington, to sit down in a relaxed setting with a senior member of the administration, to share private thoughts and feelings, to hop off the merry-go-round of our lives for an hour or so and be fully relaxed. The house was so quiet and secluded that Madeleine Albright, in those days the U.S. ambassador to the United Nations, who had arrived dead tired and gone to bed early, exclaimed the next morning, "Boy, I haven't slept that well in years!"

Sitting by the fire also turned out to be a great way to get to know Canada's new cabinet ministers and their spouses. In fact, when we were leaving the post, one of them said, "We don't know what we're going to do for a good restaurant when you guys are gone." Roy and Lee MacLaren were regular guests; John Manley, the Ottawa-born industry minister whose portfolio included commerce, consumer affairs, rural and regional economic development, space, and part of telecommunications, came with his wife, Judith; Allan Rock, the minister of justice, and his wife, Debbie, became friends as did our first guests, MP Jim and Heather Peterson; and I had my first real conversation with Paul and Sheila Martin over dinner in the house. That didn't happen until December 16th, what with my tour of Canada, the election campaign, the APEC summit, the American Thanksgiving holiday, and the never-ending unpacking of boxes. Paul had also been settling into his new job as minister of finance, the second most powerful position in the Canadian government but perhaps the most onerous and despised. He was facing a horrendous deficit projection and had a budget due in February. "By next year," he laughed, "I'll be the most hated man in Canada." Despite that, he was expected to succeed Jean Chrétien as prime minister someday.

I knew him as the son of Paul Martin Sr., the revered Liberal cabinet minister in the fifties and sixties whom I had met on several occasions when he was the mp for Windsor and a good friend of G. Mennen "Soapy" Williams, the Democratic governor of Michigan from 1948 to 1960. I often described Paul Martin Sr. to Americans as the Hubert Humphrey of Canadian politics. Paul confirmed that his father had really admired Humphrey as well as Adlai Stevenson. He himself thought that Franklin Roosevelt and Harry Truman had been the last great American presidents of this century.

We had barely sat down in front of the fire when he asked, "So what's with the Detroit Lions? Do they like to lose?" (Lion fans would have appreciated his observations.) He had grown up in Windsor, of course, and still paid close attention to the fate of the Lions in football and the Detroit Red Wings in hockey.

A few days later, on December 21st, we had Canada's new foreign minister, André Ouellet, over with his wife,

Edith. They showed up with a homemade sugar pie. "Boy," said Janet, "I can't imagine Warren Christopher coming to the door with a cherry pie." As well as being a knowledgeable cabinet veteran, Ouellet also proved to be a devotee of American baseball and American politics. He listed Bobby Kennedy as well as Sir John A. Macdonald as his heroes, and he had followed Clinton's presidential campaign closely. We also discussed the Quebec issue at length. He mentioned that Chrétien had asked him to handle relations with Quebec as well as foreign relations. He was obviously a committed federalist, though he had supported the Meech Lake Accord when Trudeau and Chrétien were against it. He was convinced that Quebeckers would never knowingly vote to leave Canada.

It was at that point, speaking for myself during a freewheeling private conversation in front of the fire, that I first raised the idea that the United States should perhaps reassess its traditional position regarding the independence of Quebec. In effect, ours was a passive position, one that maintained that the United States has always enjoyed excellent relations with a strong and united Canada and it was up to Canadians to decide their own political future. But now I wondered whether we shouldn't move at least a little farther toward a more supportive statement defending a united Canada as a successful model of peace, justice, and diversity for the whole world to emulate. Our "it's up to you" response seemed rather lukewarm, if not actually cold. And once I had raised the thought, I couldn't shake the desire to do something about it.

— 5 —

BORDER SKIRMISHES

"Why do we need an ambassador to Canada at all?" I was sometimes asked. "We get along well, don't we? What do you do up there, pour a lot of champagne?"

It was a good question. From one angle you would think that Canada is the last place in the world where the United States would need an ambassador. We have shared the longest undefended border in the world for more than a hundred years. Millions of people travel back and forth across it to work, study, play, visit relatives, and do business. They define the relationship better than any politician or diplomat can. And the relationship is a good one. From another angle, however, no two countries on the face of the planet have a more intricate, multifaceted, overarching relationship. That requires the management of an ambassador.

We cooperate on an endless list of matters each day. At every moment of every day dozens of American officials are in meetings or on the phone with their Canadian counterparts (not to mention their counterparts in all the provincial governments). They're tracking the Russian Mafia on the west coast, talking about pollution in the Arctic, building a space station. Even before I left for Ottawa, I found myself caught up in discussions about NAFTA, NATO, Bosnia, and more nitty-gritty trade issues involving dairy products, poultry, wheat, and sugar.

The work of an ambassador is always more substantive than social. Very few ambassadors to major countries can survive merely by sending and receiving messages, and even the ambassadors to small countries lose respect and the potential for advancement if they're nothing but human fax machines. Most ambassadors help originate, shape, and implement policy in ways that each particular country finds useful and acceptable. Diplomacy isn't usually a matter of treaties and wars. It's a matter of getting things done in subtler ways that advance the best interests of the United States. And it is the responsibility of any ambassador worth the certificate on the wall to oversee all the day-to-day, government-to-government connections and make sure that no disputes inadvertently or unnecessarily explode.

In my own case, of course, I didn't want to be U.S. ambassador to Canada simply as a reward for past services. I wanted to make my mark, just as I had as a congressman and governor. In that sense I saw the job as building a career rather than capping it. And I had particularly wanted Canada because it offered a blend of economic, political, and military issues. With Ottawa in easy reach of Washington and in the same time zone as Detroit, I could stay in close touch with what was happening back home, utilize my skills and connections by dealing with the most senior levels of the American government, and still have a great time. "This job is the best kept secret in all the U.S. government," I used to say to Janet.

An ambassador to a major country can actually have a wider range of authority and activity than all but the most senior cabinet members. Even though housed and paid by the State Department, he or she is, as chief of mission and the president's personal envoy, technically in command of all the dealings of the United States government with the host country – with the exception, of course, of the military during war. That means he or she works directly with the White House, the entire cabinet, and every single department and agency. This coordinating role is central to the ambassador's job.

Every department or agency, if left to itself, is likely to fight for every small advantage it can get with Canada, even at the risk of harming the general relationship. Particular interests pushing the dairy dispute in the U.S. department of Agriculture could have aggravated Ottawa's dealings with Quebec at the time of a referendum, for example, because Quebec is the major beneficiary of Canada's dairy supply management program. Middle-level officials in Commerce could cut a deal with their Canadian counterparts that might be completely at odds with getting NAFTA approved. The last thing any ambassador needs is to have dozens of people acting independently and without his or her knowledge in ways that create trouble.

In a real sense, therefore, our ambassadors are the only Americans who worry full-time about the complete relationship with a particular country and how best to weigh all the competing foreign-policy and trade issues. Nobody else does. Even the secretary of state and his or her assistants are bound to be preoccupied with the latest crisis or perennial hot spots, whether the Middle East, Bosnia, Northern Ireland, or North Korea. So they expected me to let them know if there were any major problems with Canada, but otherwise to go ahead and manage the files, work with the White House, with State, and with every other department and agency so that no one did anything contrary to the overall interests of the United States.

When John Kenneth Galbraith, the Canadian-born Harvard economist, was ambassador to India, he was asked to comment on a proposed directive that ambassadors should no longer communicate directly with the president, as he had been doing on a regular basis with Kennedy, except through the State Department. "Communicating to the White House through the State Department," he cabled back, "is like fornicating through a mattress." The order was dropped.

I could – and did – communicate with President Clinton directly on a number of issues. My ability to call up the president was one of the reasons I had been chosen for the job in the first place. But I didn't tell him anything I wouldn't have told Warren Christopher. I had nothing to hide from the State Department. On the contrary, I always kept it informed of what I was doing, because I wanted it to work as an ally with the National Security Council. My purpose in going directly to the White House, to cabinet members, or to the officials in Commerce, Transportation, Defense, Energy, or Interior was to get action, not to get a different result than State wanted or push a different point of view. Why should I bother Secretary Christopher with the details of NAFTA when Mickey Kantor was clearly in charge of the file? And Christopher, while responsive when I needed him, was happy to let me manage the Canadian relationship. He realized, too, that my connections to the White House and the other departments helped State from time to time.

Before leaving Washington for the post, I deliberately met with eleven cabinet members, as well as a dozen members of Congress and more than two dozen other senior officials. I wanted to get to know them individually; I wanted them to feel comfortable about contacting me if problems arose; and I wanted to find out what files they had outstanding with Canada and what personal connections they had, whether an uncle in Toronto or a honeymoon in Montreal. These courtesy calls were not part of the regular preparation every ambassador goes through, but I felt that Canada is more tightly entwined with more departments than most countries and I wanted to get its issues on the radar screen.

In most cases, I discovered, Americans and Canadians were working well together. Conflicts were the exception. But they did happen, and when they did, they tended to get blown out of all proportion. The media in Canada watch our every little move intensely, and they like to describe every little dispute with us as a war. You don't see that in the United States. "War" is used very sparingly in the American press. But Canadian journalists talk routinely about wheat wars, lumber wars, beer wars, and magazine wars, which is odd when you think of Canada's reputation as a non-violent, peacekeeping nation. It all goes back, in my opinion, to the War of 1812.

Most Americans think of the War of 1812, if they think of it at all, as a war with the British to prevent them from reclaiming us. Harry Truman called it a damn foolish war that never should have happened, and in truth it didn't accomplish much. So it usually comes as a surprise to us to hear Canadians describe it as a war to prevent the annexation of Canada by the United States – which Canada won! "You guys burned Toronto," they say, "but we showed you. We went down and set fire to the White House!"

I got a kick out of going to the Canadian War Museum in Ottawa. The exhibits put a lot of emphasis on incidents and heroes of the War of 1812 – in stark contrast to U.S. military museums. The legacy of that war remains a deep-rooted suspicion on the part of many Canadians that we still have designs on Canadian territory and like to push Canadians around.

Jim Walsh warned me early on that, even though we work cooperatively with Canada on hundreds and hundreds of issues, we have to manage them very carefully. Little, seemingly insignificant bits of business can explode into huge, high-profile trouble. A disagreement over salmon fishing on the west coast can flare into an angry blockade of a tourist boat, then some guys burn the American flag and the U.S. Senate pushes through a resolution condemning Canada. The situation gets out of hand, a deal gets harder and harder to find, and everybody on both sides – including the fish – is worse off.

At least half my job turned out to be about helping manage these trade "wars," which wasn't surprising given that Canada is the United States's largest trading partner. We do more trade with Canada than with all of Europe combined, for example, and we get more energy from Canada than from any other country. Roughly 95 percent of that trade goes back and forth without any problem under the Free Trade Agreement and NAFTA. Unfortunately, they don't adequately cover everything.

The oldest and most intractable disputes have to do with agriculture and fishing. We have basically agreed to disagree on them, precisely because they have always been so contentious: the one because of too much supply, the other because of too little. Part of the barrier impeding a settlement was precisely that many of the same officials on both sides had been arguing about the same things for years. I began to wonder if they hadn't become biologically incapable of agreeing. Nothing was likely to happen, I concluded, if it didn't happen at the top.

"In the bowels of the Canadian bureaucracy," one of our key trade negotiators observed, "are a bunch of guys who want to pluck a feather from the American eagle. When they get out of hand, we whack them hard and they run for cover."

The classic free-traders would say that the Americans shouldn't be clamoring for protection from Canadian wheat and sugar, while the Canadians shouldn't be allowed to protect their dairy and poultry producers from U.S. imports. These are sensitive domestic issues, magnified by the fact that farmers around the world have enormous political power, far out of proportion to their numbers. They also have a certain historic and even moral clout in the United States and Canada because they are viewed as the founding settlers, the original pioneers, the heart and soul of society, the guardians of old-fashioned values, the self-sufficient and hard-working backbone of the nation. As a result, they are often able to have their way with governments of all stripes and ideologies. The disputes between American and Canadian farmers (though kin in spirit and often even by ancestry) have been raging for most of this century. "One of the problems," I used to tell both sides, "is that you guys are an awful lot alike."

The official U.S. policy is that we would be happy to have free trade in all agricultural sectors, including dairy, poultry, wheat, and sugar. Until that's achieved, however, the United

States and Canada are going to respond on a commodity-by-commodity, case-by-case basis to protect their farmers. The Canadians claimed that the new global trade agreement – the so-called Uruguay Round that created the World Trade Organization (WTO) – permitted them to maintain prohibitively high duties that protected their dairy and poultry interests, even though the equally new NAFTA between the United States, Canada, and Mexico outlawed the imposition of new duties and would eliminate all existing duties by 1998. Our lawyers were convinced that was nonsense, not even debatable, open and shut, and they proceeded to challenge it – though not until the Quebec referendum was over in the fall of 1995, because we didn't want to stir up any trouble between Ottawa and the Quebec dairy producers. As it turned out, to our complete bewilderment, a WTO panel sided with Canada, and the battles have dragged on.

Regarding the wheat that was coming into our northern states from Canada and thus stirring up the wrath of our farmers in North Dakota and Montana, I and wiser minds than mine kept pushing for a negotiated settlement, based on voluntary restraints, before the whole issue raged out of control. We feared that the dispute would escalate to the point where both sides got locked into another no-win situation in which the interest groups and their lobbyist lawyers would make it politically harder to ever reach a deal. The longer we talked, the more likely it was that Canada's western farmers would accuse the minister of Agriculture of selling them out to assist the dairy and poultry producers in Ontario and Quebec, the more likely that American farmers were going to put pressure on Congress to offset the indirect government subsidies they saw reflected in the lower price of Canadian wheat. And that would have an adverse effect on all the other areas of our relationship. "We've got to solve this thing," Roy

Romanow, the Saskatchewan premier, warned me. "It's going to get ugly."

On January 8, 1994, the day Virginia Kelley was buried (and fittingly, as President Clinton reminded me during a phone call that evening, Elvis's birthday), I went to Toronto to participate in a round of negotiations held at the Airport Hilton between Mike Espy, our secretary of Agriculture, and his Canadian counterpart, Ralph Goodale. Espy was ready to make a deal by which the United States would accept a gradual phase-out of Canada's supply-managed dairy and poultry regime if Canada would accept caps on the amount of wheat and sugar it could export into the United States. Espy threw out some numbers that he thought were low enough for the American farmers to accept, but fair enough to the Canadians.

Finally, after three or four hours of hemming and hawing, Goodale said, "I need some time to think about this, but I'm very pleased. I think we've made a good deal of progress."

"I don't think we've made any progress at all," Espy snapped back. "This meeting has been a total waste of time." And the meeting ended.

When I got into the elevator with Espy, I said, "Maybe your play-acting will help push Goodale to a deal."

He looked at me with fire in his eyes. "I wasn't play-acting. It was a waste of time. These guys aren't serious."

The breakdown reflected, in my opinion, a difference of style between Canada and the United States. Canadians prefer to negotiate. Whether they are any good at it is another matter. They want to deliberate for days, if not weeks or years. They're also hopeless, helpless, shameless nitpickers. Under the guise of negotiation, they've been nitpicking themselves to death over the status of Quebec. And they're horribly cautious about making any deal with the

Americans, just as I think Quebec's nationalists are almost biologically allergic to a deal with English Canada. Americans, in contrast, are deal-makers. We like to cut quick deals. In that regard, we're more entrepreneurial, more innovative, more creative. Things move faster in the United States.

"I wasn't rejecting his offer out of hand," Goodale explained to me afterwards. "I couldn't just agree to it. Let him know I'm thinking about it." I passed the message along, but Canada never got such a good offer again. And, within a few days, American farmers started blockading Canadian wheat at the Montana border.

The following April, in fact, my whole strategy of toning down the rhetoric, turning down the temperature, preferring the gentle nudge over the hard punch, almost went off the tracks on the eve of a phone call between Clinton and Chrétien, intended in part to get the agricultural negotiations moving again. On April 20th, in the midst of a congressional hearing, Senator Kent Conrad from North Dakota joked that the United States ought to aim the three hundred Minutemen III missiles in his state toward Canadians. "Maybe that will get their attention," he was quoted as saying in newspapers and on talk shows across Canada the next day.

"I've got good news and bad news," I said when Conrad phoned to explain. "The good news is that I've only received one irate call. The bad news is that no one in Canada is speaking to me anymore." But the fact that we hadn't been able to resolve these problems was no laughing matter. We at the embassy were embarrassed we hadn't been able to bring the issue to an end months before.

Things only deteriorated. On May 24th, on a trip to Brazil, Secretary Espy reportedly said that the United States was going to help the Brazilians file a complaint against Canada for dumping wheat. The same day, by coincidence,

Roy MacLaren gave a tough speech in Washington lambasting the United States over the number of lawsuits and appeals that had been launched over trade issues. It didn't sound like Roy, and I assumed he was merely playing politics for the home audience, but it wasn't helpful. During a meeting immediately afterwards, Mickey Kantor expressed his frustration. "This is crazy," he told MacLaren. "We're willing to give you complete free trade in agriculture. Let's just go right to it." Canada wasn't ready to do that, of course. I wasn't sure we were either, but that was our official position.

The next day, with the headlines all about MacLaren's tongue-lashing, I decided to give an interview to CBC-TV to remind Canadians that trade between the two countries was growing by leaps and bounds, that Canada had a surplus of exports over imports, and that the disputes were a very small part of a very big picture. I also underscored the fact that we supported complete free trade in agriculture, so the Americans weren't the culprits in the stalled negotiations. As for Espy's remarks, I pointed out that he had not been authorized by the president to instigate trade complaints by Brazil against Canada. Getting a third country to move against a friend wasn't the way the United States normally operates. Not only was it my job to protect the president, that happened to be the truth.

Thinking I had got my message across, I happily flew off to Toronto with Janet and drove on to an opening night gala at the Shaw Festival in Niagara-on the-Lake. The following morning, while eating breakfast in the garden room of the Prince of Wales Hotel, I was greeted by Sylvia Ostry, one of Canada's leading economists, who congratulated me for making the front page of *The Globe and Mail*. I was surprised, because none of its reporters had interviewed me. Then I was shocked. "U.S. envoy sides with Canada," read the headline, and the Washington-based story implied that I was supporting Canada's position on wheat.

"This is a big problem for me," I noted in my journal. "I hope it's a one-day story. I don't mind appearing sympathetic to Canada here, but I do mind having my vigorous advocacy of U.S. interests ignored." Jim Walsh also feared that it made me look as though I had developed "clientitis," the foreign-service term for becoming more loyal to the country where you're serving than to your own government. And my friend David Weiss, one of Mickey Kantor's trade negotiators, warned me to cover my tracks in Washington. "Jim," he said, "you may be right on the substance, but, remember, in a spat between a cabinet secretary and an ambassador, a president usually has to side with his secretary."

"Jim, Mike Espy is not a happy camper," Kantor himself told me. "Please call him."

Fortunately, from my first campaign for governor in 1981 to my last day as ambassador, I kept my own tapes of every media interview I ever gave as a safeguard against being misquoted. So, back in Ottawa, I sent the transcript of my CBC interview to Kantor, Espy, the State Department, and various media outlets to try to nip the *Globe*'s distortion in the bud. I also tried to phone Espy to explain my position. I only got one of his assistants, who rambled on about how rotten the Canadian Wheat Board was. "It really sounds like they want a wheat war with Canada," I noted. Nor was that the end of it. *The Washington Post* picked up the story, and even though it now had the full transcript too, it took the same angle. "U.S. Envoy Backs Canada on Wheat," read its headline.

"This is real trouble," I wrote. "Thank God it's on page 30. Obviously grossly misleading. The article is bound to stir up problems with Congress."

Sure enough, by the time I phoned Senator Conrad, it was too late. "A bunch of us senators have already sent a letter to the president complaining about you," he said. "But, don't worry, I talked them out of calling for your resignation."

Great, I thought, here it is, the first anniversary of my appointment to Canada, and my gift to the president is a wheat controversy. I felt badly about adding to his woes. Then I looked out my window and – I couldn't believe my eyes – it was snowing on May 27th! "I've gone a year without controversy," I noted to myself, "so I suppose, in the tradition of the Clinton Administration, that's been far too long." As a bit of damage control, I issued a statement supporting Espy's negotiating position on wheat, without mentioning that I still thought he was wrong to use Brazil as a stick with which to beat Canada.

On May 28th *The Globe and Mail*, again without any member of its staff having interviewed me, ran the headline "U.S. envoy backtracks." I hadn't backtracked, of course; I had merely corrected the initial erroneous report. That report, it turned out, was based on a snippet of tape recorded by the CBC and shopped to the *Globe*'s Washington bureau by staffers in the Canadian Embassy. "Between CBC taking two small comments out of a fifteen-minute interview and *The Globe and Mail* writing a front-page story based on third-hand reports without talking to me," I wrote, "this has been my initiation to the crossfire of U.S.-bashing. I knew it would happen eventually, but wondered when. Oh Canada."

A month later, on June 27th, Kantor and Espy met with MacLaren and Goodale in Chicago to try once again to solve the wheat dispute. I received reports that they had discussed different levels of caps, a blue-ribbon commission, and a one-year deal in lieu of a utopian comprehensive, long-term settlement on all agricultural issues. As one of our veteran negotiators once explained to me, "With these agricultural issues, you're better off cutting a short-term deal with the hope that the weather changes or something else drives the prices up. That usually takes care of the problem by itself."

That's more or less what happened. On August 1, 1994, the United States and Canada announced they had reached an agreement on wheat. In the end Canada agreed to an export cap of 1.5 million tons of wheat, considerably lower than the 1.7 million Espy had offered Goodale the previous January. "Of course," I noted, "no matter what the deal is, these poor Canadian negotiators will always be accused of caving in or backing down."

I didn't expect to get an angry phone call from the prime minister, however. "What's going on, Jim?" he asked, sounding really ticked. "This guy Kantor has caused so many problems for me, all for nothing. I thought we had a deal on this. We made an agreement with you, and then you don't keep your word. How can we trust you guys?" He wasn't mad at me personally. He was mad, I think, because the press coverage about the wheat deal wasn't good.

Nor had things been going much more smoothly over on the fish front. In many ways, Canada is more of a maritime nation than the United States. Canadians think of their country as reaching (in the words of their national motto) *a mari usque ad mare*, from sea to sea. They eat more fish than Americans. And the federal fisheries portfolio has been prestigious and important enough to be seen as a springboard to the highest offices of the land. Since the United States doesn't even have a fisheries minister, and responsibility for the industry is spread across several agencies, I often had to act like one in my dealings with Brian Tobin, affectionately known as the Codfather, alias the Voice of the Fish, alias the Tobinator, who held that post in Chrétien's cabinet for most of the time I was in Ottawa. Bright, amusing, with the florid rhetorical style of the Irish politicians I have known in the United States, he was extremely likeable and we became fast friends. He did occasionally, however, get carried away by his Canadian patriotism to a degree that made some people in Washington nervous.

The Canadian government had had to impose strict rules prohibiting the fishing of cod, which had been brought to the edge of extinction off the coast of Atlantic Canada by a combination of more mobile fleets and more efficient technology. (Newfoundlanders also blamed the international campaign against seal hunting, since seals eat a lot of cod, thus making the bars of St. John's among the very few places in the world where men don't like Brigitte Bardot.) The fishing communities were economically and socially devastated. Yet fleets were still coming north from New England to fish just beyond Canada's territorial waters, as were trawlers from Portugal and Spain, and Canada wanted the U.S. government to help prevent that. I remember one meeting of New England governors and Atlantic premiers in June 1994, during which Newfoundland premier Clyde Wells, normally a cool and cerebral type, was practically in tears as he compared the destruction of the cod stock to the Holocaust. I thought the analogy was extreme, but it apparently played well in Newfoundland.

Though we were sympathetic to Canada's arguments and wanted to be helpful in supporting some sort of binding global convention at an upcoming United Nations conference, we couldn't go along with Tobin's proposal for Canada to unilaterally extend its control over fishing beyond its established boundary waters. If we recognized the precedent set by such an arbitrary extension, our navy would be rendered useless in straits and passages all over the world.

Such a unilateral action, I remarked, would be unbecoming to a nation that prided itself on multilateral cooperation and belonged to every multilateral organization known to man. But he could do it, Tobin quipped back, because he had grown up on a U.S. air base in Newfoundland. He seemed pleased to have our support at the UN conference, however, and when he went to "war" in March 1995 in defense of the lowly turbot, which were being fished out by Spanish trawlers using illegal methods just beyond the two-hundred-mile range, we actually helped him by keeping silent, to the surprise and umbrage of the Spaniards.

I was hoping, in part, that our silence might earn us a bit of good will in an ongoing dispute that had broken out the previous year. This one involved the destruction of the Pacific salmon fishery along the west coast. That was a tougher problem for us to manage because it required us to find a consensus among the federal departments of State and the Interior; Congress; the states of Alaska, Washington, and Oregon; and a multitude of Indian bands. When negotiations bogged down in May 1994, Brian Tobin predicted that the Canadian fishermen would form a "wall of death" north of Vancouver Island to prevent any salmon from reaching American waters. On June 10 he announced plans to slap a $1,500 fee on U.S. fishing boats entering Canadian waters, even though the inside passage between Washington State and Alaska off the coast of British Columbia has always been considered international waters. "This is bound to trigger talk of a fish war," I noted. Within hours, I had a call from Senator Frank Murkowski (R-Alaska) wondering whether we shouldn't send the Coast Guard to escort our boats.

Instead, I was hoping for a tough and quick response from the State Department, to follow up my private complaints. Otherwise, Tobin would assume we were feeling guilty about our fishing practices or didn't care. But, because we didn't have a high-level Washington official in charge of fishing issues, no formal objection came until June 14th. I passed it along to Tobin immediately, along with a plea to resume negotiations.

"Why should we negotiate with you while you're increasing your fish catch as we speak?" he retorted.

I offered to try to get our side to agree to catch no more fish than in the previous year if he would lift the fee and go back to the table. Tobin saw that as a new proposal and seemed receptive to it. Indeed, he was delighted to get a call on June 30th from Katie McGinty, the president's environmental adviser, saying the White House was willing to consider just such a freeze in exchange for new talks. "It's a tough problem," she told him, "but we're happy to work with you on it." I assumed he had threatened the fee precisely to get that kind of attention.

The next day, July 1st, Canada's national holiday, I exchanged several faxes with Tobin's assistant about a mutually proposed agreement on Pacific salmon. I thanked Tobin for trying to work it out with us when I ran into him later that morning at the Canada Day celebrations on Parliament Hill. Thousands of people joined the governor general and the prime minister there on a perfect summer's day for a patriotic show of song and dance and a few brief speeches. After the entertainment was over, I walked across the street to my office for a conference call with the White House and the State Department to finalize our approval of the agreement. Janet even typed up a revised joint statement at home, we faxed it off to Tobin, and by 5:15 we had a deal – for forty-five minutes!

At six o'clock I got a call from Tobin's deputy, Bill Rowat: the deal was off. The minister, he explained, had just been informed by a Canadian reporter that Senator Murkowski, who had been included in the White House consultations with concerned members of Congress, had already issued a statement. "I'm glad to see Canada's finally come to its senses," it declared, "and removed the highly illegal, inflammatory license fee." Not only had Murkowski pre-empted the announcement that Tobin was supposed to make simultaneously with us, he had done so in a way that suggested that the Americans had managed to convince the Canadians of the error of their ways. Tobin went ballistic. He said he had to cancel our agreement for fear the fishing industry would think he had made a final deal without consulting them.

I reminded Rowat that the Clinton administration didn't control Frank Murkowski, he wasn't even in the same party. Blaming us for what he did would be like our blaming Chrétien for something a member of the Reform Party did. The leak was too bad, but it was part of a problem that the executive branch of the U.S. government must always deal with: it has to consult Congress on this kind of foreign-policy matter, not just because the members of Congress have a constitutional role in foreign policy, but because they have constituents with vital interests and legitimate concerns. Yet consultation carries the risk of leaks and spins.

"I know all that," Rowat said, "but Tobin has totally flipped out."

"But for the sadness of the situation," I replied, "it's almost comical."

I called Katie McGinty and gave her the news. She was aghast, of course, and really angry at Murkowski's staff. "Why don't we both phone Tobin and say we're sorry?" I suggested. "And I'll phone Eddie Goldenberg and ask for his help."

Though Tobin was grateful for our calls, he insisted he couldn't go forward with his meeting with the fishermen the next day if they thought he had already made a deal. I suggested he go ahead and take his kids to the fireworks on Parliament Hill, have a good evening, and we would talk in the morning. "Okay," he said, "but I'm not going to change my mind. Maybe in a couple of weeks, but not now."

Then I called Eddie. "I don't want the wheels to come off this buggy," I said. "We've got to manage this thing. We don't want a big explosion out there on the west coast." He promised to work it out. All I could do at that point was go off to the fireworks myself.

"U.S. remarks heat up salmon war" was the next morning's headline in *The Globe and Mail*. "Tobin calls Alaska senator a 'gnat.'" The minister's full quote was "Murkowski is an equivalent of a gnat flying around the horse. All you do is give a swish of your tail and it usually vamooses."

A temporary deal to lift the fee and fish more responsibly was worked out within a day or so, and three weeks later when Vice-President Gore came to Ottawa, he brought with him a new proposal for ending future disputes over salmon. Gore asked Prime Minister Chrétien himself to consider it carefully. At one point during the luncheon in honor of the vice-president at 24 Sussex Drive, Tobin chimed in and started complaining about fish, but Gore cut him off. He wasn't angry or rude, as the Canadian papers later reported, but he was curt. "We've just given you a new proposal, I've just talked to your prime minister about it, and we'd like you to look at it." As it turned out, however, the process didn't produce any lasting results, and new negotiations had to be scheduled.

All was quiet on the fish front when suddenly, on July 24th, while I was relaxing after a Sunday-afternoon croquet game on the front lawn, another controversy popped up. Canada was about to arrest two vessels from New Bedford, Massachusetts, for fishing for Icelandic scallops right on the edge of the boundary waters off Newfoundland. The person in charge of fishing issues in the State Department was away on vacation and no one else was ready to issue an immediate caution to Canada not to do it – which I feared would make Tobin think he could get away with it. Unlike the cod and salmon disputes, this one hinged on the biological question of whether these scallops were mobile like fish or stationary. If mobile, Canada had no case. If stationary, Canada had jurisdiction, because the scallops were tethered within boundary waters but had drifted into international waters. The Coast Guard had warned New England scallopers against going so close until the question was settled. Weeks later, in fact, the State Department concluded that the scallops were stationary and, therefore, Canadian.

In the meantime, however, we Americans didn't like seeing two of our fishing boats being seized at gunpoint and escorted into St. John's harbor by a Canadian navy destroyer. I immediately sent Roger Meece, my consul general in Halifax, over to Newfoundland to find out what was happening and help arrange bail for the two captains. Senator Edward Kennedy, who was in a tough senatorial race that coming fall, phoned to express his concern. "This is crazy," he said. "We don't want anybody held up there, and we want our boats out as soon as possible."

"I'll do whatever I can," I said.

"Who is this guy Tobin anyway?" Kennedy asked. "Murkowski tells me he's a nut. Tobin called him a flea or something."

"Brian's not a bad guy," I said. "It's just that he can get carried away at times. Don't worry, we'll figure something out." And I suggested he call the Prime Minister's Office to ask for Chrétien's help.

That night Kennedy called me back, furious. He felt he had been given the brush-off by a PMO staffer. "They weren't helpful at all," he fumed. "You know, our family loves Canada. The Kennedys have been about the best friends Canada's ever had in Washington. I'm probably considered Canada's best friend in the Senate. So what the hell's going on up there?"

"They have this thing about standing up to the U.S.," I tried to explain.

"Well, I'm not going to call them back," he said. "You deal with them."

"I'm happy to," I replied. "That's why we have an ambassador up here."

Meanwhile, the bond for the two fishing boats had been set at $1.6 million and $1 million. Though Tobin couldn't interfere with the justice system, he said he would try to get it lowered, and eventually it was reduced to $100,000 each. He also managed to get the fishermen's trial delayed, by which time emotions had cooled and the prosecutors decided to drop the charges. We counseled the two captains to grab the offer and get their boats out of Newfoundland as quickly as possible, which they did on August 5th. I was happy, Teddy Kennedy was happy, and the Scallop War was over.

— —

It didn't take me long to learn that, if one side feels severely aggrieved in a trading relationship, it doesn't really matter what the legal agreements say. Some compromise has to be worked out. For example, the American softwood lumber industry, which is centered in southern states such as Georgia, Mississippi, Alabama, and Louisiana as well as the northwest, has persistently argued that their competitors in western Canada are able to sell their lumber in the United States at a cheaper price because they enjoy an unfair government subsidy. Canadian companies cut most of their trees from public lands and pay a fee that in no way corresponds to the real market price. In contrast, most U.S. lumber is cut on private land and sold at market prices. For U.S. companies to cut trees from public land, they have to bid at auctions where the prices inevitably reflect the real value. In addition, the Americans argue, Canada's environmental practices are less restrictive, and therefore less expensive, than those in the United States. So the industry puts pressure on the White House, Congress, and the Commerce Department to apply duties to compensate for the unfair advantage enjoyed by Canadian companies. For years there has been litigation, with one countervailing duty case after another.

"We own the land," the Canadian government responds, "and we have a completely different system. You need Canadian lumber and we think this is a fair price. If you really believe in free trade, it shouldn't matter."

"Yeah," the American lumber companies reply, "but we're being put out of business because your guys undercut us with your government subsidies. It's awful."

In August 1994, after Canada had challenged a Commerce Department duty levied against Canadian lumber subsidies, a NAFTA appeal panel ruled two-to-one in favor of the Canadians. The duty had to be eliminated, and the Canadian companies wanted to get back about $800 million in paid tariffs with interest. It was a huge story in the Canadian media, but received almost no attention in the United States. Nevertheless, the American companies, heavily influenced by their lawyers in Washington, continued to threaten new litigation.

Such was their unhappiness that they even filed a court case challenging the constitutionality of NAFTA itself and the NAFTA dispute settlement process.

I and most of our trade officials preferred to get rid of the constitutional challenge, refund the money, and cut a new deal, particularly since the Canadians, being negotiators rather than litigators at heart, seemed to be willing to give a little for the sake of stability in the market. Eventually we struck a framework whereby the constitutional challenge was dropped, the duties were refunded, and the two sides agreed to enter discussions aimed toward a longer-term deal. After a dozen years of feuding and litigation, the distrust on both sides was intense, and the talks dragged on. But that distrust was matched by the persistence of the negotiators, and they were able to conclude a five-year truce before I left Ottawa in March 1996.

Canadians are particularly sensitive about their culture – or what we in the United States call popular entertainment. It's something that we Americans dominate worldwide. So, when you're a nation one-tenth the size living next door to the United States, you would naturally demand to have your own TV, radio, magazines, newspapers, movies, plays, and books. How else can you preserve a sense of nationhood or a national identity without strong, independent vehicles of culture and communications? That's why Canada insisted upon – and got – a cultural "carve-out" from NAFTA, meaning that Canada could take actions otherwise prohibited by the agreement in order to preserve and protect its cultural programs. As part of the deal, however, the United States kept the right to retaliate on an equivalent basis whenever Canada invoked the carve-out.

Yet laws and policies designed to promote or shield Canadian culture still risked running afoul of the spirit, if not the letter, of free trade, especially as the Canadian government found it easier and cheaper to try to keep American products out of the country than foster home-grown material and institutions. At that point American businesses started complaining that such laws and policies had nothing to do with cultural issues and everything to do with commercial protection. And since entertainment is the United States's number-one export, our government is reluctant to allow any country to raise barriers against it. The Canadian situation in itself might not be a big problem, but there was a fear in Washington that a soft line regarding Canada would set a precedent that France, Germany, or China could use against us.

In 1995, for example, the Canadian government slapped an 80 percent tax on advertising in the so-called split-run editions of American magazines. It was aimed, in particular, at *Sports Illustrated*, which wanted to produce a Canadian edition. The Canadian magazine industry argued that, since most of the content would be the same as the U.S. edition, *Sports Illustrated* would have an economy-of-scale advantage and would therefore be able to sell Canadian advertising at a cheaper rate to the Canadian industry's detriment. Yet it was odd, I thought, that no Canadian had ever had the idea of offering Canadians, who are among the greatest sports fanatics in the world, a weekly sports magazine of their own until *Sports Illustrated* tried to do it. It was one thing to encourage Canadian magazines; it was another to suppress ours. The quarrel ended up before a WTO dispute-resolution panel, which eventually ruled in favor of the United States. Interestingly enough, the United States brought the case to the WTO in part so that Canada could not use its cultural exemption under NAFTA.

Country Music TV involved another nasty fight. The Nashville-based specialty cable channel had been on the air in Canada for roughly a decade when, all of the sudden, the Canadian Radio-television and Telecommunications Commission (CRTC) awarded its slot to a company that was specifically formed to grab the very audience that Country Music TV had cultivated. From our point of view, the Canadians simply stole the market from the Americans. I complained loudly to the Prime Minister's Office and anyone who would listen.

"Too bad," the CRTC said in effect. "You knew that this might happen if and when a directly competing Canadian company arose in that market." To which we answered, "Yeah, maybe, but if this is how you treat your best trading partner, then you guys are not very honorable." I talked to some of the board members of the CRTC, and they clearly had no idea that our reaction would be so strong. There were even rumors they were going to do the same thing to the Weather Channel. (Thankfully, they didn't.) Meanwhile, Mickey Kantor was threatening all sorts of retaliation. Roy MacLaren, I think, basically agreed that this was a crazy policy, but he argued that the government had no control over the CRTC, which is an independent agency.

On May 30, 1995, Janet and I flew to Toronto for a reception and dinner hosted by Peter Munk for the international advisory committee of his gold company, American Barrick. There were a lot of dignitaries present, including George Bush, Brian Mulroney, Conrad Black, and my predecessor, Ed Ney. I thought Bush looked really good and told him so. "Oh, I'm all right for a guy that's been defeated," he said. "It's tough to lose an election." This was some two years after the election.

"Well," I said, "you're not the first guy who's ever lost an election." David Peterson was standing beside me and we were laughing. "You know, Americans liked you. They thought you were a good president. That's not why you lost. You should feel really good." I didn't mention that he had been irrelevant to the economy at a time when people wanted someone to worry about the economy.

But when he got up to speak, he was still full of self-pity. He talked about how nobody cared about him, how popular his wife Barbara was, how her book about their dog Milly sold better than his presidential memoirs, how he was just some guy who once threw up in the lap of the Japanese prime minister. The tone surprised me.

Brian Mulroney was a study in contrast. He had a 17 percent approval rating in Canada. Nothing good was being said about him in newspapers and coffee shops across the country. Yet he got up and gave a tub-thumping speech as though he were the most popular man in the world. You would have thought he had just been re-elected by an overwhelming majority and was about to lead millions across the waters of Lake Ontario. On the side he had been telling me, "Your guy Clinton is doing really well, really well." But moments later, on his feet, he was describing George Bush as probably the greatest U.S. president in this century. I wondered how to interpret the apparent contradiction, and concluded it was just a bit of Irish charm, all well intended.

At that dinner I talked with Ted Rogers, the cable-TV magnate who owned a piece of the Canadian company that had pushed Country Music TV aside. "I don't know what we're going to do about it," he said. "This is crazy. It's not worth the aggravation. Why don't we just give the Americans a 20 percent interest in the Canadian company and solve it that way? Call me."

So I called Phil Lind, his vice-chairman who's in charge of government relations, and said, "Ted thinks this is crazy and that there's got to be a way to fix it. Why not give the

Country Music TV people a share of the business that was basically stolen from them?"

"Well, it's not as simple as that," Phil said. "We don't control these guys. They're independent and they think they won this thing fair and square. They also think they've got the government and everybody else by the short hair by playing the anti-American card. But we have some leverage with them, so let me get to work on it."

Over the next few months – and it was months – between Phil Lind's maneuverings and Ted Rogers's support and Mickey Kantor's pressure, the Canadians ended up giving the Nashville company 20 percent. It was better than nothing, and I think we made our point to the CRTC. I would like to think that they will be reluctant to de-list any more U.S. stations. Once we realized there were people in Canada who agreed with our position and were trying to help us, we backed off from making any retaliatory threats. It helped too that we had received a letter from Roy MacLaren indicating that the government had launched a review of their broadcasting and telecommunications practices, which led us to believe there would be little or no likelihood of any further de-listing of non-Canadian specialty services. And in August 1996, a few months after I left Canada, Kantor announced the final approval of Country Music TV's new joint venture and restoration in the Canadian market.

~ ~

All these so-called wars obscured the fact that the United States and Canada have never taken up arms against each other, unless you include – as most Canadians do – the War of 1812, when the colonists of British North America, still British subjects, were caught up in a military feud between the mother country and the United States. Though our governments have occasionally differed on foreign policy issues, from the Vietnam War to Cuba, the two countries are remarkably close allies. We share the defense of North America through the North American Air Defense Command (NORAD). We helped found the North Atlantic Treaty Organization (NATO). We are partners in the Organization of American States (OAS) and other organizations. And our national security and intelligence services cooperate seamlessly on a vast array of low-key, day-by-day classified matters, sharing both human and electronic information from around the world.

I was constantly amazed by how many military and intelligence personnel, from all ranks and both sides, were moving back and forth across the border. Ottawa, it turned out, is the only place in the world where all the U.S. Joint Chiefs of Staff are allowed to travel together. Every other year or so they fly up to discuss outstanding issues with their Canadian counterparts. The fact is, from the dawn of the nuclear missile age to the end of the Cold War, the major conflicts between the United States and the Soviet Union were much less likely to have been fought in the battlefields of Europe than in the skies over Canada. As a result, of all the departments and agencies, the military and intelligence agencies of our two countries had the fewest number of disagreements by far.

During my three years in Canada, Cuba was the focus of the only real, measurable difference between our foreign policies. Even Cuba was mostly a dormant issue until near the end of my term, when Canada was caught up in a congressional action against Cuba following the shooting down of two small Cuban-American planes in February 1996. The incident happened just as it appeared that moderate forces in our government were trying to engage Cuba in various ways, on the grounds that a commercial and cultural engagement would eventually lead to the collapse of Communism as it had in Eastern Europe. Cubans would get a taste of money, a taste of consumerism, a taste of freedom, and the entire system would begin to unravel. But, in the emotional aftermath of the killing of the Americans, legislation that had been previously introduced by Senator Jesse Helms and Representative Dan Burton was moved quickly through Congress with the support of the president and signed into law. The Helms-Burton law now exposed foreign companies investing in previously American-owned property in Cuba to the threat of American lawsuits. It also allowed the U.S. government to deny visas to their CEOs and officers. To members of Congress it seemed an appropriate protest against Cuba's lawlessness. Few paid much attention to its details. Passage of the bill generated only modest press coverage in the United States, except perhaps in Florida.

In Canada, however, Helms-Burton was a headline story in all the newspapers and TV reports, because it looked as though Canadian companies and their executives were being told what to do by the American government. It became a sovereignty issue: the big bad Yankees were telling the poor little Canadians whom they could trade with and how. Around that time Raymond Chrétien, the nephew of the prime minister and a seasoned diplomat who was then Canada's ambassador to the United States, hosted a dinner in honor of Janet and me at his residence in Washington. About two dozen people attended, including some senior American government officials and corporate leaders. When Raymond went on and on about the evils of Helms-Burton, they all began looking at each other as if to say "What the hell is he talking about? And why's he ranting about it?" They were genuinely surprised and perturbed to learn that we had actually passed such a bill.

If we didn't have the difference over Cuba, the Canadian government would probably have to invent something else. It's difficult for Canada's political class to go down the line with the United States on everything. From time to time Canadian politicians have to show their people that they're overseeing a sovereign nation, not just rubber-stamping the policies made in Washington. That's increasingly true for Europe too. With the end of the Cold War and the rise of globalization, leaders everywhere are going to have to find ways to differ from us in order to prove to their voters that they aren't just errand boys for the United States. And we, as the last remaining full-service superpower, are going to have to be sensitive to that reality. We can't expect our allies to bend to our will on everything, nor should we be disappointed if they don't.

An important part of my job was to help maintain and enhance our harmonious relations on security and foreign policy. I became engaged, for example, in discussions with Canada about what the United States could or should do to stop the "ethnic cleansing" going on in Bosnia. Some Americans argued that it was too late for the United States to intervene or it was none of our business. Some allies, particularly Britain and France, saw the situation as a European problem that they preferred to handle themselves. Others were counting on the United Nations peacekeeping force to stop the genocide and arrange a truce. But as the months went by and the slaughter of hundreds of thousands of people continued, the pressure mounted on the U.S. government to launch strategic air strikes against the Serbian artillery and placements in the hills surrounding the besieged Bosnian capital of Sarajevo.

Most Americans don't want the United States to be the world's policeman. In many respects we're an isolationist nation. But we've also learned that, when there's major trouble, we're probably going to be part of the solution. So we are willing to ride like a lone sheriff into Dodge City, be it Bosnia or Haiti, but usually only if our allies want us to. Yet, I believe, because of our unique combination of economic and military strength, we're going to have to lead, like it or not, even if that causes some resentment and tension among our friends or discord at home. That may be difficult politically, not least because we Americans like to be loved and want to be respected, but it may be what we must do for the sake of peace and freedom.

In the case of Bosnia, Canada would have preferred a United Nations solution. Canadians have always joined and promoted multilateral organizations – largely as a way to avoid being overpowered in a one-to-one alliance with the United States – and they were concerned about the safety of their troops who were on the ground with the UN peace-keepers. It took a lot of lobbying, including a series of conversations with Prime Minister Chrétien and Foreign Minister Ouellet, to get support for U.S.-led NATO air strikes. The initial plan was presented by Steve Oxman, the assistant secretary for European and Canadian affairs, during a visit to Ottawa on February 8, 1994. The idea was merely to threaten the strikes if the Serbians didn't pull back their guns within a week, while opening a new diplomatic initiative at the same time. But Oxman himself confessed to not knowing what would happen if the Serbs ignored the threat. As I warned him, the senior Canadian officials in Foreign Affairs and Defence weren't enamored of the scheme, in part because it might jeopardize the Canadian peacekeepers and upset the Russians.

André Ouellet and Eddie Goldenberg were more positive, however, which surprised me. I could only guess that they didn't want Canada to be the sole hold-out among all the members of NATO. "We'll try to work something out with you," Eddie said. That evening Janet and I attended the governor general's skating party, a century-old tradition that takes place under the stars on an illuminated rink surrounded by pine trees and deep snows. Afterwards we went to a dinner at the home of Tom d'Aquino, the head of the Business Council on National Issues. There, in a private conversation in a side room, I talked about Bosnia to Raymond Chrétien. "We're not going to be a problem," he said. "We're going to be helpful."

The next day, sure enough, during an hour-long meeting late in the afternoon, Prime Minister Chrétien told me that Canada was on board. He seemed both solemn and at ease with the decision, though he again expressed worries about his troops in Bosnia. And I think he was pleased that President Clinton had called him twice on the issue and shared his concerns. I thanked him, and we moved on to talk about the stalled agricultural negotiations.

Immediately afterwards, I scrawled down some general impressions of Jean Chrétien. "He is solid, self-assured, very funny, and able to make tough decisions quickly and move on," I wrote. "He is very self-confident about who he is and what he wants to do. He also appears to want to be a valuable and trusted ally of the U.S., and especially Bill Clinton. I thought as I went back to my office across the street how lucky we are to have Chrétien."

About a half-hour later the president announced the NATO ultimatum. "I sure hope my friends at the National Security Council know something I don't know," I added in my diary, "because otherwise it sure looks like we're reacting to CNN rather than using good judgment." It turned out that they were right. The Bosnian story continued to play itself out for the entire period I was in Canada. Later the United States, as part of NATO, sent 20,000 troops to Bosnia as part of a peace accord.

Once that commitment was made, I noticed a change in the way I was treated by the tight ambassadorial community in Ottawa. "I'm really glad Clinton did that" was the sort of comment I heard virtually everywhere. "You're stopping the madness. No one else wanted to or could have. It had gone on too long, and it could have spread all over Europe. Thank God you guys went in there. Too bad you didn't do it sooner."

From the time I arrived in Canada, a similar debate had been going on with regard to Haiti. The military junta there refused to recognize the democratically elected government of Jean-Bertrand Aristide, who was in exile in the United States. In this case, Canada was privately lobbying for the United States to intervene to restore democracy and stop the violence. It seemed a particular priority for André Ouellet. Haiti is important to Quebeckers as one of the few French-speaking countries in the western hemisphere, and there were tens of thousands of Haitian refugees in his own Montreal constituency. He was convinced, in my reading of our discussions, that if we simply sent twenty thousand troops down there and rattled a few sabres, the Haitian warlords would get the hell out as fast as they could. And he may well have been right, but that was not the general perception at the time. Many people feared that a prolonged military occupation would be needed, and many more were still counting on the United Nations.

On May 9, 1994, Madeleine Albright, then U.S. ambassador to the United Nations, met with Ouellet during an official visit to Ottawa. Her visit happened to coincide with President Clinton's move to a new, get-tough policy toward

Haiti that took the United Nations sanctions seriously. After I briefed her that Ouellet had been talking about Haiti long before anyone in Washington really cared, she skillfully told him, "We've come over to the Canadian point of view. We want to do something."

Fast on her heels came William Perry, our new secretary of Defense, for his first official visit to Canada. Haiti was again on the agenda. First, however, another issue blew up. It originated in 1983, when, after a heated debate, the Trudeau government allowed us to test the cruise missile over northern Canada, whose landscape most closely matched the terrain over which the defensive weapon would have to pass to counter an attack from the Soviet Union. The agreement was due to expire after ten years, and the United States was hoping for an extension – as much as a sign of Canada's commitment to joint defense as for the military benefits. In my initial discussions with Ouellet on February 1, 1994, a one-year extension seemed acceptable, and Eddie Goldenberg phoned me the next day to confirm that. After a year, he said, cruise testing would be made a part of the general review of Canada's defense policy.

On May 14th, however, during a weekend trip back to Detroit, I arrived home from a small private dinner in honor of Barbra Streisand (who had chatted about her admiration for Bill Clinton and her friendship with Pierre Trudeau) when I received upsetting news from Jim Walsh. André Ouellet had just announced at a Liberal Party convention that the government would not even consider renewing cruise missile testing after the one-year extension. It was a shock, a bolt from the blue, coming without warning or consultation, virtually on the eve of Secretary Perry's arrival. "I fear our defense establishment will now view the new Liberal government as flaky and unreliable," I wrote in my journal. "Talk about burning up good will. This is a classic misstep."

It struck me, in fact, as childish and insulting, especially in view of the fact that we were able to verify that no one in Canada had given anyone in our government any advance notice, and I interpreted it as a bit of anti-American grandstanding deliberately timed to coincide with Perry's visit on May 16th. I lodged a complaint and was repeatedly told it was simply a terrible accident. Even if the decision had been made, it wasn't supposed to have been announced either at this time or in this way. Defence Minister David Collenette himself apologized with the utmost graciousness.

When Perry's 707 arrived, I boarded it first and sat down to explain the situation to him and let him know how disgusted I was. The Canadians, I said, would like him to say one of two things to get them off the hook: either the Americans had never had any intention of asking for more cruise tests or he was pleased to have an opportunity to discuss the matter during his meetings. Perry was a gentleman of the old school, a gifted public servant, and a seasoned veteran who had distinguished himself in a number of fields. He just smiled. I wasn't sure what he was going to do.

After standing through the national anthems and reviewing the troops, he held a brief press conference. David Collenette was beside him. The first question was about Ouellet's announcement. "The United States is very grateful for having had the opportunity to test the cruise missile in Canada," Secretary Perry answered. "However, we were not planning to ask for any further testing in the future." Collenette and his staff beamed, and the whole thing was brushed aside. I couldn't help wondering how different the outcome would have been if the United States had done something like this to Canada. At the very least it would have been the subject of indignant editorial commentaries for months.

The United States wanted Canada to contribute a couple of hundred troops to any U.S.-led invasion of Haiti, so that it would look like a multinational action. "Forget it, put it out of your mind," I told Perry. "There's no way Canada is going to do that. They don't do invasions. They do peacekeeping. That's just the way they are. But if you appeal to their peacekeeping instincts, after we've gone in and invaded under UN auspices and stabilized the situation, they would probably send peacekeepers. Or maybe we should ask them for the Royal Canadian Mounted Police (RCMP). The Mounties, as they're known, always take pride in having people who speak French and some of them have Creole experience. That's how we get Canada involved."

In Perry's meeting with Ouellet and Collenette, I took it as my role to try to craft something that would lure them into helping us. I knew that Ouellet was bullish to do something. "Would some of the Haitians in Montreal go back if democracy were restored?" I prodded him.

"Maybe so," he answered. "They're a pretty educated group."

Perry picked up the ball. "Would some of them like to go back and help stabilize the situation?"

"Yeah, yeah," Ouellet replied. "You know what? We've got a military camp in Quebec. We could actually train them to go back." Tim Collins, a young political counselor from the Canada Desk up for the visit, slipped me a note that read, "Bay of Pigs," the site of the failed CIA-backed invasion of Cuba by Cuban expatriates in 1961. I thought we were going to crack up laughing. But David Collenette looked really worried: not too many Canadians outside Quebec were interested in invading Haiti.

The next afternoon I accompanied Secretary Perry to a meeting with the prime minister. "What's going on with Haiti?" he asked.

Perry explained that, while the president hadn't made a decision to deploy military power, he was considering ways to restore Aristide and the democratically elected government. "Our problem won't be so much removing the military rulers," he said. "We can go down there with our troops and do it. But the length of time to establish order and security for the new government will be the problem."

"Well, I don't know what we can do about that," Chrétien replied.

Perry talked about applying increased sanctions. He talked about finding a home for the Haitian refugees. He talked about getting congressional approval. And then he mentioned the need for some French-speaking peacekeepers, both in Haiti and Rwanda. We knew that would appeal to Chrétien, and it did. His face lit up. "What's seen as a problem here, having the French language," he said, "is an asset around the world."

By the time Vice-President Gore visited Ottawa in July, the UN observers had been expelled from Haiti and sanctions had been applied, but the final go-ahead for a U.S. invasion had yet to be made. "The word is you're going to invade Haiti," Prime Minister Chrétien said gravely when they met in his office.

"No, no," Gore replied. "We want the sanctions to work. The military option is just one of the options, but it's not imminent. We'll consult you on anything we do. Don't worry about that."

As the weeks went by, however, the military option increasingly became the only option. "While congressional reaction is mixed and polls show that the nation is against the invasion," I recorded in my diary on September 15th, "I believe the president has no choice but to invade. Otherwise, he will appear to raise the white flag in his presidency. He needs to take a strong position, stick to it against the popular will, and make it successful."

The next day, after Clinton had gone on TV with his persuasive reasons for invading and had mobilized a huge military operation, he suddenly pulled back. Instead, he decided to send Jimmy Carter, Colin Powell, and Sam Nunn to Haiti to negotiate the departure of General Raoul Cedras, the junta leader, and the return of Aristide. Over dinner that evening at the Café Ritz, Janet thought that a bloodless removal was a great idea. I thought it was politically terrible: Bill Clinton was pulling the plug on his best chance to show the world his strength and that of the United States. To delegate this responsibility to Carter, regardless of Carter's good intentions, was to delegate away his presidency. "I'm just sick about it," I said, "and I hope I'm wrong."

As it turned out, of course, how wrong I was. The Carter mission succeeded, and within a month Jean-Bertrand Aristide returned to Haiti without bloodshed to become its president. Among the thousands and thousands of jubilant people who lined the streets of Port-au-Prince to welcome him home, many were waving U.S. flags and cheering Bill Clinton. Though it wouldn't be enough to keep the Democrats in control of the Senate and House in the mid-term elections that November, it was clearly a triumph for the president. "He was really courageous to have accepted Carter's idea," Colin Powell told me when I saw him a short while later at a Canadian embassy dinner. "The truth is, it would have been a lot easier to have invaded. It would have been decisive, and I don't think there would have been many casualties at all on our side. But Clinton gambled on Carter and won."

All through my dealings with Canada on military matters, from Haiti to Bosnia, from the cruise missile to the enlargement of NATO, there was the underlying reality that Canada has been cutting back on its military commitments, budgets, and troops for more than twenty years. With a tenth of our population, it has about a hundredth of the number of people in uniform, and while Canadians have reason to be proud of their participation in World War I, World War II, Korea, and UN peacekeeping missions, Canada is getting to be on par with Iceland in NATO and at risk of being dismissed as a serious player. Even now, the United States pays more attention to what Canada thinks or needs than Britain, France, or Germany do.

The United States wants Canada to have a stronger fighting force as much to give it some independence from us and some effectiveness in its peacekeeping goals as to suit our own purposes. When left-wing Canadian nationalists call for less military spending, as they usually do, the practical effect of further cutbacks would be the very opposite of what they desire. It would increase Canada's dependence on the United States for its own defense, turning them into mere clients of American security, and it would render Canadian peacekeepers no more effectual than a bunch of Boy Scouts. Canada's historic military pride is already at odds with the size of its armed forces and the antiquity of its equipment. In the United States, the secretary of Defense is one of our three top officials, along with the secretary of State and the secretary of Treasury. In Canada, the Defence portfolio is considered a mid-level cabinet job, well below Finance, Foreign Affairs, Justice, and Trade.

At times, Canadians derive an advantage by not being noticed. If Americans were paying attention, we would probably insist that Canadians spend more on defense rather than hide under our skirts. Or perhaps we would negotiate even harder with Canadian businesses, Canadian farmers, Canadian culture. Or we might run around telling Canadians to lower their taxes and change some laws. Our blindness, our deafness, allow Canadian politicians to make much of Canada's independence from the United States through all sorts of outrageous pronouncements and actions without fear that anybody in the United States will respond or care.

That creates its own disadvantage, however, because it encourages some Canadian politicians and intellectuals to engage in constant, unproductive shadow-boxing. They strut around on their home stage, jabbing their fists in our direction, scowling, cursing, threatening to take us on, while virtually nobody south of the border is paying any attention. If one of their more outrageous statements and actions does get reported in the United States, Americans just look up for a moment and say, "Hey, what's going on with those people anyway?" Some of Chrétien's senior cabinet ministers have been known to make totally inappropriate or inaccurate comments during visits to Washington. But I'm convinced that they never intended their insults to be picked up or taken seriously. They were designed to impress or appease a small crowd of left-of-center Liberal constituents back home. Our leaders shrug off the remarks as the stuff of insecure politicians.

Over time, watching all these foreign policy and trade disputes erupt between our two countries, I came to realize that they always followed the same vicious cycle. Canadian politicians and their advisers would get lured into showing how tough and independent they really are, and would usually end up walking the plank. The final deal, no matter how advantageous to Canada, could never be good enough for the Canadian press. Whatever the ultimate compromise, they lambaste the politicians and negotiators as spineless weasels who have sold out to the Americans or been taken to the cleaners. If an American politician or negotiator has a problem with Canada that becomes highly publicized, however, he or she is generally viewed as ineffective, maybe even morally deficient. Generally speaking, Americans have a feeling if you can't get along with the Canadians, you're probably inept or downright wrong.

That's why, I concluded, high-profile disputes between the United States and Canada are no-win propositions for both sides. They're best resolved calmly and without publicity.

— 6 —

OPEN SKIES

Dialing down the disputes and dodging new contro-
versies absorbed a lot of my time, but I also wanted
to accomplish something positive and lasting while
I was in Ottawa. And that meant zeroing in on a couple of
things and giving them everything I had. In January 1994, once
NAFTA was secured, I turned my attention to the most glaring
problem I saw between the United States and Canada. It was
glaring, in part, because I repeatedly experienced it myself.

There was, for instance, the awful propeller plane
between Ottawa and Boston. It looked smaller than the
one used in *Casablanca*, was jam-packed with thirty-three
people, and reeked of the lavatory. There was the other old
prop between Washington and Montreal via Philadelphia, in
which the passengers were treated as though they were
either deportees, forced to leave the United States under
duress, or refugees desperate to get to Canada by any means

at all. Then there was the five-and-a-half-hour marathon between our two great capitals: 9:00 a.m., depart from Ottawa to Toronto; 9:55 a.m., arrive Toronto, change terminals, transfer luggage, clear customs; 11:00 a.m., depart Toronto; 12:15 p.m., arrive Boston; 1:10 p.m., depart Boston; 2:35 p.m., arrive Washington and put in claim for missing luggage. Each and every one of these flights was a painful testimony to Air Canada's grip on the government of Canada. Neither the bureaucracies of our two countries, nor the politicians apparently, had realized what a modern transportation system could actually do for people and commerce.

Another time, en route from Washington to Ottawa via Pittsburgh, Janet and I saw people turned away from the plane even though there were six empty seats. "The reason," the pilot announced from the cockpit, "is due to the bilateral aviation agreement between the United States and Canada. We're only allowed to have a certain number of passengers on this plane. If we filled those seats, not only would the United States run afoul of the agreement, but this airline's access to the bilateral would be jeopardized."

All aviation relationships between countries are governed by a bilateral treaty or agreement that regulates the carriers and number of flights in and out. The United States and Canada had one of the longest and most extensive aviation relationships in the world, of course, but they were operating under an outmoded, highly restrictive regime. Thirteen rounds of negotiations had failed to significantly update it in two decades. There had been three attempts within the past ten years, and both sides had totally given up trying.

Things weren't always so difficult. John Kenneth Galbraith once told me how the existing regime had come about. Before it, he explained, passengers traveling between the United States and Canada often had to take a flight to a border city, then hop on a national carrier for the remaining trip. In the early 1960s President Kennedy and Prime Minister Pearson decided to negotiate a new deal. Kennedy proposed Galbraith as the American negotiator, to which Pearson responded, "He's really a Canadian, I'll take him too." It was the easiest set of negotiations Galbraith had ever conducted. "I went into a room," he said, "I talked to myself, and I came out with a deal."

Now, however, the number of direct flights between our cities was limited to the point of ludicrousness. There were no scheduled flights from Ottawa to Chicago (let alone Washington), no scheduled flights from Vancouver to New York, no scheduled flights from Montreal to Miami, and only three nonstop flights from Halifax to the United States. It was unbelievable. As things stood, two-thirds of the existing flights were operated by U.S. airlines, primarily U.S. Air, Delta, and Northwest. Two-thirds of the remaining third were controlled by Air Canada, which had been 100 percent government-owned until 1989. And two-thirds of all the major airport cities in both the United States and Canada were not benefiting from a nonstop service between the two countries. Everybody had got used to the status quo, it seemed, so that the market wasn't growing in spite of positive trends elsewhere and obvious consumer demand. Canadian tourism suffered, in particular, because so many Americans prefer to fly to their vacation destinations, but will go only if the flights are short and direct.

My ambition was to instigate a policy of "open skies," which would allow any American or Canadian airline to fly international flights into any American or Canadian airport. Someday, perhaps, that could be extended to domestic flights too, but the first step was to open up the cross-border routes. And that meant overcoming the skepticism of the American officials, who had abandoned all hope of ever getting a new deal with Canada, and combating the resistance of the Canadian officials, who feared that any change would harm the two major Canadian airlines and somehow compromise Canadian sovereignty.

"That's a great idea," Jim Walsh said when I told him what I had in mind. "We really need it; it's twenty years overdue. Besides, you can spend all your time here spreading good will, but every ambassador does that. When you look back someday and ask what you accomplished here, it would be nice to have something specific to point to."

Others on my staff worried that I was way out in front of the administration on this issue – and I was, at least with respect to the State Department, which is in charge of negotiating foreign treaties, and the Transportation Department, which needed to sign off on a new aviation agreement. But I figured I had been sent to Canada to achieve just this type of necessary improvement, and I didn't doubt I could convince Bill Clinton to do it. That was the advantage, again, of having an ambassador who knows the political people.

I first raised the issue with Federico Peña, our Transportation secretary, before I even left for Canada, and he was very supportive. The United States was already thinking about negotiating Open Skies with Britain and Germany, but no one had thought about Canada because of the failure of the recent negotiations. To succeed, I argued, the project needed a high-level political commitment and an entirely new process. By the time I left Washington, I had the blessing of both State and Transportation to find out whether the will to do something existed in Ottawa.

On February 23, 1994, I raised it with Doug Young, Canada's new minister of Transport, a gruff, practical, nononsense businessman from New Brunswick and baseball fanatic whose idea of a vacation was to watch the spring training games in Florida with his children. I told him what I had told Peña, that there was no point in rehashing the old, fruitless formulas with half-hearted offers and protracted counter-offers. I also argued that it was futile to involve the same bunch of career civil servants who had been around for decades under all kinds of political leaders and, as a result, saw themselves as the permanent agents of the Crown rather than the obedient servants of the people's representatives. In the United States, all the top officials change with every change of government and are selected by the president, but the senior Canadian officials almost always stay no matter what party wins the election. What we lose in continuity, we gain in accountability.

It always amazed and appalled me how much power the bureaucrats have in Canada. They're referred to by journalists and academics, often with respect, as mandarins. Canadian cabinet ministers don't like making decisions that are at odds with the information and judgments supplied by their departments. Ministers, as good politicians, set the target, but they too often seemed to submit to the advice of their underlings on how to meet it. I found it particularly disheartening when newly appointed ministers took the fall for mistakes made by some bureaucrat months, even years, before they assumed office. No U.S. politician would ever tolerate such nonsense. In Canada, one could say, politicians easily become captives of their officials. In the United States it's more likely the officials who become captives of the politicians.

If Open Skies were left to the Canadian bureaucrats, I decided, nothing would ever get done. I wanted a clean slate of people who knew how to cut a deal and the go-ahead from on high to do it. And I got enough encouragement from Young to dash to Washington the next day to encourage

Peña, who didn't need any persuading, and Dan Tarullo, the assistant secretary of state for economic affairs in the State Department.

Young had cautioned me, however, not to raise expectations for a speedy resolution. It soon became clear to me, however amenable he himself might have been to the initiative, that his bureaucrats were actively fighting it. I came to suspect that they thought of themselves as flight attendants for Air Canada because it had been a Crown corporation for so long. Sure enough, the first set of talking points Secretary Peña received from the Canadian government a few weeks after my meeting with Young were simply a rehash of the 1992 negotiating positions that had gone nowhere. The Canadians seemed absolutely stuck, without any sense of urgency or a fresh approach to move an agreement forward.

"This has convinced me that we will need to build political support, grassroots support, right here in Canada," I noted in my journal. But I also realized that for the U.S. ambassador to campaign for a Canadian public policy was difficult. In my own way, however, I did raise the issue back and forth across the country, dozens and dozens of times, at every possible opportunity. My pitch resonated in Ottawa, in particular, where the new high-tech businesses were in need of better air service, were fed up with having to go through Toronto all the time, and had a powerful political ally in the person of John Manley, the Industry minister and local MP. Eventually, with considerable support from airport communities across Canada and the United States, to the great satisfaction of our embassy staff, we were able to help push our Transportation people and Doug Young's department toward a new deal.

The plan was for Peña and Young to issue a joint statement on the need for a new bilateral agreement at their meeting in Washington on April 29, 1994, without actually saying what it would look like or how it would happen. Then we would get a couple of high-level people to begin private discussions to explore what a framework might look like. If they could agree and get the political leaders to agree, then their framework would be passed to the negotiators for technical discussion only. I was excited, but Young wanted to see how his meeting with Peña went before releasing the statement. He asked me to take out the word "quickly." Given the difficulties he foresaw, he didn't want to put too much pressure on his government to achieve a result.

"He's obviously being very careful as he maneuvers around his bureaucracy," I wrote, "but if we can get the statement announced, it will allow us to get moving."

Meanwhile, rumors were rampant that the bureaucrats Young had inherited were fit to be tied over his interest in the subject and his private meetings with me. In fact, our bureaucrats, having experienced infinite delays and time-wasting games from the Canadians over the years, kept telling me I was wasting my time. "You don't know what we've been through," they said. "These are terrible people. You'll never get anything." But everything was set to go. I had lunch with Young and his political adviser, Fred Drummie, before the meeting, and there was not the least indication of any problem.

The meeting was held at the State Department. Peña began, as scripted, with a few remarks about the need for a new agreement. Young responded by joking that he wished the U.S. ambassador to Canada would show a little more interest in this issue. Then he mentioned that the previous negotiations had been difficult, that we should explore the grounds for a new deal first. When Peña nodded to me, I piped up, "Are you ready to issue the statement on the need for this agreement?"

Suddenly the Canadian bureaucrats on the other side of the table started fidgeting in their seats and shaking their heads, as though they were going nuts. "Well, um, I'm having second thoughts about this statement," Young said. "I'm afraid it will raise expectations. So I don't think we should issue it." Then all his officials settled back in their chairs, relaxed, and smirked at me.

Our people just raised their eyebrows and looked at me. "You idiot," was the message. "You don't know these people like we do. But now you've learned your lesson."

I was stunned. Without so much as a warning or decent excuse, these guys had derailed a very general, apple-pie statement about wanting better air service for our two peoples. "I must say I haven't had this happen very often in my entire life in politics, not to mention my adult life," I lamented in my diary afterwards. "Score one for the permanent bureaucrats in the north and give zero to the public interest and modern transportation. Oh Canada."

In retrospect, that might have been a bit harsh, but I was floored. I still think Young himself really wanted to go ahead, but he had been persuaded that it would be unpopular, that Air Canada would be angry at him, and that we were going to trick him somehow. So, in spite of his tough-guy manner, he had backed away. And that confirmed before everyone's eyes the conviction of our Canada watchers that the Canadian Transport officials were hard-headed, dishonorable, and controlled by Air Canada.

Earlier Young had invited me to fly back to Ottawa on his government plane and I had accepted. Now I begged off. I wouldn't be able to confer with him privately, I figured, and I might not have been civil to the bureaucrats on board. I left them to celebrate their sabotage and caught a – horrible – commercial flight back. I was furious.

The only way we were going to get this going, I decided, was to continue to travel up and down Canada selling the idea to Canadians. So I took my crusade to the major airport communities from Vancouver to Halifax. Everywhere I spoke about the need for a new agreement. I found almost every community keen, if not desperate, for Open Skies. The significant exception was Toronto, perhaps because it was better served than other Canadian cities and its airport was in the grip of Transport Canada. My deputy started to worry that Doug Young wasn't going to like all the favorable publicity my speeches were attracting. It might look like undue pressure from the United States. I agreed to tone down the pitch; I knew ultimately I would need Young's help and I felt he agreed with me. At the same time, I didn't want the Canadian airport communities to think – as they were being led to believe – that we had lost interest in the issue. We wanted Open Skies, most of our airlines wanted Open Skies, and we were ready to move on it.

In August 1994 I met with Hollis Harris, the Georgia-born CEO of Air Canada. "Look," he said, "we'd love Open Skies, but we're going to need a phase-in for Toronto. There's no way we're going to be able to compete right off the bat." By phase-in, he meant that the Canadian airlines would get a head start for a limited period in order to establish their services between the two countries before the bigger, stronger, richer American airlines moved in. Harris struck me as a sincere and gracious individual, and his argument made sense for his company, but I was never sure it wasn't a strategy by which some people in his organization hoped to prevent an agreement. They probably assumed that we wouldn't go along with a three-year phase-in for Toronto, still less the additional two-year phase-in for Vancouver and Montreal that was later proposed. However, I had privately convinced our officials that we could live with it, if that's what was needed to get a deal. So I thought my meeting with Harris had gone well, though I didn't know for sure: no one gets to become the head of a major airline without knowing how to play poker.

The issue finally came to fruition when Secretary Peña was invited to give a speech in Toronto to an aviation group. He asked me if this would be a good occasion for him to meet again with Young, without appearing to be pressuring him. I thought it was a great idea. As a result, on September 27th, the two men met in Toronto to see if they could get beyond the disastrous meeting of the previous spring and launch discussions for a new agreement. The first step was still to develop a framework that would then be handed to negotiators for the final details. It was a make-or-break moment. I was determined to be in the room, even though the Canadian officials had said they wanted Peña and Young to be joined only by their designated representatives, Steve Kaplan and Geoffrey Elliot – "nobody else." They were obviously referring to me. So I raced out of a breakfast meeting, where I had given a particularly dull speech on the environment to a rather sleepy crowd, and sped downtown to get to the meeting place before the Canadians could get me barred. I had learned my lesson, and I wasn't going to be fooled again.

We had a friendly and productive session, as it turned out, and it was followed by a communiqué in which Peña and Young announced exploratory talks between Kaplan and Elliot to see if there was the basis for further negotiations. "Finally," I noted, "we have launched a process." It had been like pushing an elephant up a hill. And it never would have happened if Peña hadn't come to Toronto and lit a fire under the Canadian government.

From then on I started receiving regular reports from Steve Kaplan about his meetings with Geoff Elliot. Fortunately, both of them had experience in the field and seemed to get along well together. At their first encounter in September, Elliot confided in Kaplan that Open Skies wasn't a big priority for either Doug Young or the government of Canada. If they could reach a deal that satisfied the airlines, fine. Otherwise, forget it. So Kaplan and I decided we had to systematically eliminate Transport Canada's excuses for obstructing a deal. I was going to have to keep marshaling outside support, particularly with the Ottawa-area business community, John Manley in the cabinet, and Eddie Goldenberg in the Prime Minister's Office.

On October 25th I got a second report. Young was willing to do Open Skies, but he didn't want to be blamed for its failure. Most of all, he wanted the airline companies to support it. They, rather than the airport communities, would be in the driver's seat. Meanwhile, the two representatives were making progress. They had already sketched out a viable framework: phase-ins for Toronto, Montreal, and Vancouver, perhaps some free slots in Chicago and Washington, and a few secondary issues relating to cargo and mail.

By mid-December, it was clear that they had established the framework for a negotiated agreement. In exchange for the phase-ins, the American carriers would be allowed a few more flights into Toronto, Montreal, and Vancouver. Then, after three years, there would be complete Open Skies across the border, subject only to how many slots the American and Canadian airlines could buy in any particular airport. I was really excited, and I congratulated Steve Kaplan on doing a great job. He had achieved something that our Open Skies negotiators with the United Kingdom and Germany had so far failed to do.

The next step was to announce the breakthrough before the end of the year, hand the framework over to the negotiators, and order them to come up with a final agreement in time to be signed during President Clinton's visit to Ottawa two months later. On Tuesday, December 20th, as I was preparing to get back to Michigan for the Christmas holidays, Kaplan called to say that everything was on track. The framework was down in writing; the joint statement was being prepared. However, between calls to fend off the rumors that I was about to be named the new Democratic National Chairman and a courtesy visit from the Pakistani ambassador, I remained concerned whether Doug Young was seeing everything the same way as Kaplan. So I phoned Young.

"This thing is all worked out," he assured me when I phoned. "Our plan is to do the announcement on Thursday."

"Have you seen the proposed press release?" I asked. "I think we should issue exactly the same press release so that there's no disagreement as to what it means. Otherwise, we might have to go back to renegotiate something."

"Yeah," he said, "Kaplan's sending it over. My people will look at it, but it's all worked out."

"That's really great," I said. "Boy, what a wonderful Christmas present!"

But, because of my previous experience, I was still worried. First thing the next morning I called Kaplan again. "Have they signed off on the language of the press statement yet?"

"No, but they say they will. We're now going to go with the announcement at noon tomorrow – Doug Young in Ottawa, myself in Washington. They've agreed to that. It's all set." I was thrilled.

However, just as I was about to leave for my Christmas vacation, I was informed that another major announcement, involving Canada's proposed legislation to tax split-run magazines, was also going to be made the next day. Oh-oh, I thought. Our landmark agreement on Open Skies is going to be blown off the front pages by yet more headlines from the Culture War. Then and there I decided to call up the five key reporters who had been following the aviation discussions and give them a "confidential exclusive" about the forthcoming announcement. That would allow them to get their stories ready and in the can, so that they wouldn't be trumped by the magazine tax story.

So, winding through the woods and lake country of Ontario, with Janet driving our Jeep, I phoned *The Toronto Star*, *The Globe and Mail*, *Ottawa Citizen*, Canadian Press, and the Southam news service and told them what had been going on. "This is embargoed until tomorrow noon," I emphasized.

"Sure, no problem, don't worry, we'll keep your confidence," they all said.

That evening we were the first overnight guests at David and Shelley Peterson's newly renovated country house in the Caledon Hills north of Toronto. And the next morning, as we were preparing for the four-hour leg to Detroit, David said, "Hey, you got some great stories in the papers today about this new Open Skies stuff." And there, on the front page of *The Toronto Star* and in the business section of *The Globe and Mail*, was my embargoed news, attributed either to me by name or to "a senior U.S. government official." Too bad, and not very Canadian in its ethical principles, I thought, but at least it wasn't blown out of the water by the culture story.

In fact, it almost blew the Open Skies agreement away. I got a call from the embassy, which had just got a call from Transport Canada: the deal was off again. Maybe next year, maybe never, but they felt they had been sandbagged by the news leak and weren't going to sign now. They blamed me, of course, for breach of faith and so on. And Doug Young apparently felt that his honor had been hurt, even though the stories had been very positive about him and his deal.

"So what are we going to do?" I asked Steve Kaplan.

"Well, I don't care, I'm going ahead and announcing this thing anyway," he said. "This is crazy. We've been sitting on it for days. And you were right to do what you did. We have an agreement, and I'm going to release it."

Finally, around two in the afternoon, after a lot of to-and-froing, Transport Canada relented, and the joint statement was issued. Thank God, I exclaimed sheepishly to Janet. I later heard that this whole business had been a last-ditch, last-minute maneuver by some of the Canadian bureaucrats to stall the announcement until the new year or the president's visit, in the hope of postponing or killing the final negotiations. Weirdly, therefore, my leak may have inadvertently forced their hand and saved the deal. At the very least, it prevented a lengthy delay.

As it was, on February 24, 1995, with President Clinton and Prime Minister Chrétien looking on, Secretary Peña and Minister Young signed the agreement. And less than four months after that, on a warm and sunny day at the start of May, Janet and I drove to Ottawa's aviation museum for a reception to celebrate the arrival of the first nonstop commercial flight from Washington, D.C. It was truly a happy moment, made happier by the surprise announcement the same day that Northwest was going to start a direct service between Ottawa and Detroit, the airline's hub. Within the next three years, U.S.-Canada passenger traffic increased 37 percent, over forty new pairs of cities received direct service for the first time, and traffic levels between many old markets such as Toronto-New York or Vancouver-Los Angeles increased dramatically. The number of passenger seats per year between our two countries increased by 3½ million. The combined net economic gain for both countries in activity and jobs was estimated in the billions of dollars, and all the airlines entered into creative joint ventures that resulted in better customer service and higher company profits.

There was one other small but related irritant I wanted to clear up before I left Canada. It was high time that the nation's capital had its own pre-clearance facilities so that U.S.-bound passengers could go through U.S. customs and immigration in Ottawa. It would open Ottawa travellers directly to any airport in the United States, rather than just the handful of international airports big enough to have our customs and immigration facilities, and that would give the people of Ottawa a much more efficient service and a real independence from Toronto. But it also meant convincing our customs and immigration services, at a time of mounting cutbacks in the public service and rising demands along the Mexican border, that they should spend the extra money required to install ten or twelve new people in Ottawa. Clearly they had to get something in return.

What, I suggested to them, if we could get status and privileges from the government of Canada for all the 250 or so customs and immigration officials already posted in Vancouver, Edmonton, Calgary, Winnipeg, Toronto, and Montreal? Would you then sign off on a major new facility in Ottawa and the budget authority to do it? They said yes. So I went to the Canadian department of Foreign Affairs and said, "We're not asking for diplomatic immunity. We understand that you don't want to give customs and immigration people that. But they want some sort of little card that says they're officially in Canada on U.S. government business. It would exempt them from the provincial sales tax. It would let them bring a car into the country without paying a huge duty. It would spare them from having to put their kids into French schools in Quebec. It would help make sure that their U.S. health-care plans are honored at the local hospitals. That sort of thing."

It was a win-win proposal and it made sense, but the negotiations dragged on for more than twice the time it had taken us to get the Open Skies agreement. There wasn't much motivation on either side of the border, except among the people of Ottawa and (by extension) the staff in our embassy. "This is a testimony to two phenomena prevalent in, but not unique to, Canada," I moaned in my journal after nine months of talks. "One, the less important the issue, the more difficult and acrimonious negotiations become. The lower the stakes, the more petty and bureaucratic the tactics. It's because it's left to mid-level and lower-level bureaucrats who are often afraid to make decisions and resentful of their powerlessness. They seek revenge on their opposites across the table. The second phenomenon is that Canadians have a completely different sense of time than Americans. They expect and really want to take much longer to accomplish most everything – and they do. And nowhere is that more obvious than with the securely employed government bureaucrat."

Just as we were getting close, the Canadian negotiators gummed up the works by demanding something new at the last minute. They wanted us to allow U.S.-bound transit passengers from third countries to come into Vancouver International Airport and proceed directly to U.S. customs without having to go through Canadian customs. I knew it was a deal-breaker. Besides the added expenditures, there were law-enforcement problems. If a drug carrier were to arrive with a suitcase full of cocaine, for example, and our agents asked to look in the bag, he could simply say, "Oh, I've decided to stay in Canada," and walk away. We wouldn't be able to arrest him, because he was on Canadian soil, and there was no guarantee that an RCMP officer would be willing and able to apprehend him.

Canadian bureaucrats routinely said to me, "You Americans just want to have your own police, with their guns, making arrests on our soil."

"No," I said, "we just want a Mountie with a gun somewhere nearby to help us, and we want the authority to stop people and arrest them if they're going to violate our laws. We trust your screening, but if you're not going to screen anybody, then we will have to." So the negotiations degenerated into an argument about whether Canada would give us the legal authority to arrest, inspect, and detain. If not, would they have someone there to do that for us?

I was going crazy. It became clear to me that the Canadian airlines didn't really want a pre-clearance facility in Ottawa, because it would encourage competition against their hourly flights to Toronto. It also became clear to me that Transport Canada was behind this maneuver, probably because they foolishly believed that pre-clearance was a favor to the United States. Most of all, it became clear to me that the best interests of Ottawa Airport, the city of Ottawa, and the traveling public were not important to these negotiators at all. They seemed very smug about jeopardizing any agreement and basically said, "Too bad, it's not going to happen." I even yelled at a couple of them who were needling me at a cocktail party. I suspected they saw this as pay-back time for my having gone behind their backs on Open Skies and won.

"These guys are really getting to you," Janet said. "I've never seen you do that."

"Well, I just want them to know how angry I am. I want other people to hear about it. I don't know what I can do, but they need to wonder."

Then I swung into action. I called Eddie Goldenberg at the PMO, John Manley's staff, and Sergio Marchi, the Immigration minister, to tell them what was going on. "Look," I said, "we're happy to recommend a pilot program for the in-transit passengers in Vancouver, but that means working out some thorny questions of territorial sovereignty and law enforcement. We don't have time right now. Let's work it out later." They all promised to help.

On November 30th, Eddie called to tell me he had talked to a couple of senior officials and the logjam should be broken. Then Marchi phoned to say he had made some calls too. I felt a lot better. At noon two of our senior embassy people, Marshall Casse and Vlad Sambaiew, reported from the all-day negotiation session that nothing had happened yet. Then, at six o'clock, they walked into my office with big smiles and announced, "We have an agreement!" The chief Canadian negotiator had begun getting calls "from all over" during the afternoon, to the point where he complained that his instructions kept changing every ten minutes. "This is a victory of the politicians over the bureaucrats," I wrote. "We've won. But the people are the real winners."

~ 7 ~

I LED THREE LIVES

All through my stay in Canada, I kept thinking of the title of the 1950s television show, "I Led Three Lives," because that was the way I felt. Besides my duties as U.S. ambassador, I had inescapable responsibilities as a former governor of Michigan and continuing ties to Washington as a former congressman and later as a lawyer with Verner, Liipfert, Bernhard, McPherson and Hand. I couldn't completely sever all the connections to my past simply by moving across the border as a diplomat, particularly since I was in the same time zone and only a brief flight (thanks to Open Skies) away. My friends and supporters in Michigan, as well as the public and media, expected me to do certain things, from attending the funerals of leading citizens and commenting on important issues to receiving visitors from my home state in Ottawa. And my friends and colleagues in Washington often called me for help or advice, which I was glad to offer as long as it was appropriate to the office of an ambassador. Early on, indeed, I made sure to consult with the State Department about the degree of political involvement that was permitted. Among other things, an ambassador must not engage in partisan politics while on duty.

Even though my three lives involved separate expectations by others – and, for that matter, by myself – they usually complemented each other. My effectiveness as ambassador was enhanced by my being well-known in Michigan and well-connected in Washington. My eight years as governor of Michigan helped give me a knowledge of Canada, as well as political and media experience. My friendship with the president and vice-president lent some stature to my appointment in the eyes of Canadians and some weight to my words. For all the risks entailed in my being pulled in different directions, or caught in the crossfire of competing interests, I found there were many more benefits.

A perfect example of how my different lives were intertwined was the G7 Job Summit, which was held in Detroit in March 1994. At one level, because of my Michigan connections, I was involved in suggesting appropriate locations for the events and making sure the top leaders from Michigan, as well as Clinton's original supporters, were invited to the public events. Delays at the White House over guest lists could have resulted in a half-filled room for the president's big reception if Janet, I, and a few friends hadn't got on the phone and frantically called a couple of hundred people the day before it happened. At another level, I was thinking about how the president could get maximum public support for the summit. And, on the third level, as ambassador, I was giving nonstop interviews to the local media to ensure that the Canadian issues got lots of attention and working hard to have the Canadian delegation, which included Paul Martin,

John Manley, Herb Gray, and Lloyd Axworthy, especially well taken care of.

Not that there weren't conflicts between my three roles. I met one of the toughest within weeks of arriving in Canada. On September 28, 1993, while Janet and I were still on the second leg of our cross-country tour, I phoned my secretary in Ottawa from Halifax, Nova Scotia, to see if there were any calls. "Haven't you heard?" she said. "We've had about thirty press calls from Michigan. Senator Riegle's announced he's not going to run again. And everybody now thinks you're going to run."

"You've got to be kidding!"

"No," she said.

Holy mackerel, I thought.

I had talked to Don Riegle the previous spring about whether he was going to run again. He had been a dynamic and effective senator, but he'd had some problems and been cited by the Senate Ethics Committee for bad judgment. He felt it was a relatively minor incident. That's not how it was viewed at the time by his critics and opponents. "Don," I said, "you've had three six-year terms in the Senate. If you run again, they're going to spend a lot of money calling you names. You're a young man, so you could still have another life. And if you're going to leave, you ought to control your own destiny. You know, in my own interest, I'd rather have you stay. I'm headed off for Canada, and I don't want people calling me to come back to take your place. But I think you ought to think twice about it. Quit while you're ahead, make some money, enjoy life."

More recently, we had seen the Riegles at a Canadian embassy dinner less than a week before Don's surprising announcement. Don had just hosted a Perot rally in Lansing and beaten up on the president and on NAFTA – which seemed odd behavior for a Democrat – and he was rather defensive about it, but he was still insisting it was full steam ahead. His wife Laurie even implied to Janet that Don was definitely ready to run again. Now, for personal and family reasons, he was out.

In the wake of his announcement, a lot of people assumed that I would be in the race for his Senate seat. If I hadn't just been made ambassador to Canada, I probably would have run. It would have been a golden opportunity to get back into politics and make up for my defeat in 1990. The polls were showing I was still well-known and well-liked. Virtually every party leader in the state called or wrote to assure me of support. People who had been less enthusiastic about my seeking a third term for governor were now encouraging me to run. It was quite possible that the voters themselves wanted to correct what was probably a low turn-out fluke in 1990. And, unlike then, I now had a friendly mayor of Detroit and a friend in the White House. Michigan attorney general Frank J. Kelley said to me, "This is it. If you've ever wanted to be a senator, this is your best chance – and it may be your last chance as well." And he may have been right. If I ever run for office again, I may never have a campaign where all the ducks are lined up quite as perfectly as they were then.

"If you run for the Senate," said another close adviser, "you'll know what you're going to be doing with the rest of your life. You'll be a senator until you retire, probably, and that's where you ought to be. It's a great place for you if you're ready to go now."

But Riegle's decision came at the wrong time for me. Though I might not have asked for the Canadian post if I had known he wasn't going to run, I really wanted to be an ambassador. I had just arrived in Canada. I was already excited by the place. I was just then telling Canadians that I wanted to get to know them better and wouldn't take them for granted. As well, we were right in the middle of the NAFTA battle. I thought of myself as a dedicated public servant, and I didn't see how I'd ever again be confirmed by the Senate as an ambassador – or anything else – if I walked away from Canada after less than two months on the job.

I got a call out of the blue from Brian Mulroney, who clearly had lost neither his political instinct nor his knowledge of the United States, advising me not to go. "The timing is very bad," he said. "Being an ambassador will only add luster to your reputation if you still have political ambition." I appreciated Mulroney's judgment.

I also realized, however, that I owed it to those who had spent energy and money supporting me over sixteen years not to dismiss their encouragement too quickly. I talked to my old pollsters. I thought through the themes I would use in a campaign. But the best way to deal with it, I decided, was to let the dust settle, do my job, then go back to Michigan for the Thanksgiving and Christmas holidays to consult with my key people. I couldn't do that sitting in Ottawa, not least because nobody in the embassy knew anything at all about Michigan politics. So I told the press, "I've got this wonderful job, and I have no plans to run." And I told my friends, "Look, I'm happy to look at it, but I'm not going to decide till later this year." And I told all the people who phoned and wrote, "Thanks for your support. I'll keep you in mind, and I'll let you know."

Somebody said at the time, "It's an embarrassment of riches. You're either going to be ambassador to Canada or you're going to be a United States senator." But I'm not sure it would have been that easy. Nineteen ninety-four turned out to be a very bad year for Democrats. Shortly after the word was out that I might run with the whole party united behind me, the Republicans made a Freedom of Information request, through a friendly reporter, asking how much my train trip had cost the American taxpayers. The State Department called me and said, "They're already after you." Since I had nothing to hide, I was amused.

As October passed into November, and November into December, the pressure kept building. The longer I delayed announcing my decision not to run, the more people assumed I would. When we returned to Michigan in mid-December, Janet got tired and depressed with virtually everybody telling me I had to run. The polls were good, their feeling was positive, and they thought I was wasting my time up in Canada pouring champagne. But Janet knew the job was important and exciting, and she was really finding it interesting and fun. At that year's White House Christmas party – which was a great success, despite the fact that many of the key Michigan supporters had been invited late, the computers broke down, leaving everyone shivering in line out in the cold without coats for an hour, and the president looked like walking death because of his allergies to Christmas trees – a lot of people encouraged me to come back. Afterwards, at a dinner with leading Democrats from Michigan, one after the other got up and gave a speech about why I should run. It seemed almost orchestrated, and it was the kind of testimonial that any politician would die for, but I remained noncommital. And it was followed by a call from David Wilhelm, the Democratic national chair, who said that everyone in the White House, up to the president himself, was ready to pave the way for me if I wanted to run. I was still reluctant.

On January 8, 1994, I got the call from President Clinton at my hotel in Toronto. "I'm calling about Michigan," he said. "It's such an important race." The consensus of the people around him was that I should be the candidate. It would be a chance for me to stage a comeback just as he had done in Arkansas in 1982. "If you run, I'll do everything I can to elect you. If you're beaten, I'll help you out. But you can't win if you really don't want to do it. You've got to decide what's in your gut." But it certainly sounded as though he preferred I run.

A short while later, Bruce Lindsey said, "Let us know when you make your decision, because we're going to have to begin looking for a successor."

I suppose I could have said, with the president's backing, NAFTA won, and a few more months under my belt, that I had done enough in Canada. But, on January 22nd, Janet and I went to the White House to tell Bruce that I had decided to stay in Canada, and I officially announced my decision to the press two days later. Most of my closest friends – except Janet – were surprised, if not shocked. But, more than my doubts about whether I had enough time to develop a theme, get around the state, and raise the money necessary for a successful campaign, I had been guided by my feelings about the importance and excitement of the job in Canada. And, in the back in my mind, I thought I might have another chance in 1996 if Michigan's other Democratic senator, Carl Levin, stepped down (though he had warned me, in no uncertain terms, not to count on it). Not only would that allow me to serve as ambassador for three years, it also would probably be a better time to be a Democratic candidate. I knew that the Democrats were going to have a tough year in 1994, though I didn't know how tough. In fact, if elected, I would have been the only new Democratic senator to win that year. Bob Carr, who ran because I didn't, lost by nine points.

In the end, Michigan Democrats did very well in 1994, because the state was prosperous and its people were in a good mood. Every Democrat incumbent in Michigan, with one exception, was re-elected, as did every Republican incumbent in Michigan, with one exception. Even so, as I often said, there are a hundred U.S. senators, but only one U.S. ambassador to Canada. And while I was ready for the prominence of being a U.S. senator, I had already done that kind of job for eight years as a congressman. Worst of all, I now know I would have traded being in the minority in the Senate for the incredibly interesting experience I had in Canada at a critical time in its history.

━ ━

Even though the State Department guidelines gave me some small latitude, I steadfastly refrained from partisan comment or involvement during the 1994 election season. At times it was hard to hear my Republican successor claim that he had done a great job considering all the problems he had inherited, when in truth he had inherited a $422-million surplus and enjoyed a free ride with the Clinton economic recovery. But, whenever I said anything, I set myself the CNN test: "What if this gets carried on CNN in the U.S.? Are the Republicans going to feel that I'm their ambassador, too, or are they going to think I'm just sitting up in Canada worrying about the Democrats?" So I went out of my way to be fair. Other than telling people that I thought Clinton was doing a great job, I didn't criticize the Republicans. In reality, I didn't mind the sabbatical from U.S. politics. It was great not having to get pulled into the campaign and, given the results, I felt kind of safe.

"Why is it," Bo Cutter and Bruce Lindsey both asked me around this time, "that whenever I talk to ambassadors like you, you're all having such a great time, while we're getting the crap kicked out of us back here in Washington?" Of course, I reminded them how hard I was working and how complex the issues were, but I actually felt almost guilty about how much fun I was having too.

In early August, however, I did compose a private memo to the president about what I thought he needed to do in advance of the November elections. I had it in my pocket when I saw him on August 6th at a fundraiser in Detroit. He was very low in the polls, everybody was saying that he couldn't do anything right, and he looked tired, but he gave a terrific speech that left his audience in better spirits. I rode with him afterwards to the airport. He was even more tired and so hungry that he ate the better part of two huge meals during the forty-minute drive. I wanted to buoy him up, but I also wanted to deliver a stern message. Bruce Lindsey had encouraged me to do so.

It had long been apparent to many of Clinton's friends and supporters that he wasn't being well-served by some of his White House staff. They had shown their incompetence in countless ways, creating ethical, substantive, and public relations problems, even with his key supporters. One friend told me of going to a White House meeting that was presided over by a young person sucking a lollipop! As a result, even when the president was doing well on the big issues like NAFTA or Bosnia or the budget, the little things often made him look sloppy. The worst disease of the Clinton administration was really a Washington disease: a steady stream of young, arrogant, officious staffers who flatter and pamper their bosses, demonstrate their loyalty by pushing other people around, think nastiness and rudeness are signs of strength and effectiveness, and devote almost all their energies toward pleasing their superiors instead of reaching out to Congress, party activists, friends, or the American people. The Clinton White House seemed overrun by these types, whom I consider the parasites of democracy, and I didn't think the president had any real idea of what was going on in his name.

"You've got to reorganize the White House staff, now," I said during the drive to Selfridge Air Base. "Don't wait until after the election. It could be a disaster, you know. Generally a party in power loses seats mid-term, so you're likely to be viewed as having had a setback. If you don't reorganize now, it'll look like you're just reacting to the election rather than taking charge and cleaning house. Because you need a better staff. Don't be discouraged. Remember, Reagan was low at this point in his presidency too."

"Yeah," Clinton said, "but the economy was in bad shape when he was unpopular. It's in great shape now and we're still low."

"That's another thing," I said. "You haven't been talking about the economy. You got it going with your recovery program, but you haven't been making a coordinated effort to take credit for your economic achievements. You've got to showcase your strengths. You're on TV every day – way too much, in my opinion – but if you're talking about every little thing, it's hard for people to know what's important to you. They want you to succeed, but you don't have a lot of time."

The president agreed that he was overexposed, but I felt bad about the conversation. I worried I was invading his privacy, adding to his burden, kicking him when he was down. But I thought he needed to hear from a friend, someone who wasn't on his staff or asking for anything. My only goal, I told him, was to be part of a successful Bill Clinton administration.

Near the end of our chat he looked out the window and spotted a river in the dark. "What's that called?" he asked.

"It's the Clinton River," I said, and we both laughed. Then, until we arrived at the air base, we talked about old times, his visits to Michigan, a possible trip to Canada, and his affection for Jean Chrétien. He slipped out of the car, shook a few hands, climbed up the stairs of Air Force One, and was gone. To my intense disappointment, he did not give his office the shakeup it needed before the election.

What happened, of course, was that the Senate changed hands to the GOP and the House, to everyone's surprise, became Republican for the first time since 1952. It was a disaster for many fine Democrats. But I wasn't sure it was a disaster for Bill Clinton. "The real issue now is how will the president react to this setback?" I wrote in my journal. "Will he seize this as an opportunity, or will it be the beginning of the end for the Clinton presidency?" On November 9, 1994, at the request of our embassy personnel who were interested in my interpretation of what had happened, I took time to analyze the voters' message at our weekly meeting. I also indicated that since the president had been blamed for not getting things through Congress anyway, because the southern Democrats had often been voting with the Republicans, he was better off with the voters knowing that he didn't control Congress. They would be less likely to hold him accountable for what happened there.

After the meeting I wrote a memo to the president urging him to use the situation to his advantage. I decided not to send it, but a couple of weeks later, on November 20th, I spoke with him on the phone. "Look," I said, "the election, however regrettable for a lot of our really good Democrats, probably gives you a great opportunity to renew your presidency. Now you're going to be able to define yourself in ways

Above: Meeting with
Quebec Premier Jacques
Parizeau in Quebec City,
December 1994.

Right: With the Speaker of
the House of Commons,
Gib Parent, and Lucien
Bouchard, at Kingsmere,
September 1995.

Below: "Hard at work" with deputy, Jim Walsh, in the
embassy, January 1995.

Above: Watching Lucien Bouchard on television, with the president, Bruce Lindsay and Mike McCurry, moments after the family room meeting, February 1995.

BARBARA KINNEY / THE WHITE HOUSE

Below: Deputy national security adviser Sandy Berger (left), Blanchard, and speech writer Bob Boorstin (far right) with the president as he puts the finishing touches on his speech to parliament, February 24, 1995.

OFFICIAL WHITE HOUSE PHOTOGRAPH

President Clinton and Prime Minister Chrétien in the House of Commons, Ottawa, February 1995.

OFFICIAL WHITE HOUSE PHOTOGRAPH

Above: The president, prime minister, ambassadors Jim Blanchard and Raymond Chrétien celebrate the conclusion of a successful state visit at the Canal Ritz.

OFFICIAL WHITE HOUSE PHOTOGRAPH

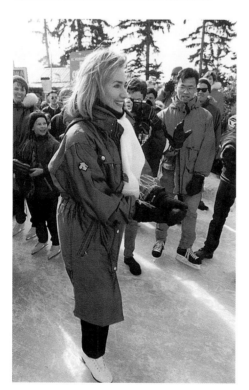

Left: Hillary Clinton skates like a champ on the Rideau Canal.

Above: The president putts during the "Great Golf Match," Halifax, July 1995. Looking on, from left to right: a security man, Blanchard, Erskine Bowles, John Rae, and the prime minister.
OFFICIAL WHITE HOUSE PHOTOGRAPH

Right: A watchful moment at the tee.
OFFICIAL WHITE HOUSE PHOTOGRAPH

Below: Moments after a near miss: the prime minister and the ambassador, August 1995.
JANET BLANCHARD

Top: Doug Young and Federico Peña sign the Open Skies agreement while the prime minister and president look on.
OFFICIAL WHITE HOUSE PHOTOGRAPH

Above: An overhead view of the incredible "No" rally in Montreal, October 27, 1995.
JIM BECK / MONTREAL GAZETTE

Above: A final visit to the prime minister's office. The Prime Minister, Janet, Eddie Goldenberg, Blanchard, March 1996.

J.M. CARISSE / OFFICE OF THE PRIME MINISTER

Below: Janet with the prime minister in Ottawa, March 1996.

J.M. CARISSE / OFFICE OF THE PRIME MINISTER

Above: At the prime minister's farewell dinner at 24 Sussex Drive. From left to right: Jay, Jean Chrétien, Janet, Aline, and Jim Blanchard.

J.M.CARISSE / OFFICE OF THE PRIME MINISTER

Below: Secretary of State Warren Christopher surprises Blanchard with a citation at the State Department on his last day on the job, April 1996. Ambassador Raymond Chrétien and Foreign Minister Lloyd Axworthy look on.

STATE DEPARTMENT

you haven't been able to in the last two years. You've got somebody to contrast with. You're playing a game of chess with Congress, not water polo or volleyball, so take your time, say as little as possible for the moment. Relax. Listen. Let the Republicans talk, talk, talk. Quit trying to analyze and respond to everything. You're the president. Be presidential. There are a lot of reasons for what happened, and you're not the prime minister of a party that's just lost its majority. It's a totally different situation. You're the president." He was quiet until I reminded him that Eisenhower, Nixon, and Reagan, had all fared better electorally than Carter, even though Carter was the only one who had a majority of his own party in Congress.

"Yeah," he said, "but Carter accomplished more than they did."

"Perhaps," I replied, "but he didn't get re-elected. Look, you've got to shut down all this side talk about the elections from your staff. Just worry about the economy. Highlight what you've done. Let the Republicans shoot their mouth off. Remember, you don't have to win every battle to win the war here. Some good defeats could help you, as long as you look strong. And you've got plenty of time to show these guys as extremists. You'll get re-elected if you do this right."

"I know, but all the Democrats are blaming me. I went out and raised all this money for them, and now they're blaming me. We've won every battle and we've just lost the war."

"No, no, no, it's just round one," I insisted. "Go out and sell your record for the next two years. That shouldn't be a problem." But President Clinton sounded besieged, hassled, defensive.

A month later, on Christmas Eve, Janet's mother told me that President Clinton had been trying to reach me at her home in Williamston, Michigan. I figured he was going to offer me another job, at best in the cabinet, at worst (and more likely) with the Democratic Party. My name had been bandied about to be chair of the Democratic National Committee (DNC). In the wake of the huge defeat in November, there was a general belief the DNC had been weak, and the hunt was on for a new chair. But it wasn't a job I wanted and I had already planted a story in the press that I wouldn't take it if offered.

The next day we were at my sister's home near Lansing for Christmas dinner with the whole family, all of whom wanted to talk about the president's fortunes. They're very political and big liberals – I'm probably the most conservative of the lot – and they couldn't understand why Clinton was being so harshly criticized. At 6:00 p.m., just as we were about to have dessert, the phone rang. It was the White House. I dashed down to the basement to take the call. After a few preliminary remarks, I asked, "How can I be helpful?"

"Well," the president said, "who do you think should be the chairman of the DNC?"

"Governor Bayh would be good, Governor Baliles would be good, Senator Dodd would be good."

"Why not you?" he replied.

I gave him a lot of different reasons why not. Number one, I didn't want to be a party official. Having been a congressman and governor, I never wanted to do that. And it's a big fundraising job, which is something I don't enjoy. I didn't believe in taking a job I didn't want. Besides, I was concerned about the situation in Canada and felt I could be of better use to him if I stayed.

"Yeah," said the president, "but I've checked around with members of Congress, businesspeople, governors. You could really help me. You're one of two or three key people who could really do a good job."

"Maybe," I said, "except I'd rather be ambassador to Libya!"

"You may have to be!" he lashed out.

I hung up feeling depressed that I hadn't been able to say yes to the president, and when I went up and told my relatives what had happened, they were aghast. "We've just been sitting here talking about how we're going to help the president," they said, "and you told him no?"

"I really don't want that job," I explained, "but I told him I'd think about it." I don't know who put the president up to calling me, but I didn't appreciate the fact that nobody in the White House had warned me. If Clinton had been getting good advice, his staff would have known that I would say no. So I felt really bad. I worried that I was being selfish and maybe not as loyal as I should be to the president.

However, I did feel a duty to consider accepting the post out of deference to him, so I called a few people the next day. They all confirmed my doubts. The party had a $4-million debt, the chair was essentially a fundraising job, and the White House would expect me to be kind of a staff member. "You won't be free to run things as you see fit," I was told. "It's a thankless job. Most DNC chairs are treated like dirt." Almost everyone thought that I shouldn't touch it with a ten-foot pole.

I phoned the White House a couple of days later. The president was out, but I spoke to his chief of staff, Leon Panetta. Janet and I will be happy to help on the campaign, I said, and we are willing to come back from Canada in time to be helpful. But, not only was I enjoying Ottawa, I had a lot on my plate, especially with the threat of a referendum on Quebec. Panetta seemed to understand.

～　～

At other times, the three-way connections between Ottawa, Michigan, and Washington were subtler than a presidential phone call. On April 17, 1995, for example, I was in

Marquette, Michigan, to give a speech to its Economic Club on Canadian-American relations. While there, I got talking to some old friends about the rise of the right wing in U.S. politics, and they told me how disturbed they were about an ad hoc, paramilitary, grassroots group calling itself the Michigan Militia. Apparently it had been training up in the northern woods in preparation for a United Nations invasion, which it feared was coming to impose a world government on Americans. I was really quite surprised. I had never heard of the group before.

My surprise turned to shock three days later, on April 20th, when I heard about the Oklahoma City bombing, the worst terrorist act in U.S. history. The next day, at a friend's house in Connecticut, I was called by Ed Rabel of NBC News, who told me there was evidence linking the Oklahoma bombing to some outfit called the Michigan Militia. Did I know anything about it?

"This is the damnedest thing," I thought, and I told Ed what I had heard a couple of days before in Marquette. "So it sounds like a pretty wacky group to me."

At Ed's request, I phoned some people I knew at the Michigan State police and other law-enforcement agencies to learn more. They confirmed that they had been monitoring the Michigan Militia, which they described as a paranoid, paramilitary group always hanging around the police and sheriff offices wanting to be deputized. Some of them meant well, but had bizarre beliefs. They viewed the government, the president, and the United Nations as enemies, and were sure Russian troops were training in northern Michigan. I obtained some of their literature and passed it on to both the FBI and NBC News.

The impact of the Oklahoma blast reached even Ottawa. By the time I returned to Ottawa, the RCMP had decided to give me direct security, which meant I was now driven around town by a confusing rotation of Mounties instead of by Vaughn Cameron. More unhappily still, the designs for the new United States embassy in Ottawa, which I had been discussing on the morning of the bombing, were dramatically changed in a way that replaced aesthetic considerations with security ones.

A month earlier, I had been phoned by Billy Webster, the president's scheduler, asking for a favor. He was wondering if I could help arrange for the president to speak at my alma mater, Michigan State University in East Lansing. I was delighted to help and fortunately had known its president, Pete McPherson, since my college days. Even though he was a long-time Republican, I felt comfortable about phoning him in the strictest confidence to see if he could – and would – get Bill Clinton invited to give the spring commencement address. Pete was honored to receive the president on his campus, as I guessed he would be, and it was easily arranged for May 5th.

On May 4th, thanks to Open Skies, I boarded Northwest flight 1831, direct service from Ottawa to Detroit, flying time one hour and thirteen minutes. (I was pleasantly surprised to see that the flight was half full, not bad for the fifth day of a new run.) And the next day, up in East Lansing, Janet and I drove over to Michigan State University. We attended a big brunch reception, which included about two hundred people whom we had recruited to help Bill Clinton win Michigan in 1992. The reception was held in the Duffy Daugherty Football Building, an incredible facility with what seems like miles of locker rooms, training rooms, fitness rooms, steam baths, classrooms, computers, everything, including a huge indoor football field with synthetic turf. From there we were going to be driven a couple of blocks over to Spartan Stadium, which holds about 72,000 spectators, for the president's speech.

A few days earlier I had talked with Bob Boorstin and David Shipley, the White House speechwriters, and said I didn't think the president should shy away from taking on the Michigan Militia or talking about the Oklahoma bombing. Most Michiganers were really embarrassed and offended to have had their state's name associated with it, and many of the state's prominent politicians had been pussyfooting around the issue, sometimes because they were afraid of the gun lobby, sometimes because they had inadvertently honored the Michigan Militia as a civic association. I thought the people of Michigan would appreciate a bold response from the president.

So, at the pre-commencement brunch, Clinton got up and, among other things, talked about the bombing. "This Michigan Militia and these paramilitary groups are not the real Michigan," he said. "The real Michigan is right here. It's Michigan State. It's the auto industry. It's the Detroit Tigers. It's the Detroit Lions." All of a sudden the people in the arena went wild. The event turned into a kind of pep rally. It was clear that he had struck the right chord and was soothing the wounds of the psyche of our state.

As we left the brunch, he shook some hands, then walked toward a back room where he was going to take a nap. His eyes were red, and he looked really tired. En route he pulled me over in the hallway. "What's that place where we had our first rally during the campaign?" he asked.

"Battle Creek," I said.

"Yeah. And what's that company there?"

"Kellogg's."

"Yeah, Kellogg's Corn Flakes. That's the real Michigan, Jim. What are some other examples like that?"

"Well," I said, "how about the Great Lakes? Or the UP? Don't say Upper Peninsula, say UP, that's what everybody calls it."

"Yeah. And what's that place where we had our NGA meeting? Traverse City, cherries. That's the real Michigan."

He was obviously working through his commencement speech in his mind. I later found out he had been up past midnight writing because he knew he was going to take on the Michigan Militia. It wasn't unusual for him to rework the drafts from his speechwriters, superimposing his own voice and thoughts onto their words. While he was resting, rumors swept the campus that he had taken ill, but they were dispelled when he emerged in high spirits an hour later for the drive across the campus to the stadium.

There were about forty thousand people waiting there under a sunny sky, and they went wild when Clinton walked out wearing his Yale robes. My mother thought he looked like a Greek god. I was happy to see the kids so enthusiastic. And the president wowed them when he went after the paramilitary groups.

"There is nothing patriotic about hating your country," he declared, "or pretending that you can love your country but despise your government. There is nothing heroic about turning your back on America or ignoring your own responsibilities. If you want to preserve your own freedom, you must stand up for the freedom of others with whom you disagree, but you also must stand up for the rule of law." The applause was polite. But then he launched into the theme he had been thinking about. "And I would like to say one word to the people of the United States. I know you have heard a lot of publicity in recent days about Michigan and militias. But what you have seen and heard is not the real Michigan." Now there was serious applause. "*This* is is real Michigan!"

The applause was thunderous, and it continued in waves as he recited the list he had made. It was an inspired and inspiring speech, and the press coverage that night and the next day was as good as he had ever received in Michigan. We were all proud of him.

Up until that point, I was worried that he was going to have a tough time getting re-elected. But, from that day on, I began to think that he was actually going to make it. Bill Clinton, I decided, was the Indiana Jones of American politics: he'd get himself into one tough scrape after another, grab a vine at the last minute, and swing free and victorious with a great big grin on his face.

— 8 —

THE BEST OF FRIENDS

Nothing brings into sharper focus the relationship between the United States of America and another country than a presidential visit. It's the high point, we were taught at the State Department's "Charm School," of any ambassador's term. And, given that Bill Clinton's favorable rating was at 75 percent in Canada, I had been urging the White House to schedule a visit to Ottawa before the debacle of the mid-term elections. It would have garnered the president a lot of good press in the United States and boosted his spirits to be surrounded by applause and warm crowds.

"I want to go early in the fall," Clinton himself had told me in April 1994, "so that it's warm enough to play golf with Chrétien."

"That'll have to be real early," I said. Ottawa is the second coldest capital in the world.

It was decided, however, that a trip wouldn't be possible until early in 1995. Eventually the White House chose February 23rd and 24th – one night shorter than hoped for because the Clintons wanted to be back in Washington for their daughter Chelsea's birthday on the weekend. I didn't know how warm the crowds would be on a freezing February day in Ottawa, and a golf game was clearly out of the question, but that was our first and best opportunity.

On January 9th I went to a meeting at the White House to plan the trip with staff from the National Security Council, White House scheduling and advance, the White House press office, and the State Department. We met in the Situation Room, the site of so many presidential crises in peace and war, and discussed the overall schedule, the major events the president would attend or host, the themes we would stress, and the politics of U.S.-Canada relations. Then we went over a lot of details, from how many of the U.S. cabinet would be coming to what we could do with Hillary. I urged everyone not to do too much, to keep things simple. He was going to be extremely well-received and they shouldn't worry. But most of these people had an absolute bunker mentality about everything at this point in the White House.

The president was getting beat up right and left, and he was walking around like a whipped dog. ABC's Sam Donaldson was predicting Clinton wasn't going to run for re-election. Newt Gingrich was king of the town. Leon Panetta and Mike McCurry were just starting to get control of things. I had to convince the White House that Canadians loved the president, so nobody had to create any goofy stuff.

The principal event would be the president's address to Parliament, and I was happy to hear that Bob Boorstin was going to be writing it, not least because I had worked with him on the Clinton campaign in Michigan. The main theme

was to celebrate Canadian-American relations as a partnership that works. I also knew we were going to have to deal
with the question of Quebec. As Jacques Parizeau had predicted in his first meeting with me, the Parti Québécois had
won power in Quebec in September 1994, after defeating
Daniel Johnson's provincial Liberals, and Premier Parizeau
was promising to hold a referendum on independence within
a year.

Saying that the future of Canada is for Canadians to
decide was fine so far as it went, but I had been in Canada
long enough to know that the separatists took this to mean
the United States could live with any result, or didn't care, or
secretly favored separation. The fact was, whenever a president of the United States had been pressed, his answer was
always "Yes, sure, we want Canada to stay united." Then the
State Department would jump in and say that wasn't our
official position. So I wanted to go farther in order to dispel
anyone's belief that we were indifferent or that the break-up
of Canada was somehow in our political interests. And I was
confident that Warren Christopher shared that view. He had
implied as much on February 25, 1994, during a meeting
with André Ouellet.

When Ouellet was asked what position Canada wanted
us to take with regard to Quebec separation, he answered,
"We want your support for a unified Canada."

"It's there," Christopher answered without any hesitation.

Indeed, I found, when I talked about moving the United
States toward a more open support of a united Canada, that
there wasn't really anybody in the State Department who
argued against it. Though Prime Minister Chrétien was
delighted to hear that we were thinking about being more
emphatic (and no doubt guessed that we weren't about to do
something unpredictable), he hadn't asked us to get involved.

He didn't expect it, nor did we promise him anything. As things progressed, of course, I did talk to Eddie Goldenberg about how we could be helpful without appearing to be meddling or looking like we were prompted by the federalists. And, as we got near the time of the trip, I ran some language by him to make sure he didn't see any problems with it. But no one in Ottawa was really sure what we were going to do until we did it.

Connected to the Quebec issue was the issue of what to do with Lucien Bouchard, the leader of the separatist Bloc Québécois, which was now the official Opposition in Ottawa. I had expected him from the outset to ask for a meeting with Clinton during the president's visit. The leader of the Opposition in Parliament has usually requested, and often obtained, such a meeting. On the other hand, the leader of the Opposition has never before been a fervent separatist dedicated to the fracture of Canada. My concern, if we turned him down, was that the Quebec nationalists would blame Chrétien and portray it as a rejection of all Quebeckers. Having miraculously survived a flesh-eating disease, which cost him a leg and almost took his life the previous December, Bouchard had ascended into political sainthood.

"There's no fixed rule," I told Eddie Goldenberg on February 5th, less than a month after Bouchard had been photographed emerging from the hospital on crutches. "There have been occasions in the past when American presidents have met with Canadian opposition leaders. Kennedy met Pearson when Diefenbaker was prime minister. Reagan met Mulroney. So you ought to think this through, and you've got to be careful. Sure, we could lend him some legitimacy if we say yes, but we could make him a hero if you say no. Let us know what you want us to do, and don't worry, we're not going to make any decision until we talk. We know it's a problem. We'll figure out how to finesse it."

For my part I concocted the idea of getting Preston Manning to request a meeting too, then hold both meetings at my house, safe from the eyes of the press and cameras. That way, we could honor the tradition of meeting with opposition leaders, give Bouchard the respect his office deserved, yet not give him any special legitimacy or media attention. Our people figured it was a good scheme, but the prime minister still thought it was too much and wasn't pleased. He had to be convinced to go along by Eddie Goldenberg and Raymond Chrétien and never felt totally happy about it. So I phoned Manning and said, "How would you like to meet with the president?" He thought it was a great idea, of course, and was happy to ask for a meeting just like Bouchard's. Later I called Bouchard and said that the president would be delighted to meet with him, with the stipulation that we weren't going to allow any press at all.

"Can't I have a photograph?" he asked.

"I'm not sure," I said. "We don't want to get in the middle of any referendum." I knew, of course, that a photograph of Clinton and Bouchard would be on every telephone pole in Quebec during a referendum, because I was aware how popular Clinton was in Quebec. He had a 74 percent favorable rating in Quebec, compared to 60 percent for Parizeau and 45 percent for Chrétien.

But Bouchard seemed happy anyway. "I don't want to embarrass the president," he said. "I want to deal with Canadian issues, I want to tell him what's going on in Quebec, and I want to tell him we're friends of the U.S. We're pro-NAFTA. I want to give him a glimpse of what a separatist really is."

Meanwhile, every presidential visit brings with it myriad logistical and social issues: How many at a luncheon or a dinner? What to do at Government House? What time would the president speak? Where would he prepare for the speech? Janet and I were pushing for a "spontaneous" public event in which Hillary Clinton and Aline Chrétien would go skating on the Rideau Canal. Everyone thought it was a wonderful idea, but nobody would give it the final blessing. But the thorniest problem was how the Secret Service and the RCMP would guard the president and who would be in charge. Theirs was a historic feud. Unlike the FBI and the RCMP, who usually get along very well on matters of cooperative law enforcement, the Secret Service viewed the Mounties as rather clumsy on security issues, and they argued that no matter where the president goes, they're in charge of his safety. The RCMP tended to see the Secret Service as arrogant and pushy, and they noted that they have never lost a leader yet – a claim the Secret Service could not make. To complicate matters further, the Mounties have a rule prohibiting anyone but themselves carrying guns, which was in obvious conflict with the fact that the U.S. president always travels with a phalanx of armed guards.

I was caught in the middle of this fight, which dragged on until the very eve of the visit. On the one hand, I hadn't been very impressed by the Mounties during Vice-President Gore's visit the previous summer, especially when they pushed me around in the crowd because they didn't know who I was. On the other hand, I didn't want to insult them on Canadian soil. So we came up with a compromise that had three huge guys from both forces squashed into the front seat of the president's car, and an understanding that the RCMP would ignore all the weapons the Secret Service were toting into the country. But there still remained an argument over who was going to drive the car and who controlled the ground rules in the event of a problem. It was comical.

"Crazy calls from the embassy, from Michigan, from Washington, from the Prime Minister's Office and the White House," I wrote on February 7th. "It seems like we have a full moon. Both the Prime Minister's Office and low-level spokesmen from the NSC caused confusion regarding a meeting with Bouchard. Secret Service and the RCMP continue their fight over who would really guard the president."

Adding to the madness were the sudden rumors that our Budget department (OMB) was about to propose a border fee on commuters and visitors as a way of collecting some revenue for expanding immigration and customs facilities. I suspected that it was really aimed at controlling the influx of people from Mexico, but it would hit Canadians and U.S.-Canada relations with a devastating impact. It was a classic example of someone in our bureaucracy coming up with a "great idea" that completely overlooked Canada.

"It will make the U.S. and the president look foolish," I wrote to the State Department. "I can already see the cartoons in Canada and hear the jokes in New York, Michigan, and Washington. How do we warn the White House that this is crazy?" Paul Martin raised it as a serious problem with Bob Rubin during the G7 finance ministers' meeting in Toronto in early February. I eventually had to call Leon Panetta and the president himself to beg them to get it stopped before the visit.

"I don't know who came up with that idea," the president said, "but I'm hoping it will die." As it turned out, it didn't die until the very eve of his arrival. The OMB settled for a local option in which communities who wanted it could have it. Nobody, of course, did.

At long last, on February 10th, two weeks before the visit, we got a sign-off from the White House for the schedule we had proposed weeks before. But we still couldn't get final approval for the guest list I had drawn up for the breakfast the president was going to host at the National Gallery for Canadian political and business leaders. By the time I did get the go-ahead, it was too late to mail the invitations, so my office had to phone and fax 175 people on short notice. No sooner was that done than the White House social office called to say that they would prefer to make the calls. "If my previous experience is any guide," I noted at the time, "everyone will be invited on the day of the event." As it turned out, the printed invitations didn't arrive from the White House social office until it was too late, so we had to send most of them out as souvenirs after the president left.

On February 15th I started doing the round of media interviews that always precedes a presidential trip. They were intended to tell the press and the general public what to expect, what not to expect, what's important, why it's even necessary. I was especially careful not to signal that the president might say something different about Canadian unity, because if it's in the paper before you do it, it's never enough. It was another case where it was helpful to have a political ambassador who was media-seasoned and knew how to answer questions without raising expectations or causing problems. Even before the interviews began, I had let the press know that President Clinton was going to meet with Lucien Bouchard and Preston Manning, so that the issue wouldn't become the focus of speculation. And I used an interview on the "McNeil-Lehrer Report" to lambaste the *Wall Street Journal* for an editorial comparing Canada to a Third World country. Anybody who knew anything about Canada wouldn't compare it to a Third World economy.

There were still many irritants, major and minor, to fret about. On February 17th, I heard that some White House people were actually talking about delaying the announcement of the signing of the Open Skies agreement until early the following week. "Unfortunately for them," I wrote in my journal, "it's been in the press for two months. Clearly someone down at the White House or the NSC is totally out of it." And then I received the trip directory of the forty-five or more people from the White House, State, NSC, and Transportation who were coming to Ottawa with the president. That's when I got really angry, for the planners had not seen fit to invite three of our most valuable people: David Weiss, the head of trade for North America, Lynne Lambert, the director of the Canada Desk, and Jim Tarrant, our official Open Skies negotiator. So I had to get on the phone to get them included. "I'm going to let the president know about this bullshit," I noted to myself, "but probably only after his speech to Parliament. I want him in a good mood."

I realized that I was feeling a lot of stress because of the visit, stress unlike any I had ever felt when I was governor or a congressman, even on the eve of an election or before a major debate. "It could be my advancing age," I wrote, "although usually fewer things bother me at fifty-two than forty-two or thirty-two. It's more likely that I do not have the kind of confidence in the White House and the president's operation to make me feel good about this significant trip." One of my top deputies said this was the most disorganized and least professional White House operation he had seen in twenty-five years. "My first congressional campaign and all succeeding efforts as a congressman and governor were significantly better organized," I noted. "I feel for the president, the loyal people who get left out, and the people who look to Bill Clinton for an affirmation that government can really help people and lift the country."

At one point, just days before the trip, Leon Panetta actually threatened to cancel it if the RCMP wouldn't go along with our Secret Service arrangements. They were still arguing with us about who was going to drive the president's limousine and control the ground rules. It all blew up again during a last-minute meeting when someone asked the Mounties, "What happens if there's a problem and the president says, 'Move out?' Do you listen to him or do you listen to what's in your ear from RCMP headquarters?"

"RCMP headquarters, of course," they replied, and everything dissolved into chaos. It proved the Secret Service's point that they should drive, but it was tough to get the RCMP to change their answer. It remained a source of tension. One day, I remember, while I was walking back to my office from lunch, I saw a motorcade moving slowly in front of the Chancery. The RCMP had decided to hold a practice run! We couldn't believe it. Any assassin could have watched where the president was going to be down to the second. It was laughable, but our Secret Service agents were practically weeping.

Security was also the big issue at our house. In the past, American presidents tended to stay at Rideau Hall, the governor general's residence. But Janet and I assumed, since we knew the Clintons, that they might feel more comfortable with us. We hosted Bruce Lindsey, too, as well as the White House physician, the president's naval attaché, and Hillary's personal assistant. As a result, we had Secret Service and RCMP agents swarming all around our grounds with snowmobiles, high-powered rifles, and binoculars. They were on our roof. They were in our garage. They installed a huge communications center with thick cables in our basement. They turned my second-floor study into a super-secure room in which no conversation could be overheard by any type of device known to man. They put bullet-proof material over the beautiful picture window from which I overlooked the world every morning. They tried to put huge plants in front of it to block the view until Janet yelled, "Enough is enough!" They did aerial reconnaissance by helicopter. They wanted to position men in our walk-in linen closet, my exercise room, and every single bedroom. Eventually they settled on having a guy standing guard all night on the stairways between the floors.

The whole of Ottawa felt like it was being invaded by U.S. forces. Every few days more arrived: eighty, then a hundred, then three hundred, then five hundred, to the point where the Chateau Laurier Hotel was absolutely full with our people. Every event, large and small, from the gala at the Museum of Civilization to Mrs. Clinton's trip to a children's hospital, had its own coordinator and staff; every stop had somebody from every Canadian and U.S. agency; and virtually everybody in our embassy had some job or other, whether driving a White House advance person to an event or making sure there was a supply of food and coffee for the Secret Service. Every night for the last ten days there was a countdown meeting to go over all the details. It was a huge undertaking, led by Jim Walsh on my behalf and Steve Bachar, the lead White House advance man.

At the final countdown meeting, everyone was feeling pretty good. It was the calm before the storm. After the meeting I went back to the office, because the White House social office wanted Janet and me to suggest a seating plan for the president's breakfast. I had sworn it was a job I would never do as ambassador, yet there I was doing it. I had to laugh at myself, but I really wanted every last detail done properly.

February 23, 1995, came at last and Air Force One landed right on time at 10:30 in the morning at Ottawa's Macdonald-Cartier International Airport. Governor General Roméo LeBlanc, a French-speaking Acadian from New Brunswick and former Liberal cabinet minister who had just succeeded Ray Hnatyshyn as Canada's head of state, greeted the Clintons and escorted them, along with his wife, Diana, Janet, and myself to the welcoming ceremony in a nearby hangar. Then we all got into cars for the drive to Rideau Hall. I had warned the president not to expect wild crowds. He was popular in Canada, people were excited he was coming, but Canadians are undemonstrative and it was, after all, the middle of winter. So I was surprised to see, as we went along Sussex Drive, large crowds out in the cold waving signs and cheering.

After a brief tête-à-tête with the governor general and Diana and a round of photographs, the Clintons joined a large gathering of Canadian dignitaries for a luncheon in the ballroom. This was followed by a ceremonial tree planting, similar to the one in which John Kennedy had reinjured his back and forever after blamed John Diefenbaker for causing it deliberately. Then Janet and I rode with the president and Hillary to our embassy, where the president was going to go over his speech to the House of Commons in my office with several advisers, including Sandy Berger, Tony Lake, Erskine Bowles, Bob Boorstin, and myself. When we got there, I discovered that the Secret Service had pinned all the curtains closed for security reasons, blocking both the light and my magnificent view of Parliament Hill. With the president's permission I unpinned them at once.

We all sat around the table for about forty minutes while the president worked over the draft of the speech that had been prepared for him, including a quotation from Harry Truman I had found while researching every presidential statement ever made about Canada or Quebec. "Canada's eminent position today is a tribute to the patience, tolerance and strength of character of her people," Truman said in 1947. "Canada's notable achievement of national unity and progress through accommodation, moderation, and forbearance can be studied with profit by sister nations." I wanted to use it to show that there were indeed precedents for what Clinton was saying.

"So our plan is to do more of a tilt toward supporting a united Canada, right?" the president asked.

"Absolutely," I said. "And this will do it. We don't want to meddle, or appear to be meddling, but we do want to make it clear that we're in favor of a united Canada."

The key lines in the draft were "In a world darkened by ethnic conflicts that tear nations apart, Canada stands as a model – not only to the United States but to the entire world – of how people of different cultures can live and work together in peace and prosperity." Then the Truman quote, followed by "I am sure I speak for most Americans in expressing the hope that the people of this great country will settle their differences and stay together. At the same time, we recognize that Canada alone must decide its political future."

It was a powerful statement. In fact, Tony Lake was worried that it would look like we were really hammering the separatists. He didn't want either Canadians or Quebeckers to think that we were telling them what to do. "Let's take the traditional statement at the bottom and move it up," Lake suggested. "That way, nobody will think we've made a major departure. Then you can follow with the Truman quote."

With that and a few other changes made, we drove over to the Parliament. Outside there was another large, enthusiastic crowd cheering and yelling, "We love you, Hillary. Welcome, Bill, you're the greatest," as we passed and a couple of dozen stern-faced protesters with pro-Cuba signs. Hillary waved to them, and to her astonishment they waved back. "These are the nicest, friendliest protesters I've ever seen," she said.

"That's Canada," I said. "They don't agree with us on this issue, but they're polite."

As soon as we arrived at the Parliament Buildings, the president was whisked away for a short, one-on-one meeting with the prime minister, while Hillary and the rest of us were taken on a brief tour. The House Speaker showed us the chair in which Yousuf Karsh had taken his famous photograph of Winston Churchill. "I hope we're going to have a chance to see Karsh," Hillary said. Janet had guessed she would want to. He had photographed Hillary once, and talking with Karsh had been one of the highlights of Tipper Gore's visit to Ottawa with the vice-president the previous summer. (Tipper, who is herself a photographer, had delighted in taking *his* picture.) Hillary's White House staff, who had pooh-poohed the idea, now looked at us sheepishly. The Karshes were like family to Janet and me by this point, so Janet gave them a call and sent Vaughn to pick them up. We regretted that the meeting hadn't been properly arranged beforehand, though they were as gracious as ever.

Then we all marched into the House of Commons and were seated on special chairs set in the wide aisle between the opposing rows of wooden desks, with the government MPs on one side and the opposition parties on the other. When

Clinton and Chrétien walked in, the place turned into bedlam, with everyone cheering and applauding like mad. It was extraordinary, and the president seemed genuinely surprised after I had warned him how reserved the Canadians might be. The prime minister introduced him by adapting a piece of trivia I had given Eddie Goldenberg: no American president who addressed the Canadian Parliament was ever defeated for re-election, every president who did not was defeated.

"I thank the prime minister for his history lesson," Clinton ad-libbed when he stood up. "I have never believed in the iron laws of history so much as I do now." Everyone laughed.

When he got to the unity part of the speech, he improvised slightly. "In a world darkened by ethnic conflicts that literally tear nations apart, Canada has stood for all of us as a model of how people of different cultures can live and work together in peace, prosperity, and respect." The applause was thunderous and sustained, it sent tingles up my spine, but none of the Bloc Québécois members clapped. They all took their cue from Bouchard. Then Clinton went on, "The United States, as many of my predecessors have said, has enjoyed its excellent relationship with a strong and united Canada, but we recognize, just as the prime minister said with regard to your relationships to us a moment ago, that your political future is, of course, entirely for you to decide. That's what democracy is all about." Everyone cheered again, except this time it was the Bloc members who were clapping the loudest.

Clinton saw it and started laughing. "Now, I will tell you something about our political system," he ad-libbed. "You want to know why my State of the Union address took so long? It's because I evenly divided the things that would make the Democrats clap and the Republicans clap. And we doubled the length of the speech in common enthusiasm." Everyone was laughing and applauding by this time. Then he quoted Truman, and they all cheered again. All in all, it was a wonderful, electrifying speech, and the reaction to it was better than I had hoped. All my frustrations and worries, all the sloppy planning and petty feuding were forgotten. As he did so often before, Bill Clinton had risen to the occasion.

Immediately after the speech, a group of us went up to the prime minister's office for a three-on-three private meeting: Chrétien and Clinton; Tony Lake and his Canadian counterpart, Jim Bartleman; and Raymond Chrétien and myself.

"We've really got good relations between our two nations, and between you and me it couldn't be better," Chrétien began. "We have a few disagreements once in a while because of our large trade, but relations are good and things are going well."

"Well, why don't you give me a list of things you don't think have been adequately handled," Clinton replied, "and I'll look into it."

Then the two leaders got off on a discussion about the international financial markets, precipitated by the recent bail-out of the Mexican peso. "We need to look at that as a case study," the president said, "because this type of thing could happen again."

"Yeah," said Chrétien, "these guys are going to repeat this globally, just like your S&L crisis and your junk bond crisis. You know, it's a real problem. I go to bed at night feeling good, then I wake up in trouble because some guy at the *Wall Street Journal* decides we're a Third World country."

"We've got to be careful what we say about this at the upcoming Halifax G7 meeting," Tony Lake warned. "We don't want to scare the markets into thinking we're going to start regulating them."

"But our Federal Reserve and the Bundesbank think that inflation is a greater threat than it really is and they're scaring people," Clinton said. "They don't understand the deflationary impact of open markets and the deflationary impact of increased productivity. They're erring on the side of caution, and they could cause a lot of trouble. The economies are better disciplined now. What we need to do in Halifax is raise this issue to see whether our assumptions are still correct about inflation and international economics."

"A lot of this is ideology anyway," Chrétien added. "Why do we let these guys run our lives? Look at your deficit. Jimmy Carter had a $55-billion deficit, and they pissed all over him. But Reagan had a $270-billion deficit and they didn't do anything. It was ideologically driven. Something needs to be done. We can't permit this gambling on currency trading. And I think the IMF has lost all credibility. People really resent them. How are we going to restore credibility with the IMF?"

I thought it was interesting that neither leader wanted to dwell upon his own political situation or even the trade issues. I found the fact that they wanted to deal with long-term, big-picture issues really heartening. Certainly everybody was in a great mood.

Then it was time to go back to the residence for the president's closed-door meetings with Bouchard and Manning. The prime minister and André Ouellet continued to be unhappy that we had agreed to receive Bouchard, and they really wanted one of their own people to sit in on the meeting in case he said something outrageous. I didn't know how to do that without looking as though they were spying on Bouchard, until Raymond Chrétien offered to help. "I'm close to Bouchard," he said. "We don't agree on the issue of independence, but we're friends. We went to school together. I've helped him when he was ambassador to France. So I don't think he'd mind if I were there. I know him well enough that I could just ask him myself." Sure enough, during the luncheon at Rideau Hall, Raymond pulled Bouchard aside and asked if he could sit in on the meeting. Bouchard said fine. So it was all worked out – or so I thought.

For security reasons, the Secret Service decided they didn't want Bouchard's car pulling up to the front door of the house. They wanted him to get out at the front gate, then walk the remaining hundred yards or more. It was a farce. I tried to explain to them that Bouchard had just got out of the hospital, he had one leg, he was still learning how to use crutches, the driveway was long and uphill, and it was icy. "Sorry," they said, "but that's the way it is." Furthermore, when he got to the house, they wanted him to climb to the second-floor study that had been secure against bugging.

"You guys are crazy," I said. "First of all, you're going to kill him. Secondly, it's disrespectful. Thirdly, it's going to look as though we're deliberately harassing him. We can't do that." Reason eventually prevailed, and both Bouchard and Manning were allowed to arrive in an RCMP car and meet Clinton in our family room-cum-library on the main floor.

When Clinton walked in for his briefing, he immediately spied my humidor. He went right over, opened it up, and said, "What are we smoking these days, Jim? It wouldn't be Cuban, I don't suppose," and he took a handful of cigars.

"Now, here's the situation," I said. "No matter what you tell this guy, he'll interpret it as support for separation. If you tell him it's a nice day, he'll go out and tell the press you're in favor of an independent Quebec. So you're going to have to watch it. I would say as little as possible. Ask a few questions, be real nice. He's a decent guy, he's beloved in his province, but he wants to be the king of Quebec. He wants to lead the parade wherever it's going." And when I saw the White House photographer coming in, I added, "No, no photos, none. I want you to disappear. I don't want him to even see there's a photographer around."

Then Lucien Bouchard, his chief of staff, and Raymond Chrétien came in, and we all sat on sofas and chairs around the fire. Bouchard chose to sit right next to Clinton. "I wanted you to see in flesh and blood, first hand, a separatist," he began. "For most Quebeckers, Quebec is first, not Canada. And every time there's a problem, the differences crack Canada farther apart. We're a different nation." He talked for a while about the background to the founding of the Bloc Québécois. "We're democratic. We're peaceful. And we don't like the perception in the U.S. that we're troublemakers. Nothing is going to change when we separate. We're going to have good relations with you. We're going to be one of your major trading partners. We're still going to be part of all the alliances and treaties. We're free-traders who supported NAFTA. We love Americans. We share the same values as the rest of Canada, but we want to end the duplications and the antagonisms." Then he stopped. There was a long pause. Bouchard seemed surprised that Clinton didn't say anything in response.

Finally Clinton said, "How many people are there in Quebec?" It was probably the quietest Bill Clinton had been in his entire life, but it was exactly the right thing to do.

"Seven million," we all answered at once. Then more silence. Raymond didn't say anything. Lake didn't say anything. So I chimed in and said, "I want to remind you that we met with you because you're the leader of the Opposition, not because you're a leading separatist. When do you think the referendum is going to be held?"

"I don't know," he said. "It could be the fall. It could be the spring. But if it succeeds, my party disappears. There won't be any reason for it after that."

Then Clinton asked, "How is your illness?"

"Oh, I'm doing okay," Bouchard answered. "Thank you." Then he got up and left.

Preston Manning came in. He clearly enjoyed meeting the president. "I've got this letter for you," he said. "We want to work with you on these different issues that are important to Canada. I'm going to be going to Washington. I'd like you to help me out with some contacts." Then they had a free-wheeling discussion on the deficit and interest on the debt. Manning felt that Canada should follow the United States on tax rates. And they talked about health-care expenditures, free trade, and what Manning called a new federalism. "In that sense," he said, "we agree with Quebec that we need a new approach." It was a pleasant meeting and lasted, like Bouchard's, about twenty minutes.

Hillary came bouncing in from her round of visits. "You guys have a better home than we do," she said. It was true to the extent that they were trapped on the third and fourth floors of the White House, as though they were under house arrest. Bruce Lindsey joined us for a while too. We were all just sitting around, chatting, about to get cleaned up for a gala dinner, when the phone rang. It was my staff assistant Greg Fukutomi, informing me that the White House social office wanted to make changes in my seating plan for the next morning's breakfast.

They were getting pressure from somebody in the White House to replace some of the Canadians at the president's table with their American buddies. "Get them on the line," I snapped. And when I got through, I started yelling, "This is crazy. It's all been carefully worked out. You guys don't know what you're doing. Just leave it alone."

Clinton was across the room, sitting on the sofa talking to Janet. He was in a great mood because his speech had been so well received. "What's going on?" he asked.

"Oh, it's your White House social office," Janet said. "They're trying to change the seating we worked on till midnight last night."

"Bruce, grab that phone," Clinton barked, "and tell those people to do what the ambassador says." So I passed the phone over to Lindsey. After a bit of argument, we heard him say, "I'm with the president. Would you like to talk to him? Now do what the ambassador says. Thank you very much." And, boom, he hung up. Ah, I thought, the burdens of the presidency!

After freshening up and posing for more photographs, looking as though we were all heading for a high-school prom, we were driven across the Ottawa River to the Museum of Civilization in Hull for the prime minister's gala dinner. "Tonight," the president said in his toast, "in celebrating our countries and what unites us, let us work together and let us say long live Canada. *Vive le Canada.*"

—   —

When I got up the next morning, I learned that the president had already charged out of the house for a three-mile jog along the river in very, very cold air. He had apparently slept for about five hours, which is all he usually needs. So I went over to check on things at the National Gallery and was embarrassed to find a large crowd of politicians and business leaders already gathered there for our 9:00 breakfast reception. Some had been instructed to arrive as early as 7:30, because they had to pass through metal detectors and other security measures. It turned out that the RCMP and the Secret Service were trying to outdo each other, so we ended up with twice as much security as we needed in one of the safest countries in the world. Worse, they had insisted on pulling down the curtains over the huge windows in the gallery's great hall, so that no one would be able to see the breathtaking view of Parliament set in brilliant sunshine and bright snow. We worked out a little compromise, which allowed the curtains to be up until the moment before the president's entry. It wasn't great, but it was better than nothing.

After breakfast, at which the people who really make things work for our two governments and our businesses were treated to good brief speeches by the president and the prime minister, Clinton and I got in the president's limousine for the short drive to Parliament Hill for an expanded meeting of ten cabinet members and officials from each country. We were alone. He immediately began working through the *New York Times* crossword puzzle with rapid-fire speed, while asking me what was going to be discussed at the meeting. Haiti, Bosnia, trade, the usual stuff, I told him. Then he asked, looking up, "What am I going to do about the election campaign?" He was looking at me. "Who am I going to get to run it?" His mind was on three things at the same time.

"I don't know," I said, "but I really didn't want to do the DNC thing. And we've got a lot going here. There's going to be this Quebec referendum and things could blow apart. I've got to be here to help out. After that, Janet and I will come back and help out on the campaign. I don't want to run it, but we'll come back and help."

The meeting was held in the cabinet room and lasted a little over an hour. It included people like Federico Peña, Mickey Kantor, and Sandy Berger on our side (but not, unfortunately, Warren Christopher, who was in an Ottawa hospital with a bleeding ulcer), and Deputy Prime Minister Sheila Copps, André Ouellet, Roy MacLaren, and Doug Young with the Canadians. Everyone was in a relaxed and happy mood. The speech had gone well. The press coverage was great. The gala and the breakfast had been a success. When I reflected back fifteen months ago to Clinton's first meeting with Chrétien in Seattle, the difference was amazing. Then things had been cordial, but stiff. Now they were warm and mutually supportive in almost every respect. Despite the impression in the media that we were in there arguing about dairy, poultry, and sugar, trade wasn't even mentioned until one hour had passed.

I'm not sure Canadians would want to hear that. They prefer to think of their leaders pointing the finger at us and pressing Canada's case. But their negotiators are pressing Canada's case every day. The leaders don't need to do that when they're together. Indeed, when we finally got to trade, they both concluded that relations were much better than in November 1993 and they would just keep consulting. There was a brief discussion about Country Music TV and *Sports Illustrated*.

"We're worrying about split-run editions," the prime minister said. "We're nice guys, but do we have to become a son of a bitch once in a while to get our way?"

"On a lot of these issues, the less said, the better," Mickey Kantor replied. "We're sensitive to your needs and we're going to try to work things out."

André Ouellet said he was was worried about the timing of any U.S. protest against Canada's dairy and poultry regulations, because of its possible effect in Quebec. "Look," said the president, "we're going to work with you on this. We don't want you to lose the referendum."

Mostly, however, we discussed Bosnia, North Korea, Russia, the Ukraine, Haiti, support for the UN, the upcoming G7 meeting in Halifax, and the environment. The prime minister went off on a tangent about China and a trip he had once taken to Siberia. He had climbed over a fence and gone to a beer hall with a person who spoke Russian. There were dancers from Leningrad Ballet doing the twist in this bar, and they asked him to send them some records by the Animals, a group he had never heard of. It was his way of explaining how trade and market economies will bring about democracy. "Once you give people the goods and try to take them away, they'll revolt," he said. "And modern culture and communications will have the same result."

Afterwards, we all paraded into a large and beautifully decorated reception hall, the Confederation Room, for the signing of the Open Skies agreement. It was a proud moment for me, of course, even if it was a mere formality by this stage. Doug Young and Frederico Peña signed with Clinton and Chrétien standing behind them. I had no doubt that the president's trip had forced everyone to get the treaty done. The night before, the prime minister had publicly acknowledged my role. I detected the hand of Eddie Goldenberg. "Everybody here knows how much you were involved with it," Eddie said, "but we wanted to make sure the president knew too."

The press conference itself was a bit of disappointment, in my view, because the president insisted on taking questions that had to do with American domestic policy. I had argued against it with Tony Lake and Sandy Berger. "He's here in a foreign country. He doesn't need to do it. And it's, like, rude. He should restrict himself to questions about U.S.-Canadian relations. He should highlight the Open Skies agreement. He should just tell the White House press corps that he'll be happy to answer their other questions when he gets back to

Washington or on the plane." But Berger insisted that would be tough to do.

Sure enough, after side-stepping further comments about Quebec, he got a question from Helen Thomas about affirmative action, to which he gave a long, drawn-out answer. Then there was one about Newt Gingrich accusing the administration of a smear campaign. Clearly the U.S. media had already tuned out Canada, and the president was being pulled back to Washington before we could even focus on the enormous success of the trip. It proved my point. I didn't know whether it was because Clinton thought he was going to please the press by answering whatever they asked, or whether he was like the kid in class who always needed to show he had the answer, or whether he was getting bad advice, but I thought he should change the policy. I passed a sharp note to Tony Lake saying that I thought this was "unnecessary, undiplomatic and off message." He wrote back, "What do you really think? You have a point."

Near the end of the news conference the prime minister was asked if he still had such a business-like relationship with the president that he called him Mr. President rather than Bill.

"When we are with other people," Chrétien replied, "I call him Mr. President. When we are alone, I don't call him William Jefferson. I call him Bill." All the journalists laughed, and Chrétien glowed. At last, I thought, there was a public recognition of the closeness that existed between the two men in private.

Now the fun began. All that was left was lunch and the farewell ceremony. Nothing could go wrong now. The prime minister, the president, Ambassador Chrétien, and I got into a limousine to go to lunch at the Canal Ritz. Hillary, Aline, Kay, and Janet were going to join us after their "spontaneous" skate on the canal. On the way there, Clinton saw a sign saying "Beaver tail," and he started laughing. "What's beaver tail?" he asked.

"It's a cinnamon-like dough shaped like a beaver tail," I said. "It melts in your mouth. It's a Canadian snack." And the prime minister was not sure why we were roaring like adolescents. We were just giddy from relief from the tension of the trip, I think.

We arrived at the restaurant, which was built like a ski chalet and beautifully bright, and everyone ordered beer. We had a table by the second-floor window for the eight of us, separated from the president's security and staff by a curtain. Before long we could see our wives coming along the canal, with Hillary skating like a champ, trailed by a huge crowd of people and a mob of schoolchildren, all of whom had broken through the wooden barricades the Secret Service and RCMP had erected. When they came inside, Hillary had a great big smile we hadn't seen for a long time.

For an hour and a half, with no interruptions, we laughed, talked politics, and told stories – nothing serious – while crowds of people gathered outside in the bitter cold. It was a perfect ending to the visit. "Tell me why we didn't do this earlier!" the president exclaimed, obviously delighted by the whole experience. The president and Hillary Clinton shook all the hands on the way out, then we headed for the airport, where he shook more hands and posed for more photographs with our embassy employees. Then, while the air force band played and a winter storm blew in, Bill and Hillary got on the plane and, at precisely 3:30, flew off.

Somebody once said about a presidential visit that you're happy when he arrives and you're happier when he leaves. It requires such an enormous amount of planning and co-ordination. But, for all the stresses and strains, I really believed that this one couldn't have gone any better, except for Warren Christopher's untimely illness. We were higher than kites from fatigue and joy. It felt like the day of a successful election campaign. I could hardly sleep that night, and I was up early the next morning to savor the mountain of news stories about Open Skies and color pictures of Hillary skating, all as positive as they had been all week: "Best Friends" – "Friends Forever" – "U.S President Welcome to Return Anytime" – "Bill and Hillary Charmed Us All."

"Vive le Canada!" I found myself shouting.

~ 9 ~

TOO GOOD TO LOSE

On September 11, 1995, Quebec Premier Jacques Parizeau announced the kick-off of his much-delayed referendum campaign. The vote – upon which rested the fate of Canada – was to be held on Monday, October 30th. The question was deliberately vague. It never mentioned independence. It didn't define sovereignty. There was no reference to separation from Canada:

> "Do you agree that Quebec should become sovereign, after having made a formal offer to Canada for a new economic and political partnership, within the scope of the bill respecting the future of Quebec and of the agreement signed on June 12, 1995?"

> "Canada, far from taking pride in and proclaiming to the world the alliance between its two founding peoples, has

instead trivialized it and decreed the spurious principle of equality between the provinces," the Parti Québécois government stated in a poetic preamble to the declaration that launched the campaign. "Continuing within Canada would be tantamount to condemning ourselves to languish and to debasing our very identity."

To my way of thinking, that kind of rhetoric was totally lacking in reality, and I didn't know an educated person in Quebec who believed it. It was merely a vivid demonstration that reason may not always prevail in matters affecting ethnic pride. Freedom, sovereignty, respect are states of mind, and to the extent that people feel them lacking, there's going to be trouble. But most Americans considered that a poor excuse to destroy a country as great as Canada. To the extent they think about it, they admire Canada and would feel really badly if it broke up. Our own Civil War was awful and bloody, and while it may not be fair or accurate to project that experience onto Canada, that's the way Americans feel. It's not subject to negotiation. As I used to tell Parizeau and Bouchard, don't mistake ignorance and misunderstanding for indifference and sympathy. Americans aren't into separations and secessions.

I once escorted a delegation of former members of the U.S. Congress to a reception the Speaker of the House of Commons was hosting at his summer residence in the Gatineau Hills. They were absolutely shocked to see Lucien Bouchard there, as though it were the most natural thing in the world for a separatist leader to be joking with senior Canadian officials and posing for pictures with fellow MPs. "Why would Quebec want to separate?" one of them asked the next day at a meeting with former members of Parliament. In reply, my American colleagues were treated to two hours of hand-wringing, moaning, groaning, and complaint that left them totally bewildered. They thought it was interesting, but none of them had any sympathy at all for the notion of an independent Quebec.

From September 11th on I continued with all my different duties – meeting with my staff, working with government and business leaders, greeting guests, going to diplomatic receptions, traveling the country giving speeches – but a part of every day, including the first thing in the morning and the last thing at night, was spent tracking the campaign. For almost two months I kept in regular contact with Eddie Goldenberg in the Prime Minister's Office; John Rae, a Montreal businessman who was the prime minister's liaison on the No campaign team; Steve Kelly, our consul general in Quebec City; and Eleanor Savage-Gildersleeve, our consul general in Montreal; as well as a host of cabinet ministers, pollsters, and journalists. I also had good contacts among the Yes forces and access to translations from the Quebec media. Meanwhile, Jim Walsh and I worried constantly about the U.S. strategy, what we could do, what we should do, and what if the worst were to happen.

On September 28th I went to Montreal and visited John Rae at the offices of Power Corporation, where he worked as a vice-president when not involved in Chrétien's campaigns. Ever since President Clinton's speech in Ottawa, I had been wondering how the United States could help the cause of Canadian unity in a way that wouldn't backfire against either us or Ottawa, and John felt it would be good for me to sit down with him and their federal pollster, Maurice Pinard, to discuss it. As with the president's speech in February, I wasn't being pushed to do anything by the prime minister or his staff. They were pleased I was thinking about it and knew that the United States would try, within reason, to be helpful again.

Based on Quebec's first referendum in 1980, Pinard assumed there was a hidden No vote of 5 or 6 percent, which comes out at the end but can't be measured beforehand. Taking this into account, he thought the federalists had a 12 to 14 point lead at that time. A harder question such as "Shall we become an independent country separate and apart from Canada?" got less than 25 percent Yes. His third observation was that younger voters seemed far less favorable to the Yes side, which meant the future trend was against the separatists. Fourth, the undecided voters were driven by economic issues. And, fifth, the U.S. position could be helpful to the federalists. Pinard confirmed my own polling information, that Clinton was well-liked and well-respected in Quebec, with a favorability rating much higher than either Parizeau or Chrétien. "If he did it right," Pinard said, "it couldn't hurt to have him say something nice about Canada."

The next day I was to give a speech to the Canadian Institute of International Affairs at the Westin Hotel in Montreal. I had deliberately chosen to address a foreign-policy forum because I wanted to highlight Canadian-American relations rather than the Quebec issue. I didn't want to inject myself or my country into the campaign. However, I expected questions about our position and I intended to use them to counter the separatists' claim that an independent Quebec would easily or automatically become a member of NAFTA. That's exactly what happened. Though different newspapers reported my remarks differently, they all got the point and the overall news coverage was helpful to the federalists.

I drove back to Ottawa the following morning, Saturday, September 30th, just in time to change and get out to the Camelot Golf Club for a game with the prime minister. It was my second with him. Janet and I had played with the

Chrétiens in early August, and they were clearly better golfers than either of us. At one point I tried to chip a shot onto the green, but instead of flying up in an arc and coming down near the pin, the ball took off as though fired from a rifle and headed straight for Chrétien's head. He quickly pulled off his cap, caught my ball in mid-air, and dropped it a foot from the hole. His RCMP security guard even started giving me tips about how to hit the ball. "No wonder you're a good golfer," I told Chrétien. "You've got your own pro here disguised as a Mountie." After he saw how bad I was, I started to get more requests to play with him. I used to joke that he used my game as a way to humble the big, bad Americans.

Chrétien had come close to being humbled himself the previous June when he and Clinton got their long-anticipated opportunity to play each other on a cool, overcast day at the conclusion of the G7 summit in Halifax. They were joined by John Rae and Erskine Bowles, Clinton's deputy chief of staff, while I led the foursome around the course with the club pro. The president teed off with a beautiful 270-yard drive straight down the fairway. Then the prime minister, who looked small beside Clinton even though he is himself a big man, stepped up with a determined expression – and hooked the ball way out of bounds. He had to pick it up and move it away from a fence. He clearly was chagrined by the inauspicious start, and his next few holes weren't much better. Soon Clinton was giving him advice, maybe do this with his wrist, maybe try that with his iron. The more the president yapped, the more the prime minister scowled in silence. By the end of the front nine, Chrétien was eight strokes behind.

Happily, though he wasn't as good a golfer as Clinton, he got control of his game and came back through sheer focus and will. Meanwhile, the president's strong, flashy drives were deteriorating into a series of missed putts. By the end of the match the two leaders had tied. Sitting under an umbrella on the golf cart, smoking a cigar, I entertained myself by pondering whether the game wasn't a metaphor for their political careers.

Now, on this beautiful autumn day, Chrétien and I were partnered against John Manley, the Industry minister, and John Richardson, a member of Parliament. For five hours we only discussed golf, except briefly when Chrétien expressed concern about getting Canada's peacekeepers out of Bosnia before there was trouble. I replied that we'd be hard pressed to send in 20,000 peacekeepers unless other nations, including Canada, were involved, even if only symbolically. I also mentioned we were hoping to sign a NORAD renewal when Foreign Minister Ouellet visited Washington on October 18th in order to underscore the alliance with Canada on the eve of the referendum.

The prime minister was confident at that point that the federalists were going to enjoy a decisive victory a month later. We all were, and the polls supported our confidence. "I think the PM likes golfing with me because he's clearly better and I don't talk him to death like the president did in Halifax," I wrote afterwards. "We won. The PM liked that, too. He likes to win at whatever he plays."

On October 5th I flew to Washington. My purpose was to get a few ringing endorsements for a united Canada in the press and make sure that nobody in Congress said anything that would inflame the issue back in Quebec. It was my first trip to the capital since May 17th, the longest I had been away from it since I was governor, and I was struck by the poor condition of the roads and all the panhandlers around town, especially in comparison to Ottawa. I was also struck by the new prevailing wisdom that Clinton was going to be elected for a second term. His fortunes had undergone a marked change for the better within five months.

My first appointment was with E.J. Dionne and John Anderson of *The Washington Post* editorial board. I found Dionne particularly interested, because his family was originally from Quebec. I briefed them on the situation and how, without wanting to meddle, we were trying to be supportive of a united Canada, what the president had said to the House of Commons, what our position was with regard to NAFTA, and the interplay of all the various arguments. Most people with whom I spoke were surprised that Canada was even allowing the vote to happen. "Well," I explained, "they got themselves trapped a decade or more ago into allowing this kind of thing to go on."

I went on, "The polls look good. It could even be a decisive victory. But we can't be sure, anything could happen. It's a very fuzzy question. It's an emotional issue. Ethnic tribalism is on the rise. Populism is on the rise. Tax protests are on the rise. Everybody's talking about the devolution of power. Central governments are being discredited all over the world. So I don't think we should assume it's all going to work out fine."

I took the same message to meetings with a half-dozen key congressional staff members on Capitol Hill that day and the next. I knew there was no Democratic or Republican position on Canada to worry about, but I wanted to alert the powerful members of the Senate Foreign Affairs Committee and the House International Relations Committee, especially, about what was going on. As one of the Republican staffers confirmed to me, "The separatists are all over Congress like a blanket these days." I warned everyone not to let courtesy meetings get turned into advertisements for independence. For the moment, I told them, things looked good for the federalists, but anything could happen. Then something amazing and alarming did.

On October 8th, about halfway through the campaign, Premier Jacques Parizeau realized that the Yes side was going to lose with him at the helm. He switched strategies. He now emphasized that a victory for the Yes campaign would mean only the beginning of a year-long round of negotiations with Canada. Indeed, his referendum question was ambiguous enough to let him interpret the vote any way he wanted.

To give some credibility and weight to his tactical retreat, Parizeau announced the appointment of Lucien Bouchard as his designated "chief negotiator." In effect, he handed over the leadership of the rest of the campaign to his hugely popular, immensely charismatic, and more moderate colleague. It was a desperate, last-ditch effort to win over the "soft" nationalists, whose support was crucial to both sides. All at once, it seemed to work. In fact, it had an enormous impact.

Back in Ottawa, I watched the electrifying effect of Bouchard's entry into the campaign. It blew everything else off the front pages, including a strong statement made by former president George Bush during a meeting with former prime minister Brian Mulroney in Colorado. "Stay united," Bush was quoted as saying. "I'm a staunch supporter of one Canada. I'd hate to see Canada divided." Everybody predicted an uptick in the polls for the Yes side as a result of the Bouchard effect, but I don't think anyone guessed how great it would be.

Meanwhile, I was at work on the agenda for the meeting scheduled on October 18th in Washington between André Ouellet and Warren Christopher. I was engaged in an uphill struggle, trying to get Canadian officials to concentrate on the big items, such as Bosnia, Haiti, and the Quebec referendum. Indeed, it had been clear since the Halifax summit that such a meeting might be a useful occasion for the United States to say something about Canadian unity, if that proved helpful and necessary, or at least to provide a symbolic photograph for the media. Now, more than ever, I thought it was a perfect opportunity to showcase the relationship between our two countries in advance of the referendum vote. However, the bureaucrats in Foreign Affairs kept wanting to talk about Arctic wildlife, an Antarctic council, and reform of the United Nations.

Even our suggestion of signing the NORAD renewal, as a way of drawing attention to an important treaty that an independent Quebec would not automatically inherit, fell on deaf ears. The lower-echelon Canadian officials were blasé about it, as if they were doing *us* some kind of favor. "The surprising thing about all these agenda decisions," I recorded in my journal, "is that it's business as usual or nitpicking business as usual by the top government bureaucrats of Canada on the eve of the referendum." It was almost as though the officials were in denial about the possible break-up of their country.

While that was going on, I got a strange message from the Canadian mission at the United Nations via our UN mission requesting a meeting between the president and the prime minister when they both were in New York for the UN's fiftieth anniversary celebrations. It was strange because I was in constant contact with the Prime Minister's Office in those days and nobody there had ever mentioned it to me. I thought, however, coming a week or so before the vote, that such a bilateral meeting might be a good idea. As it turned out, neither Eddie Goldenberg nor Jean Carle had heard of it either, but they too saw its possibilities. I told them that

I would have to move heaven and earth to get it, so they had to decide fast.

Then I went to Montreal to attend a reception for our new consul general, Eleanor Savage-Gildersleeve, in her beautiful residence on Redpath Crescent. The talk, of course, was all about the referendum. The Yes side was well-represented and sure that Bouchard had given it a favorable boost. The No side was predicting victory, but not by the 60–40 margin of 1980. Eleanor was really surprised not to find the passion and energy she had seen during political crises in the other countries to which she had been posted. "Everything is so calm," was my own impression of the city. "No crowds or graffiti. Business as usual. It's eerie. That's Canada. Even the Quebeckers appear to be restrained and orderly."

I did note, however, the headline in that morning's *Montreal Gazette,* "Cree chief says no to Quebec." Matthew Coon Come, the chief of the Cree Indians of northern Quebec, had just announced that they were going to hold their own referendum six days before Quebec's. It was a sharp reminder that separation was fraught with conflicts that could even escalate into civil war. Near the end, in fact, our consulate phones were jammed with panicky calls from people desperate to get themselves and their money out of the province.

The next day, October 14th, I flew on to Quebec City to greet Dan Glickman, our secretary of Agriculture, who was coming for the fiftieth anniversary celebrations of the World Food Organization, and also to meet with Steve Kelly, our superb consul general. On the drive into town from the airport, there wasn't a Canadian flag to be seen, but every lamppost had a campaign sign for either the Yes or No side, which gave more of a sense of referendum fever than in Montreal. Kelly, a former newspaper reporter who had spent a lot of time in Paris, was bilingual, sophisticated, and politically astute. He had recently met at our consulate with Bouchard, whom he found genuinely surprised by the dramatic outpouring of support that had followed the announcement of his new role in the campaign. That weekend's polls confirmed that the gap between the two sides was getting narrower. The big question was whether it was a temporary bump or a serious trend. If Quebeckers ended up thinking they were voting on whether they wanted Lucien Bouchard to negotiate a better deal with Canada, rather than for separation, the Yes side could win.

Since his brush with death, Bouchard had clearly acquired something like legendary status, which was abetted by his demagogic rhetoric and complex personality. He had achieved in life what René Lévesque accomplished only posthumously, and it looked as though he could do no wrong in the eyes of French-speaking Quebeckers. When, for example, he made what I viewed as a racist remark, about "white races" in Quebec needing to have more babies, he was neither hurt by it nor castigated in the province's media. On the contrary, his remark may even have helped the separatist cause by appealing to the dark, tribal side of Quebec nationalism.

Given the irrational forces at play, it was hard to counter effectively with the dry realities of economics and law, but it would have been irresponsible not to call attention to them. In mid-October, therefore, I made sure that the Prime Minister's Office and the Quebec media were aware of the nineteen-page study by Chip Roh, a trade lawyer and former USTR official, commissioned by the Center for Strategic International Studies. Entitled "The Implications for U.S. Trade Policy of an Independent Quebec," it was the most thorough analysis I had ever seen on the subject. It totally refuted the separatists' arguments. Among other things, it proved convincingly that an independent Quebec would not have automatic rights or obligations under existing trade agreements, including NAFTA, the WTO, and the Auto Pact. Quebec would have to negotiate its accession to each of those agreements.

Though I was still confident that the Bouchard effect was temporary and that the polls would settle down in the federalists' favor, the numbers were way too close for comfort. It was time, I thought, for the United States to weigh in, at least with a statement by Warren Christopher during the Ouellet visit. "Are you that worried?" I was asked by my colleagues at the Canada Desk.

"Well, we've got two things here," I answered. "One, I do think it's going to be close. I've been through a race where I was ahead 55–35 on Thursday and lost 49.8–49.6 on Tuesday. And, two, if anything goes wrong, the American people are going to wonder why we didn't say something."

On October 17th, I spoke to Eddie Goldenberg over the phone. "The polls are now 50–50, " he said, "and those are our own numbers."

"Counting Pinard's 5 or 6 percent hidden vote?" I asked.

"Yes," he said grimly. "We're dead even. The other side did very well last week."

I sensed from his voice that the federalists didn't have a fall-back position. "Well," I said, "we're planning to have Christopher make a nice statement, certainly repeat and maybe strengthen what the president said in February. But we want to make sure we say it right. We don't want to hurt you with Quebeckers."

"Don't worry about that," Eddie said. "Nothing's going to hurt us now."

The next morning I flew to Washington with Janet for the Christopher-Ouellet meeting. The lead story in *The Globe and Mail* was another blow to the No side. In a speech the day before, Canada's Finance minister, Paul Martin, had stated that a million jobs would be in peril if Quebec separated. It wasn't his intention, but it was certainly viewed as rhetorical overkill. Like others, I worried that it might hurt the credibility of the federalists' solid economic arguments against separation. I was more convinced than ever that it was time for the United States to indicate support for a united Canada. If that's what we feel, what was so wrong about saying it? Were the separatists going to stand up and denounce us? No doubt some would, but the reality is that the first place they'd run after independence is to Washington. And if they think it's Paris, then they're kidding themselves. Quebec does more trade with many U.S. states than with France, after all.

There may have been some in our embassy or the State Department who made their careers by hedging on every issue, but neither Jim Walsh nor I was among them. I would have felt badly enough living as an ordinary citizen in Michigan if Canada had broken apart, but I was damned if I was going to let it happen on my watch as ambassador without doing or saying anything that might have helped prevent it. Besides, I knew directly and instinctively that both the president and the secretary of state agreed with me. They just needed someone with political antennae to verify for them how far the United States government could go without insulting Canadians.

That was my job. I was on the ground, so to speak, and unlike the officials at the top of the State Department who were preoccupied with the hottest spots around the world, I had the time to talk with my staff and prepare our position carefully.

As soon as I arrived in Washington on October 18th, I went over to the State Department to brief Secretary

Christopher along with Peter Tarnoff, his under secretary of state for political affairs; Lynne Lambert, director of the Canada Desk; Dick Hecklinger, the deputy assistant secretary of state for European and Canadian affairs; and several other assistants. After going quickly through the other issues, the group asked me to explain our thinking regarding Quebec, and I went over the language we had prepared for Christopher's statement.

"Now tell me why we're doing this," he said.

"This referendum has gotten very, very close," I explained. "Anything we can say that's positive about Canada could help, because our polling shows that Quebeckers, including French-speaking Quebeckers, value highly what Americans think. Here we are in Washington struggling to piece together Bosnia-Herzogovina, a nation that never existed, while the fate of our best friend, closest neighbor, and strongest ally is hanging in the balance. I don't think the American people would ever forgive us if for some reason, God forbid, the separatists prevailed and we hadn't at least said, oh, by the way, Canada is a great country. As long as we do it right, it won't backfire. I've talked to the prime minister's people, and they agree. Everybody agrees. Just think of the witch hunt in the 1950s against those who 'lost' China. Now imagine what Congress would do if Canada broke apart. They'd want to know where the United States was, where President Clinton was, when the moment of truth arrived."

Christopher looked up and said jokingly, "I gather you feel strongly about this, Jim? Well, I just wanted to hear your thinking. But, don't worry, I'm there."

A short while later, at a press availability before our meeting with Ouellet, Christopher was asked as expected about the referendum. "The foreign minister and I are going to be discussing primarily global and regional and bilateral issues," he answered. "I don't want to intrude on what is rightfully an internal issue in Canada. But, at the same time, I want to emphasize how much we've benefited here in the United States from the opportunity to have the kind of relationship that we do have at the present time with a strong and united Canada. I think it is probably useful for me to say that we have very carefully cultivated our ties with Canada, and they've been very responsive in connection with all of those ties. I think we shouldn't take for granted that a different kind of organization would not obviously have exactly the same kind of ties. And I don't want to try to participate in the internal debate there in any way, but I do want to emphasize the very, very important value that we place – the high value that we place on the relationships that we have with a strong and united Canada, as reflected by the kind of personal relationships that I have with the foreign minister and that the president has with the prime minister."

Christopher's words, his delivery, even his body language were perfect. Then we all went into the Treaty Room for private talks about Bosnia, Haiti, the United Nations, and Cuba. I must have been made silly by relief, because I started laughing when I noticed that Warren Christopher, Peter Tarnoff, and I were all wearing exactly the same style of black shoes – the "Diplomat" by Church. At the end, when Christopher asked about the referendum, Ouellet replied, "It will be close, but we will win."

My next task was to work on the "press guidance" as a follow-up to Christopher's statement. We knew we were going to get a lot of inquiries about it, and we didn't want to have what he said or what he meant misreported, particularly in Quebec. Everyone had to be very careful. We operated on the assumption that it was not beyond a separatist sympathizer in the media to get some intern or janitor at the

State Department to say that Quebec is a nice place and twist it into a headline to the effect that highly placed U.S. officials favor independence.

"The Secretary's response was an extension of our long-standing position," it read. "The Secretary said this is rightfully an internal Canadian issue, but at the same time he wanted to emphasize the high value that the United States places on its excellent relations with a strong and united Canada.... The Secretary pointed out that we have carefully cultivated our ties between our two countries and that we shouldn't take for granted that a new entity would have exactly the same kind of ties."

On the whole, the media reaction was accurate, though the French-language press in Quebec tended to ignore or downplay the significance of Christopher's statement. But the next day, during a trip to Boston to meet with the editorial board of the *Boston Globe* about the referendum, I got a call from Steve Kelly. Bernard Landry, Parizeau's deputy premier and Quebec's minister of "International" Affairs, was upset. He wished to speak to me and he had a letter he wanted me to deliver to Christopher. "Mr. Secretary," it read,

> I was most interested to learn through the media of your public statement yesterday before your meeting with the Canadian Minister of Foreign Affairs and International Trade. That declaration, made less than two weeks before referendum day in Québec, inevitably attracted considerable attention here, and it was presented by opponents to the project of our government as a clear shift in the traditional position of the United States.
>
> Invariably, over the years Quebecers and their governments, federalists and sovereignists alike, have

endeavoured to strengthen their political, economic and personal ties to the American people and their government. You will recall in particular the determining role played by Québec in making free trade between the United States and Canada a reality, while the Liberal Party of Prime Minister Jean Chrétien was actively opposed to it. We are convinced that Québec's accession to sovereignty would make possible new and fruitful relations between us. A sovereign Québec would be, after all, your eighth largest trading partner.

The US government is obviously free to speak and act as it will, and your statement yesterday, Mr. Secretary, expressed American interests with all proper reserves as far as its wording was concerned.

Let me respectfully draw your attention however to the possible long-term impact of any new American government pronouncements made before the October 30 referendum.

Québec is now living a historic moment. Should American declarations be publicly perceived as a factor in the decision that Quebecers are to make, they would enter into our collective memory and the history books.

If the Yes side wins, as is now probable, Québec voters and the historians will remember that the sovereignty of Québec was achieved despite or even against the American will. That will make more difficult our task of developing with the United States the productive and friendly relations we hold dear.

If victory eludes the Yes side by a slim margin, as is plausible, those who did vote Yes – a clear majority of francophone Quebecers – will be tempted to assign responsibility to the United States for part of their profound disappointment. I do not know how many decades it will take to dispel that feeling.

In the days to come, should American declarations be more emphatic, or should they come from the higher levels of the Administration, the deeper would be the traces left in our history. At the time of the 1980 referendum, both the President of the United States and the Secretary of State refrained from making any comment during the last ten days of the campaign. And we all have every reason to believe this was the appropriate behaviour.

Québec and the United States, Mr. Secretary, will be neighbours forever. We appeal to the sense of democracy both the Americans and their government hold dear, as we invite you to let Quebecers themselves decide once again on their own destiny, in all serenity.

"This guy's crazy," I told Steve Kelly. "Tell him that you've talked to me and I will call him. It's going to make him look foolish in Washington, you know, to appear to be threatening the secretary of state of the United States. Tell him, if he's got any brains at all, he won't tell anyone he's done this or show it to anybody. Tell him I'll keep it confidential, but tell him that I think he's made a big mistake in writing it."

Eventually I sent it down to Lynne Lambert at the Canada Desk and told her to stick it in a drawer, not bother Christopher with it at all. I didn't even think we needed to answer it. "It's not like he's some foreign leader," I argued. "I mean, would the Canadian minister of Foreign Affairs feel required to answer a cabinet member from one of the states?" A couple of days later I learned that Parizeau had called Governor Angus King of Maine and Governor William Weld of

Massachusetts asking for a statement of support and faxing them a copy of the Landry letter! It eventually made its way into the press, though I never did find out how. Certainly nobody in our embassy leaked it; it's not likely that anyone at the State Department would have passed it on to the press; and I very much doubt that King or Weld would have bothered. My own guess is that Landry himself put it out, despite my advice, perhaps for domestic Parti Québécois reasons. All I know is that his letter was met with the laughter and scorn I had predicted.

I certainly wasn't intimidated by his veiled threat. That very afternoon, in fact, I began thinking that the president might have to speak up. It happened during a call from my friend Angus Reid, the Canadian pollster. In the past three nights, his numbers had gone from 49 percent Yes to 50 percent Yes to 52 percent Yes. "Momentum is building for a Yes vote," he said. "Voters don't want to leave, but they want to give Lucien Bouchard a way to negotiate with Canada. It's like giving him a strike vote to carry in his pocket. It's a protest. No one seems to be listening to the consequences at all."

"What more can we do?" I asked.

"I think the president's going to have to speak," he replied.

Eddie Goldenberg and John Rae also sounded tense and worried when I spoke with them, though their polls still had the No side ahead if most of the undecided voters came their way, as expected. I suggested to them that if they really wanted a few kind words from the president, the prime minister was going to have to ask him at the United Nations that weekend. "I can talk to the White House and try to get Mike McCurry to kind of repeat what Christopher said," I told them. "I don't think anybody's going to have a problem with that. But to actually drag in the president at this point, even though I'm sure he's sympathetic, the prime minister is going to have to pull him aside and say, 'Look, this referendum is really close. You're popular in Quebec. If you say something positive, it could really make a difference. Just repeat what Christopher said. We're not asking you to say anything more.'"

On Saturday, October 21st, the president arrived in New York, the prime minister arrived in New York, and by coincidence Janet and I were just a few blocks away. Our friend Yousuf Karsh had astonished and delighted me by offering to come out of retirement and photograph me, perhaps the last portrait he would ever do, in a temporary studio he had set up in the penthouse of the Carlton Hotel. I was on and off the phone all that day trying to make sure that Chrétien had a chance to get a quick photo and a brief word with Clinton at the United Nations reception. He did. I later heard that both the president and Hillary seemed genuinely concerned about the closeness of the campaign and wanted to help. And so, on Sunday, I began dealing with Lynne Lambert of the Canada Desk and Nancy Soderberg of the National Security Council, with regard to what the president might say.

"We've got to have something that's as strong as we've been saying, or stronger," I argued, "but it's got to be positive. If it's positive, it won't backfire. If it's negative, it could. So we don't want to do anything that looks like a threat or an exaggeration of any kind. We want to say something about Canada that schoolchildren from Newfoundland to B.C. would feel good about if they read it, would feel proud about their country. I don't see how anyone could fault us for that."

The following day, Monday, October 23rd, Lynne informed me that Warren Christopher had taken our proposed statement and actually strengthened it before sending it over to the White House. He had revised it to assert, in the clearest possible way, "A strongly united Canada has proven to be a great country, as well as a powerful ally, and we hope it will continue." We were happy and excited. Coming from Mike McCurry, it would be good. Coming from the president, it would be great.

I called John Rae. "The polling numbers have stabilized," he said. "We're not out of the woods, but we're not hanging from the tree either." I could tell from his voice that he felt the federalists had been hanging from the tree for the past few days, which was worse than they had let on to me. I pressed him on the numbers, and he said they were about 50–50, assuming the undecideds all went No.

Janet and I left New York City to drive north to Albany and catch a flight to Ottawa from there, stopping en route to tour the West Point Military Academy and Franklin Delano Roosevelt's home at Hyde Park, where Clinton and Yeltsin were in the midst of a private meeting. We stayed that night in the presidential suite at West Point's historic Hotel Thayer. It was impossible to ignore its illustrious history: General Dwight Eisenhower's autographed photo looked down on me as I sat writing my journal at the desk used by Douglas MacArthur. When we flicked on the television, Larry King was interviewing French president Jacques Chirac.

At one point a viewer from Montreal called into the program and asked if France would recognize an independent Quebec. "The French government does not want to interfere with this referendum," Chirac responded.

"But if Quebec does vote to separate, will you recognize them?" King pressed.

"We'll see," Chirac said. Then, pressed again, he added, "Well, yes, of course we would recognize the fact."

That, I thought, put Chirac right smack dab in the middle of the referendum. I phoned Jim Walsh, John Rae,

Eddie Goldenberg, and Jean Pelletier to let them know, assuming they hadn't been watching CNN just then. But the word had spread fast, and nobody was happy about it. In fact, Pelletier, who knew Chirac, had been certain he wasn't going to interfere.

The next morning, during a private tour of Roosevelt's home, I got a call from Jim Walsh. I was whisked out of the living room and up the stairs to the former servants' quarters, which looked to have been untouched for decades. I spoke to Jim on an old black phone. "The White House is now finalizing the language to say something about Canada," he said. "Maybe today, maybe tomorrow, maybe the next day. They've just called and they're really nervous, really worried. There's a front-page *Washington Post* story saying the separatists could win, so they now realize it's for real. It's got them even more interested in doing the statement the right way." Then he connected me to the State Department, and we all had a lengthy discussion about our proposed statement.

When I resumed our tour, I confided to our guide that I had been talking to Washington about how the president could help keep Canada united.

"That's really ironic," she said. "Right around the corner there's a bedroom named for a prime minister of Canada, Mackenzie King. He was very, very close to Roosevelt, you know, and he was here so often that they made it his bedroom." The continuity and humanity of history came alive at that moment, and I had the strangest sense of having a small part in it.

~ ~

The next day, October 25th, five days before the vote, I was back in Ottawa. "The fall is over," I noted in my journal. "We're going into winter." I lit the first fire of the season in my study at the residence, looked over all the newspapers, and worked the phone. "Two years ago," I wrote, "Jean Chrétien scored his greatest victory when his party took the reins of government. In today's papers, however, he is fighting for Canada's life. The stories on the opinion polls show that the Yes side is ahead. Chrétien's agreement to consider constitutional changes is viewed as a concession. Many are saying it's too little too late."

At that morning's weekly country team meeting, I remarked that the rest of Canada had finally woken up to the possibility that the Yes forces could win. "This requires that every member of our mission," I told them, "has to be sensitive to the concerns and feelings of our Canadian friends, neighbors, and your fellow employees who are Canadian. Don't joke around. Don't fool around. Anything you say, any comment might get reported in the media, so be really careful." The atmosphere in the room was tense and foreboding.

In the offices of Ottawa's bureaucrats, however, it seemed like business as usual. I couldn't believe it. The cultural ministry wanted to run with a bill to crack down on *Sports Illustrated*. Foreign Affairs notified us, on the heels of being unable to process the NORAD renewal papers in time for the Ouellet visit in Washington, that they couldn't vote with us on Cuba at the UN. I was really upset. "The U.S. government is treating the referendum challenge with a greater sense of urgency than the Ottawa bureaucrats," I wrote that day. "It would be disheartening if the average Canadian heard what I had heard today. Clearly, the same concern would be shared by the PMO, as well, but the career civil servants seem unable to prioritize the issues or interrupt their routine, and here they are nitpicking us while we're trying to help them."

The last thing Canada needed at that point was Washington angry at it over *Sports Illustrated* and Bernard Landry gloating in the press about English Canada's miserable treatment of Quebec's great friend, the United States. I eventually had Jim Walsh call House Leader Herb Gray's office and beg them to pull the *Sports Illustrated* bill, at least for a while. They did.

Late that morning, I got a call from David Johnson, a former consul general in Vancouver and career foreign service officer who was then our spokesperson for the National Security Council in the White House. "Stay tuned," he said. "Mike McCurry is going to say something about Canada during his daily news briefing." And, at 1:10, in response to a planted question about the referendum, he did.

"It's obviously an internal Canadian issue that will be before the voters and will be decided locally," McCurry said. "However, I can say on behalf of the president that a strong, united Canada has proven to be not only a great country, but a very powerful and good ally of the United States. And we hope that relationship will continue."

Would a strong but not united Canada prevent a good relationship with the United States? "Well," McCurry responded, "it would be impossible to assess that. But I would say we would hope that the relationship that we have enjoyed with a strong and united Canada would continue."

In other words, you hope the separatists don't succeed? There was laughter in the press room. "I think I chose my words carefully enough that you can catch the drift," McCurry answered. And then, among other things, he mentioned that the president was going to have a news conference on budget issues later that afternoon.

Immediately afterwards, David Johnson phoned me back. "We've got more," he said. "The president wants to do this himself. We're going to have somebody ask him a question at the news conference."

At the appointed time, I was in my office overlooking Parliament Hill, with my eyes glued to the TV and my heart pounding. Sure enough, right on cue, a Canadian reporter stood up and asked, "Mr. President, are you concerned about the possible break-up of Canada and the impact it could have on the North American economy and U.S.-Canadian trade relations?"

"Let me give you a careful answer," the president replied. "When I was in Canada last year, I said that I thought that Canada had served as a model to the United States and to the entire world about how people of different cultures could live together in harmony, respecting their differences, but working together. This vote is a Canadian internal issue for the Canadian people to decide. And I would not presume to interfere with that. I can tell you that a strong and united Canada has been a wonderful partner for the United States and an incredibly important and constructive citizen throughout the entire world. Just since I've been president, I have seen how our partnership works, how the leadership of Canada in so many ways throughout the world works, and what it means to the rest of the world to think that there's a country like Canada where things basically work. Everybody's got problems, but it looks like a country that's doing the right things, moving in the right direction, has the kinds of values that we'd all be proud of. And they have been a strong and powerful ally of ours. And I have to tell you that I hope we'll be able to continue that. I have to say that I hope that will continue. That's been good for the United States. Now the people of Quebec will have to cast their votes as their lights guide them. But Canada has been a great model for the rest of the world and has been a great partner for the United States, and I hope that can continue."

He had spoken it sincerely, without looking at a script, and it had come across beautifully. Everybody was delighted.

Jean Pelletier called me right away and said, "Well, you went as far as you could go. That was really nice. I think it will have a positive effect. Tell the president we're very happy and we appreciate it."

My only regret, which couldn't have been avoided, was that both Prime Minister Chrétien and Lucien Bouchard were scheduled to make statements to the nation on TV that night. Their speeches were watched by a quarter of all Canadians and somewhat overshadowed Clinton's own statement in the media. But the next day's reaction continued to be good. Raymond Chrétien called to say, "Quebeckers love the U.S. They like Clinton. So it has helped, and I can tell you the P.M. was really pleased." My consuls general reported that the president's remarks had received prominent and positive play across the country. And we received only four calls of complaint at our consulate in Quebec City, far fewer than we had about how to move bank accounts to the United States or how to get a U.S. passport.

The strongest editorial complaints we got, oddly enough, were not from the French-speaking press. On October 23rd the *Calgary Herald* objected to Warren Christopher's intervention, even though they agreed with what he said. "It's a question of style more than substance really. It's not a matter of what's said, but who says it. It's silly, but that's politics. It's also a family thing. Couples considering a divorce can say awful things about each other, but let an outsider, even a close family member try to intervene and, well, it's just not a good idea." In my opinion, they didn't understand how popular Clinton was in Quebec or that most Quebeckers, frankly, were more interested in what Americans thought than what Albertans thought.

Odder still, on October 27th, the pro-federalist *Montreal Gazette* accused President Clinton of unnecessary meddling.

"As right as Mr. Clinton was in substance, his remarks also were entirely out of line, because they seemed to be offered up as political ammunition for the No side in the referendum." Damn right, I thought. "Evidently," the editorial continued, "the U.S. government is worrying more about doing what it can to prevent the break-up of Canada than about irritating the sovereigntists." Exactly, I thought. I found it pretty mild criticism, especially since it repeated all the arguments that we wanted repeated. Everywhere I went, in fact, all I heard was how happy the overwhelming majority of Canadians were with Bill Clinton.

We were coming down to the final moments of the campaign. All the newspapers were full of only one subject – the referendum – and on Friday, October 27th, the pro-unity forces held a gigantic rally in the streets of downtown Montreal. Between 100,000 and 150,000 people came from all over the province and the country to demonstrate their love of Canada in a colorful, enthusiastic, and emotionally stirring show of flags and patriotic speeches. They flew in from British Columbia and Newfoundland for the day; they drove all night from Toronto and came by bus from New Brunswick; they brought their children and their hearts. It was a dramatic, powerful, watershed moment in the history of the country.

While Janet and I were watching it on TV at the residence, the phone rang. It was Prime Minister Chrétien calling from Montreal, just moments before he was to address the crowd. He sounded in good spirits. "The overnight polls show we have turned the corner since Tuesday," he said. "We were six points behind. Now we're three points ahead. I just wanted to thank you for what the president said the other day."

Then we chatted a bit about his speech to the nation on Wednesday night, Landry's letter to Christopher, and Parizeau and Bouchard. "They want to be king of a small kingdom," the prime minister said. "They're not interested in being just the premier of an important Quebec." And he talked about Canadian attitudes. "You know, Canadians are hard-working and successful, but we don't think we're as good as we are, unlike the Americans."

"Is there anything more we can do?" I asked. But he said, no, we had done more than enough. So I told him I would let the president know he had called, and I wished him good luck. It struck me as incredible that he could sound so serene, humble, and confident with the future of his country – not to mention his own political fortunes – on the line. "Here he is on the phone chewing the fat, one politician to another, friend to friend," I jotted down. "I sure hope he wins. Canada deserves it and so does Quebec."

Later that afternoon Janet and I ourselves headed for Montreal, where I was scheduled the next day to tape a future PBS panel show, "The Editors," on the subject of U.S.-Canada trade. Given the traffic caused by the rally, we decided to go by train. "The rally has finally injected some passion in the No side of the campaign," I wrote in my diary. "It will probably turn out to be a very significant moment in Canada's history." The separatists later insisted that it had backfired among francophone voters, but I believe it was the day that ordinary Canadians saved Canada. If nothing else, it energized the Montreal vote and made federalist Montrealers realize they weren't being left to die by the rest of Canada. The country cared about them; they weren't going to be forgotten. Even though the rally had dispersed by the time we arrived, the streets were still littered with leaflets and placards and we could smell the excitement in the air.

Just before going out to dinner with Jim and Heather Peterson and Sheila Martin – Paul was supposed to join us, but got so worried he stayed home making calls – I heard from Steve Kelly in Quebec City. He had just been talking to the PQ's pollster, Michel Lepage, who was depressed and practically in tears: his polls were showing 45 percent Yes, 41 percent No, with most of the undecideds still expected to go No. Lepage was predicting that the Yes side would get around 46 or 47 percent, no higher than 49, though the francophone vote would be around 58 percent Yes. Such a narrow loss, he thought, would lay the foundation for a big win later, though he conceded that a portion of the Yes supporters were really only interested in wringing concessions from Ottawa. Meanwhile, other pollsters were still predicting a Yes win, Pinard was holding to 53–47 No, and Léger & Léger was saying it was 50–50 and too close to call.

Then Preston Manning called. "It doesn't look good," he said. "I'm here with my people working through scenarios in the event of a Yes victory, and we'd like to sit down and talk with you about it at some point. We're going to need your help. We're going to need to have some kind of declaration on the intent to divide the debt of Canada. I think maybe we should have an international panel – the United States, the U.K., Japan, as well as Canada and Quebec – to think about it, and we're going to need to have the United States voice support for stability on the international markets. I'm putting this stuff together and I'll get it over to you at the embassy."

"Well, we're still hoping it won't happen," I said. "But I'm happy to look at anything you send."

"By the way," Manning added, "your president was dead on. Boy, that was good. It was a very deft touch." I appreciated that, but I still thought Manning was overly pessimistic and somewhat premature to be preparing for the break-up of Canada.

The TV taping on Saturday morning went without incident, but the off-air talk among the various panelists was fraught with speculation about the approaching vote. I found the federalists mostly pleased with what the president had done, of course, and the separatists rather quiet about it. While at the studio I met Peter Jennings, the Canadian-born ABC news anchor, who was going to do some special reports from Montreal around the referendum. He phoned me a little later for some background analysis. He was finding it hard to cover the story objectively, he said, because he was still such a proud Canadian and was worried about his homeland.

He asked me to explain the reasoning behind the president's statement and what my current guess was about what would happen. Given the history of the undecideds, Chrétien's last-minute concessions to the "soft" nationalists, and the Montreal rally, I thought the No side would win a narrow victory. If the Yes side did prevail, I added, it would be because of the popularity of Bouchard, the ambiguity of the question, the desire to protest the status quo, and the rise in populism and ethnic tribalism around the world. Later, in fact, John Rae confirmed that his overnight polls were still showing a very slight No win.

It was Sunday, October 29th, the last day of the campaign, and the mood was tense. I had a minor problem to defuse. Bernard Landry had contacted one of my senior advisers and somehow persuaded him there was a bandwagon effect moving toward the Yes side. Our guy got all excited and, without consulting either me or Jim Walsh, called down to the State Department to say he had inside information that the Yes side was about to win and the United States had better prepare a new plan.

"Well, I talked to Landry" was his lame explanation when I finally spoke to him. "I know him well, we're friends, and he told me they had polls that showed they're going to win decisively. You weren't home, Jim Walsh wasn't home, and it seemed so urgent that I thought I should call Operations Center and get them to set up a meeting or conference call to talk it over. Landry told me he had numbers. He's never lied to me before. Why would he lie?"

"You're supposed to be one of my political advisers," I said, "but let me tell you something about politicians. Occasionally, they lie. Some lie all the time."

"But Landry's never lied to me before, sir."

"Well, maybe he has such polls, but I doubt it very much." It didn't matter, as it turned out, but it didn't help my mood. I saw it as an effort by Landry, who must have known by now how foolish his letter to Christopher had made Quebec look, to try to repair relations with the United States. Either that, or he was simply indulging in wishful thinking. On referendum day, I and every other ambassador in Ottawa got a letter from him asking for diplomatic recognition of Quebec if and when 50 percent plus one voted Yes. "When the result is known," he wrote, "it would appear fitting that the international community, and more particularly the country you represent, take note publicly of the will the women and men of Québec have expressed democratically respecting their future. Then, when the National Assembly of Québec will have proclaimed the sovereignty of the new State, the moment will have come to recognize it, without this gesture jeopardizing good relations with the rest of Canada."

On Sunday morning I tried to distract myself by watching the Washington talk shows, but the endless speculations about whether Colin Powell would run for president seemed pretty boring. Later I got a call from ABC's "Nightline." They were checking me out for a possible appearance on referendum night. I also got the feeling they wanted me to say something inflammatory or they wouldn't put me on. I didn't let on exactly what I was going to say, because I didn't want them to decide to scrap me in favor of some American crazy.

That evening we tuned into Bouchard's packed, emotional Yes rally and the massive No rally held at the Museum of Civilization just across the Ottawa River in Hull, Quebec. "There Jean Chrétien gave his final plea for Canada with a grim-faced Aline standing by his side," I noted in my journal. "In Calgary and Vancouver and St. John's, Newfoundland, there are rallies. There's a massive rally in Toronto. Canadians all over the land have rallied for a united Canada and sympathy for Quebec. Church services were held all across the land praying for Canada." The tone of the TV reporting seemed very ominous.

At 10:30 p.m. I called John Rae in Montreal. "Hi, John, it's Jim Blanchard. How are you doing? How are things going?"

"Just great," he said. "Tomorrow should be okay. I'll call you during the day." And he hung up. He sounded as though he had already been asleep. Which amazed me: I wasn't sure I was going to get to sleep at all.

It was October 30th, referendum day, the making or breaking of Canada. Snow flurries were in the air. The currency exchanges in Washington State were refusing to accept Canadian money because of the heavy demand for U.S. dollars. Our household staff was trying to break the tension by teasing Roger Beauregard, who lived across the river in Gatineau, Quebec, that he would have to apply for a passport to come to work the next day. I began it by doing a bunch of early-morning radio interviews in Detroit and other places, working on a press guidance with the State Department and the White House in the event the Yes side won, and watching the CBC-TV coverage. It was terrible. The commentators all described the Yes side as having won the campaign. They trashed the federalist campaign strategy and accused the prime minister of blowing his lead. And, incredibly, every hour on the hour, they led with an accusation by Quebec's chief electoral officer that the federalists' rally in Montreal had been in possible violation of the campaign spending laws. Any objective observer, I felt, would have had to conclude that CBC was absolutely committed to the break-up of Canada.

Around midday I called Eddie for the latest. "I've got two speeches ready," he said, "but the P.M. says I only need one." That's when I found out that there wouldn't be any exit polling during the day or any bellwether precincts to watch. The ballots were paper, they would be counted by hand, and everyone would learn the results at the same time, probably around 8:45 p.m. A few hours later John Rae said he was still hoping for a 53–47 victory. His last polls showed the No side with a 1.5 percent lead and 70 percent of the undecideds leaning to the federalists.

It never got reported in Canada, and came too late to make any difference anyway, but early that afternoon Mike McCurry got some follow-up questions at his regular press briefing about the president's statement in support of Canadian unity. "The president's been criticized in circles up there for what he said here last week. It's been said that he was interfering in the Quebec election. How do you respond to this?"

"The president made quite clear, as he addressed these matters, that he recognized that this is an internal matter that must be decided by the Canadian people," McCurry stated. "He said that on several occasions, and so did I. But nonetheless, the president does have strong views on the important relationship that exists between the United States and a united Canada, and felt it was important for him to set those forth. This is an issue which has now attracted considerable attention here in the United States, particularly in states that border along Canada, and it's perfectly proper for the president of the United States, given that concern, to express himself on the issue."

"Does the U.S. government have or has it ever had a policy on recognizing Quebec or a breakaway province in Canada?"

"I'm not aware that we have a policy concerning any individual province within Canada specifically," said McCurry, "and this process by which the United States government extends diplomatic recognition is one that follows international law, generally."

"So what will you do in the wake of the results tonight? What will the U.S. government do?"

"Well, we'll watch the election returns."

"One other question on Canada. Has anybody done a legal analysis as to what would happen if Quebec seceded, in terms of NAFTA? Would Quebec be automatically a member of NAFTA? Or would that have to be renegotiated to include Quebec?"

"There has been some discussion of that issue," McCurry said. "I'm not aware of any final legal opinion that has been rendered by the State Department legal counsel, or anyone else. But we've made clear that there's no automaticity to NAFTA participation in the event that Quebec was ratified as a separate entity."

"So what you're saying is: NAFTA is between Mexico, the United States, and Canada and would be with what remains of Canada, if there were a separate Quebec nation?"

"I'm saying that there's no automaticity to adherence to NAFTA."

"Could you spell that?"

"It's a good State Department word," McCurry said, and everyone laughed. For someone who wasn't in the middle of the fray in Canada, I thought he had done a truly magnificent job.

I arrived home from the office shortly before the polls closed at eight o'clock. By now this was feeling like my own election, and I couldn't help recalling how narrowly and almost accidentally I had lost as governor of Michigan in 1990. I was really worried. I lit a fire in the family room, Gianni poured Janet and me some wine, and we had our dinner while watching the CBC coverage, which was carried simultaneously on C-SPAN in the United States. As everyone who watched the broadcast remembers, there was a type of visual monitor that looked like an old-fashioned applause meter, with a needle that moved back and forth across the dial between the blue of Yes and the red of No. Because the earliest returns were reported from the pro-separatist regions of Quebec, the Yes side began well ahead. I had a hard time digesting my food.

Nick Burns, the State Department spokesperson, kept calling throughout the evening regarding who was going to represent the United States government on "Nightline" after the vote was in. Initially the people at the top wanted me, then they wanted Nick, now it came back to me. "Whatever you want," I said, "but we've got guidance. If the Yes side wins, we're basically going to say that this is going to involve long, drawn-out negotiations – months, maybe years – and we're going to take our lead from Ottawa. There's not a clear-cut vote on separation. It's just a negotiation. And it's for the Canadians to negotiate." I was still hoping, however, that I would be able to acclaim a No win.

Minute by minute, the monitor swung back and forth. Janet and I felt sick watching it. With 50.3 percent of the vote in, the Yes side had 50.42 percent, the No side 49.56. Fifteen minutes later, with 59.6 percent of the vote counted, it was Yes 50.14, No 49.86. Fifteen minutes after that, with 64.7 percent of the vote, it was exactly 50–50. It looked as though it wasn't going to be over until every last vote was counted. Around 9:30, with 67.2 percent of the vote in, it was still 50–50.

"I'd better stop drinking this wine," I told Janet. "I've got to get cleaned up and go over to the studio and try to explain on 'Nightline' what's going on. This is wild stuff." I mean, I had to think about what I was going to say without even knowing the outcome. It was unbelievable.

Then, with 80 percent of the vote in, the No side finally took the lead, 50.23–49.77. At least it's the right direction, I thought. But, another fifteen minutes, with 90 percent of the vote in, it reversed again, 50.26 Yes, 49.74 No. Then, shortly after ten o'clock, with 92 percent in, it jumped back to 50.3 percent No, 49.7 percent Yes. Janet and I were going nuts every time the dial changed. Even with 99.8 percent of the vote tallied, the fate of Canada was suspended between 50.5 percent No and 49.5 percent Yes. It was still too close to call, particularly given the extraordinary 95 percent turnout. It looked as though the No side was going to prevail, but as I headed upstairs to shave and shower, I still wasn't certain.

I was in the shower, in fact, trying to compose my thoughts for both scenarios, when Janet rushed into the bathroom and shouted, "They've just called it! At 10:20 they've called it a 1 percent victory for the No side! They've finished all the counting!"

"Thank God!" I yelled back.

Now I was feeling great. I dashed off to the television studio and arrived just in time to go on the air at 11:30. "My sense is that Canadians are going to argue about this for a long time to come," I told Cokie Roberts, "but I don't think people should interpret this big Yes vote as a break-up of the country. It was too fuzzy."

In fact, despite the closeness of the vote, I saw it as a huge victory for the federalists. True, they had begun with a massive lead. True, the separatists had gained some ground since the 1980 referendum. And, true, Chrétien and the No forces hadn't been prepared to deal with Lucien Bouchard, his emphasis on negotiating a new deal with Canada, and the shift of the young voters. They had stuck to their low-key script of economic threats and political self-interest. But the fact remained they managed to pluck victory from the jaws of defeat against an ambiguous question, a charismatic opponent, nationalist passions, and the worldwide resurgence of ethnic tribalism. The federalists had won.

"You know," I told the prime minister when I next saw him, "I've been through nine elections and I won eight. I lost the ninth by a quarter of 1 percent. Trust me: a win is a win is a win."

I was also convinced that President Clinton's statement had something to do with that win. It may be impossible to prove or measure how much, but given the closeness of the vote, every little thing had to be seen as making a difference. Canadians saved Canada, but I felt proud and delighted (as I do to this day) about our country's contribution. The president had been right to speak up. Far from meddling, he had merely said what he believed – and what the vast majority of Americans believed – in a straightforward, positive way. As for me, I felt as though I had just won a big election of my own. Part of that, I admit, was purely selfish. I had been spared the anguish and humiliation of having to go back to Washington or Michigan as the ambassador on whose watch Canada had broken apart.

After celebrating the survival of this great country with a glass of champagne, Janet and I went to bed, exhausted, elated, and very, very relieved.

~ IO ~

THANK YOU, HAROLD DICK

The morning after the referendum vote, despite having had only four and a half hours' sleep, I still felt euphoric. I spoke to both John Rae and Eddie Goldenberg, who explained that their forecasts had been accurate, except the undecideds had split evenly instead of preponderantly No. I called to thank our people at the State Department for their team effort. I did interviews on radio talk shows in Michigan and on C-SPAN. I congratulated Quebec Liberal leader Daniel Johnson and federal Conservative leader Jean Charest for their strong supporting roles. Charest's charismatic appeal to Quebeckers was especially noteworthy. Then Bernard Landry phoned. Jacques Parizeau was about to announce his resignation as premier of Quebec and leader of the Parti Québécois – to be replaced, everyone knew, by Lucien Bouchard – in the wake of the loss and his insensitive blaming of it, during a slurred speech on TV, on "money and the ethnic vote."

"This problem is deeply rooted," Landry said. "Everybody's overreacting to Parizeau's remarks. We're not blaming the minorities. It's the system. But, the truth is, the minorities haven't integrated at all. When they do, then we'll win in every region. And I'm not sure your president is well-informed on this issue. Like all you guys, he used the words 'strong and united.' But we're not united. Now Ottawa is going to have to deliver the goods. If they start from the basis that Canada is two nations, like our grandfathers and forefathers wanted, then there might be a way to work something out. In the meantime, I think our opinions deserve more careful examination by you Americans than Mr. Chrétien's. Remember, his own riding voted Yes, and so did Charest's."

"Look," I replied, "you're a nice man, you've been very gracious to me, and I respect your point of view. But I wasn't sent here to preside over the break-up of Canada. I did what the president and the American people wanted me to do."

— —

Even though life began to return to normal, the heart-stopping narrowness of the No side's victory continued to have a dramatic, even traumatic, impact on the whole nation. The strength of the Yes vote shocked many Canadians, who had passively trusted that a Quebec-born prime minister had had the whole situation under control and was going to win with at least 60 percent of the vote. They hadn't really appreciated how unpopular Jean Chrétien was in his home province because of his love for Canada, how revered Lucien Bouchard had become, or how deceptive the question had been. Many were angry and upset by how perilously close they had come to losing their country, and they blamed the prime minister. In the weeks that followed, when his immediate attempts to make the constitutional concessions he had promised during the campaign encountered resistance from the provinces, especially British Columbia, there was a widespread fatalism that Quebec separation was after all unavoidable.

Knowing how bad the situation had really become behind the scenes of the No campaign, I gave Chrétien and his team credit for rescuing the country. They were able to adapt in mid-course by promising constitutional changes that would give Quebec distinct status and a veto power, and, more effective yet, they had injected some passion into the pro-Canada forces with the Montreal rally. So I sympathized with the prime minister when all he heard from English Canada, instead of praise or thanks, was how he almost blew it. Even a midnight assassination attempt on his life that occurred a few days after the vote was turned into another way to poke fun at him. And I couldn't believe my ears when business leaders and informed observers said, oh well, there's not much difference between winning by 1 percent and losing by 1 percent. Boy, I thought, there sure is a difference. It's the difference between the end of the beginning and the beginning of the end.

My own opinion was that Ottawa should go now on the offensive. As I suggested to the prime minister during a small dinner party on January 6, 1996, "You can be the greatest goalie in the world, but if you keep letting the other guys shoot at you, sooner or later some jackass will score a goal. You have to begin to check the other guys at the other end of the rink."

The Chrétiens had obviously been through a stressful couple of months. I don't think they are the type of people to get depressed, but I did notice how weary and disappointed they looked on TV from all the carping and abuse. That night, however, I found both of them as gracious, animated, and opinionated as ever. They were full of details about the assassination attempt. A psychotic, knife-wielding francophone from Montreal had easily slipped past the RCMP security guards at 2:30 in the morning, wandered the house for half an hour, and sneaked into the private suite where the Chrétiens were sleeping. Awakened by a noise, Aline got up and saw a grubby figure moving outside their bedroom. "What are you doing here?" she yelled in English, and quickly slammed the door and locked it. She woke her husband – "You're dreaming" was his first response – and phoned the security detachment, while the prime minister picked up a twenty-pound Inuit sculpture to use as a defensive weapon. In telling the story, the prime minister actually went upstairs to fetch the carving in order to show us how large and heavy it was. If the intruder had gone up the front stairs instead of the back stairs, apparently, he would have had immediate, unimpeded access to them. But if he had broken through the bedroom door, I think Chrétien would have beaten the daylights out of him.

The Chrétiens were still clearly livid with the RCMP both for the break-in and the subsequent efforts to downplay its seriousness and perhaps cover up what really happened. The weapon, far from being the little penknife the Mounties described to the press, had been a six-inch hunting knife. It was Chrétien himself who first noticed it lying on the floor. "Hey, you forgot this," he had to yell to the guards as they were leaving. And, even more alarmingly, Aline had had to call them twice to come from their quarters at the gates. When they finally reached the house after a 20-minute delay, they realized they had forgotten the key, so they rang the doorbell and panicked the would-be assassin!

The prime minister was even angrier with the French-speaking media in Quebec for not connecting the intruder's mental state to the venomous rhetoric Lucien Bouchard had used against him during the referendum campaign. He was fed up, in fact, with the way the Quebec media constantly overlooked the racist or semi-racist remarks and downright lies of the separatists, while treating the slightest criticism of the separatists' tactics and disinformation as another betrayal of Quebec. I found his attitude, however exaggerated, both understandable and normal. Indeed, I've never known a politician who hasn't felt that way about the press at some point. "You will go down in history as the man who saved Canada," I told him, "but you'll never read that in the newspapers. Your grandchildren will hear it, but you won't."

It was and is my firm belief that the entire world – with the possible exception of France – wants Canada to stay united. Some countries were even annoyed with Canadians for allowing Quebec to vote on separation, because they saw it as a bad precedent for their own struggles against divisive ethnic movements. And the United States, in particular, doesn't want to have ethnic tribalism, whose harmful effects it sees everywhere else, take root in North America in the form of a separate Quebec. Yet many observers were beginning to fear that it was only a matter of time before another vote was held and Quebec became independent.

As I saw it, therefore, the Canadian government needed to put everybody on notice that separation was not inevitable and Canada would act to preserve the union at all costs. Furthermore, to the extent that anyone figured it was inevitable, I also thought they should assume that large parts of Quebec, including Montreal, the Ottawa Valley, the Eastern Townships, and the aboriginal lands in the North, would remain part of Canada, since they had voted overwhelmingly No during the referendum and did not share the separatists' vision.

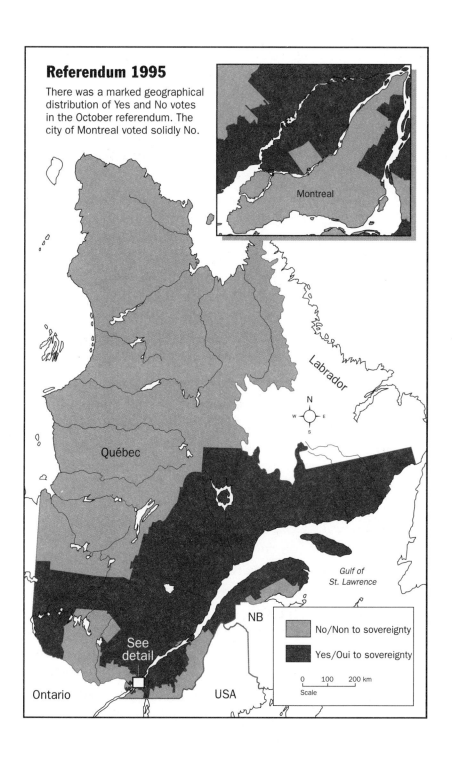

Referendum 1995

There was a marked geographical
distribution of Yes and No votes
in the October referendum. The
city of Montreal voted solidly No.

Montreal

Labrador

N
W   E
S

Québec

Gulf of
St. Lawrence

NB

No/Non to sovereignty

Yes/Oui to sovereignty

0   100   200 km
Scale

See
detail

Ontario

USA

Given how deeply Quebeckers care about what other countries think of them, not least the United States, I recommended to the prime minister that each and every ambassador in Ottawa should be contacted by a high-level government leader and told how much of a threat the separatist agenda is to the well-being of all Canadians, to all ethnic groups inside Canada, and to the Canadian traditions of tolerance and human rights. The foreign ambassadors should be asked to take that message to their governments back home, and the Canadian ambassadors around the world should reinforce it with visits to the leaders of their host countries. Credible and effective pro-Canada spokesmen such as Pierre Trudeau, Paul Martin, Jean Charest, or Brian Tobin should take the federalist arguments into the American media, to counter Bouchard's efforts to put a respectable face on the separatist ideology in international circles. I also thought that Ottawa should organize another huge rally in Montreal to thank the people for their overwhelming support and remind Quebec federalists that they aren't being forgotten or abandoned. Finally, I mentioned what I called the Jim Blanchard passport test. If the worst happened and the Yes side won by a narrow vote, I would announce that every individual Quebecker could make a choice. Those who wished to have a Canadian passport would apply to one office before a certain date; those who wished to have a Quebec passport would apply to another office at the same time; and the boundary lines of any new sovereign state would, as far as possible, reflect the results. (This, of course, was a blunt, practical, American idea that no one was ready to embrace.)

On January 24, 1996, I went to Montreal to have lunch with Pierre Trudeau, in hopes of persuading him to deliver a speech in Washington on behalf of Canadian unity. We dined alone at the Mount Royal Club, where, in one of those coincidences that continually reminded me what a small country Canada really is, we ran into Robert Bourassa, the former Quebec premier. As we sat down, I couldn't help but notice how fit Trudeau looked at the age of seventy-six: same striking features, piercing blue eyes, strong hands, sharp mind, and clearly articulated viewpoint. He seemed keenly aware of what was going on in Canada and around the world, and appreciated Clinton's statement during the referendum campaign.

Though the staunchest federalist of his generation, he hadn't been invited to participate in the No campaign, and on the whole he didn't think Chrétien's strategy had worked very well. The economic threats had worn thin, and there hadn't been enough positive said about Canada or an appeal to a higher calling. He felt it was like saying, if you want to be rich, vote No. As for his making a speech in Washington, he seemed genuinely and pleasantly surprised to hear that I thought it would stir a lot of interest and could have a significant impact. But he seemed very reluctant to come out of political retirement to do it.

The mood around our Montreal consulate was that Chrétien wasn't capable of coming up with a formula to save Canada, especially given the popularity of Lucien Bouchard. Bouchard, by this time, had resigned as leader of the Bloc Québécois in Ottawa to officially take over from Jacques Parizeau as premier of Quebec. I found some hope at dinner that night, however, when we were host to four strong Quebec nationalists – a publisher, an economist, and two trade association presidents. At first they all sounded like separatists, but as the conversation unfolded, a different picture emerged. They were worried that the rest of Canada, despite the close call, wasn't seriously addressing the issue of how to keep Quebec within Canada. They said that no one in

Quebec really wanted another referendum soon. They believed that the Yes vote had been mostly a mandate to negotiate a better deal with Canada, not to separate, and they seemed shocked that anyone would have interpreted it otherwise. In fact, they sounded as though they desperately wanted to stay in Canada. I found it fascinating and somewhat perplexing.

A couple of weeks later, on February 8th, Janet and I returned to Montreal to have dinner with Lucien Bouchard and his American wife, Audrey Best. We invited them to pick the restaurant, imagining they would suggest some discreet and exquisite place on Rue Saint-Denis, and we were somewhat taken aback when they chose the Café de la Paix at the Ritz-Carlton Hotel, the one-time bastion of the English-Montreal plutocrats. One person in the cocktail lounge even hissed as we passed, but everyone pretended not to hear. The evening was intended to be a relaxed and friendly get-together, and the Bouchards turned out to be particularly enjoyable company – talkative, open, and bright.

Both were well plugged into U.S. history and politics. Bouchard made it clear from the start that his hero was John Kennedy, along with Churchill, De Gaulle, and Roosevelt, and he appeared to have read every book ever written about the Kennedys. Audrey had just finished the new biography of Pamela Harriman. Her father was an active Republican and Steve Forbes supporter in Orange County, California. When I asked if she considered herself an American, a Canadian, or a Quebecker, she stated firmly that she was an American. She spoke of eventually sending their two young sons to college in the United States.

At one point I asked Bouchard if he had been in Montreal in 1967 when De Gaulle made his famous *"Vive le Québec libre"* speech. No, but he had seen him in Quebec City in

1960. He remembered lunging forward to shake De Gaulle's hand and being cut on the face by an invisible wire used for crowd control. He certainly made it sound like an important moment in his life.

Much more important, of course, was his near-death experience, and it occupied a lot of our conversation. He had had the same strep infection that Audrey and the children had; it just attacked him differently. When the doctors diagnosed the problem as flesh-eating disease, they were able to amputate his leg and apply the proper antibiotics just in time. He's now, he said, a case study in the *New England Journal of Medicine*. I must say we had a very enjoyable evening with the Bouchards.

The next day, February 9, I met him again, this time formally with our staffs present, and his tone was much more reserved and militant. After outlining his goals for improving Quebec's crippled economy, by reducing its $55-billion debt and launching an aggressive economic development program, he explained that his purpose was to establish a solid foundation before asking Quebeckers to vote again on sovereignty. I asked him if he thought a solution could be negotiated with Ottawa.

"You know Chrétien?" he said. "He's a good friend of yours, is he not? Do you honestly think he is prepared to work out something with us, that he is prepared to compromise?"

"Yes, I do," I said. "He's a practical man. I think he can be flexible. Even if he doesn't know it now, his advisers and the leaders in the rest of Canada will insist that something gets worked out."

"Why would English-speaking Canada be willing to help us achieve our goals when they weren't before?" he asked.

"It depends on what your goals are," I replied. "If you want to leave Canada, they won't. If you just want more respect, that's another matter. They didn't think that a united Canada was at risk before. Now they do. People take the things that are most close to them for granted until they lose, or almost lose, them."

I don't know what Bouchard thought of what I said, but he knew I would be leaving Canada shortly and he wouldn't have to deal with me any longer. Nor, with others in the room, did I expect him to show any flexibility. But I did come away with the impression that his private self was less ideological and more practical than his public persona. Like most politicians, he was a man who wanted to be admired, and it struck me that he wanted to go down in history as Quebec's greatest leader rather than as someone who took risks that ended up hurting his people.

Later, after lunch with John Rae, Janet and I found ourselves walking past Notre-Dame, the beautiful old church in Old Montreal. We slipped in and lit three candles: one for Canada, one for Bill Clinton, and one for extra measure.

A couple of days later I tested Bouchard's argument with Jean Chrétien. "The problem is," the prime minister responded, "anything we offer him is never enough. He doesn't know what he wants. He just wants to buy time. If he wants a deal, he should tell me what he wants. I might be able to help him out. I can sign a deal; I'm still popular; Canada will support me. But the separatists are afraid to sign a deal with us. They're afraid because they don't want to look foolish to later generations of separatists. So they'll never sign anything."

Unfortunately, I thought he was probably right. But I took comfort in remembering two important things, however complicated and problematic the issue of Canadian unity will always remain. One, most Quebeckers, including most French-speaking Quebeckers, are *not* separatists at heart.

And, two, the break-up of Canada is *not* an inevitability. Quebec is at the core of the Canadian personality. It has helped make Canada such an enviable and distinctive nation. But Canada is also at the core of the Quebec personality. And it too has helped make Quebec strong and unique.

～　～

Once the Quebec referendum was over and won, I began to feel that my task in Canada was done. The great battle had been fought, the forces of good had triumphed (at least for the moment), and within days I was back dealing with another bureaucratic attempt to push the bill against *Sports Illustrated* through the parliamentary system. These guys just can't help themselves, I thought, shaking my head. It was time to think about leaving.

"We can't seem to get Blanchard out of Canada," the president once said, but I knew if I stayed too long, I would effectively be retiring from U.S. politics, which I wasn't ready to do. Indeed, I had basically told the White House that once the referendum was over, I could focus on coming back to help reelect the Clinton-Gore team and worry about the Democrats in Michigan. Now Bruce Lindsey and Mack McLarty were on the line saying that the president was expecting me to play an active, if not formal, role in the campaign.

I certainly wasn't in any hurry to leave Canada, but I didn't want to be caught in a situation where, some day in March or April, I got a call from the president pressing me to be back within a week. And since I didn't want to be a paid staffer on the campaign, I needed to make arrangements to return to my old law firm. In other words, I wanted to have time to organize a smooth transition, wrap up any outstanding matters, and say my farewells properly. I wrote a letter to the president to that effect on January 11, 1996. "In view of the incredible problems the White House and Bill Clinton have had with making personnel decisions," I noted in my journal, "who knows when I will hear back."

One of the things you hear from everyone in the foreign service is that your farewell is one of the most wonderful experiences you will ever have. When word leaked out at the end of January that we would be leaving in March, and then again after I officially announced it on February 14th, Janet and I found ourselves wined and dined around Ottawa and across the country. The Martins, the Raes, the Donolos, the Manleys, the Marchis, the de Chastelains, and ultimately the Chrétiens themselves were among our many Canadian friends who gave dinner parties in our honor, as did the Italian ambassador and Mrs. Cambiaso. There were luncheons hosted by the minister of Foreign Affairs, the ambassador from Mexico, and the PMO. There were receptions organized by David Peterson, Tom d'Aquino, the Ottawa diplomatic corps, Mayor Jacquelin Holzman of Ottawa, and Peter Clark, chair of the Ottawa-Carleton Municipal Region. There was a breakfast at the National Press Club and an exhausting round of radio, television, and newspaper "departure interviews." It was like having a front-row seat at your own memorial service, and it wasn't like anything I had ever experienced before. I had always been seen in play in American politics. Even when I was defeated as governor or left for Ottawa, my competitors assumed I'd be back someday, which made them hesitate about saying anything complimentary. In Canada, however, nobody was worried about my ever running against them, so everyone felt free to go overboard. People kept saying such nice things that I joked, "If I had thought it was going to be this good, I would have left long ago."

The prime minister's dinner was held at his home on Sunday, March 10th. The Chrétiens were as warm and hospitable as the first time we visited them at 24 Sussex Drive. There were thirty-seven guests, including most of the senior cabinet ministers and their spouses, the key staff members from the PMO, Raymond and Kay Chrétien, David Peterson, Jim and Heather Peterson, Yousuf and Estrellita Karsh, André and France Desmarais, Jim and Marian Walsh, and my son, Jay. After photographs and cocktails, we were escorted into the beautifully decorated dining room for an elegant and delicious dinner, following which champagne was poured and the prime minister rose to give a toast. I could hardly believe the honor done me when he said, while I blushed with uncharacteristic modesty, "Jim Blanchard has been the best ambassador the United States has ever sent to Canada. He is a good diplomat and a good politician."

"If you have to go, this is the way to go," I remarked in reply. Then I talked about how wonderful everybody had been to us and how much we would miss Canada. It had become our second home, and we were only leaving, with deep regret, to serve a good cause: the re-election of President Clinton. Everyone cheered. "We want you to know that Canada will always be in our hearts," I concluded. "Wherever we go or whatever we do, we will stand on guard for thee." Then I proposed a toast of my own, to the prime minister, Aline, and a strong, healthy, prosperous, and united Canada.

Afterwards, as we circulated in the living room, I was struck by the sense of warmth that permeated the house. The kindness, the sincerity, the gentleness, and the genuineness of these people, the top leaders of Canada, was heartwarming. Janet, Jay, and I have never forgotten the spirit of that evening. On our way home, Jay, who had seen more than his fair share of political dinners, said, "That was very refreshing. Everyone meant what they said."

Knowing Canadians as we now did, and knowing they wouldn't leave until the guest of honor did, and knowing that most of them liked to get to bed early to be ready for work the next morning, we departed promptly at 10:30. As we stepped out the front door, we looked back and saw all our friends bunched behind us on the vestibule stairs, ready to follow us out the door. We waved, they smiled, and we knew then we would always be part Canadian.

— —

Whenever I'm asked what I have learned from reading my Ottawa journals, the answer is many things. I realized, for example, that I tended to remember the times when I had been right and forget the times when I had been wrong. My journals forced me to admit that I had been wrong about the Gore-Perot debate on NAFTA, wrong about the Carter mission to Haiti, wrong about the political resilience of Bill Clinton. I came across enough errors and misjudgments, in fact, to keep me from crowing whenever I happened to be right.

My journals also underscored how often the really interesting and important events happened outside my official schedule. My first meeting with Jean Chrétien as prime minister wasn't on my schedule, for example: it was arranged spontaneously during a telephone call with Eddie Goldenberg. Running into Brian Tobin at the Canada Day celebrations while trying to resolve the fishing dispute was hardly prearranged. Nor was coming out of a meeting with Jacques Parizeau in Quebec City to learn that Lucien Bouchard was fighting for his life in a Montreal hospital, and watching the whole city stop as the world had stopped at the moment of President Kennedy's assassination, and realizing that Bouchard had just been canonized politically.

The lesson, I believe, is that people with important jobs, no matter what their field, must always leave themselves plenty of unstructured time for thinking, reading, strategizing, moving around, and connecting with others. They need to be rested enough, flexible enough, and lucky enough to respond to whatever comes their way. I routinely began my days in Ottawa in reflective solitude in front of the picture window overlooking the Ottawa River and Gatineau Hills, and then I planned my day's initiatives and calls, all before I headed to the office. "Controlling and managing the schedule is the key to success and substance and sanity," I wrote in my journal. "It's absolutely the whole ball of wax for anybody who wants to succeed in public life or business."

My third impression was how varied, fascinating, significant, and fun the job of United States ambassador to Canada can be. I had a sense of that going in, which was why I had wanted the job, but it turned out to be even more and even better than I anticipated. A lot of Americans imagine that the duties of an ambassador to Canada must be a walk in the park. Canadians are similar to us; they're nice people; and they treat American tourists well. I've met scores of U.S. businessmen who once conquered a fishing lake in northern Ontario or dined in one of Montreal's many fine restaurants, all of whom assumed that the post was frivolous and irrelevant, a cushy reward for past services.

It's true that I could have done less traveling, played more golf, read more books, and learned how to ski. Ambassadors are free to structure their own time, after all, and given the high quality and hard work of our career foreign-service personnel, they can easily coast and leave the tough business to their staff. In my case, because I knew my ambassadorship was likely to be only a three-year experience, I wanted to squeeze every drop of activity and achievement out of it. Perhaps if I had thought I was going to be in Canada for eight years, I might have slowed down a bit and had even more fun than I did. But I could feel the clock ticking every single day, and I was very busy because the whole Canada-U.S. relationship is very busy.

Moreover, while I obviously benefited from having remarkable access to Canada's decision-makers – certainly more than any foreign ambassador to the United States can get in Washington – it meant that I felt under constant pressure to be knowledgeable, effective, and hard-working. It didn't take me long to discover that you can make a fool of yourself much more quickly in the eyes of the politicians, the media, and the general public in a small, relatively uncomplicated system such as Canada's than in the huge networks of the United States. I concluded, in fact, that every U.S. ambassador to Canada ought to travel the length and breadth of the country early and often.

The fourth impression I drew from my journals was that I couldn't have done half what I did, whether traveling to all the provinces or speaking to hundreds of groups or dealing with the prime minister and his cabinet ministers, without the superb assistance of Jim Walsh, who basically ran the embassy for me; my secretary, Joanne Holliday; and the rest of my State Department colleagues in Ottawa and Washington. Too many Americans, including too many members of Congress, have a low opinion of our foreign-service personnel, often dismissing them as high-living bureaucrats ready to sell out their country's interests at a moment's notice. On the contrary, I found the overwhelming majority of them extremely well-trained, usually multilingual, highly dedicated people, and the fact that they get rotated every three years minimizes any of the "clientitis" to which they might be exposed. Just as they start to feel attached to a particular country, they're sent somewhere else. In my experience, they're usually much more committed to advancing U.S. foreign-policy interests as a whole and have a better sense of where and when to apply pressure, where and when to ease off, than the officials of other government departments, who are mostly focused on short-term, single-issue solutions.

It's my belief that the president and the secretary of state ought to give more attention to reinvigorating the foreign service. It's traditionally been the élite of government service, attracting many of the brightest graduates in liberal arts or international relations from our best universities. From my own experience, I would advise every new ambassador to treat them with respect and as friends: they're loyal, they're helpful, and they'll make you look good. And their job is still of crucial importance to the United States, indeed to the world. However secondary foreign affairs may appear to many Americans at times, our freedom and our interests depend on the leadership and stability other countries need and expect from us. That is a duty and burden from which we must never withdraw.

But it's also my belief that the foreign service needs reform and renewal, not simply cables, lectures, and cutbacks. The State Department could use many more people out in the world and a lot fewer in Washington, where layers after layers oversee each other and do many of the same things. The personnel appointment process should be re-examined, so that so many excellent, experienced people aren't forced out at the prime of their careers because there isn't any room for them in the few senior positions. And, if my experience in Ottawa was anything to go by, the administrative division, as opposed to the so-called political, economic, or consular "cones," is in the greatest need of an overhaul.

Bright young people who go into the foreign service to analyze politics or apply economics or see the world aren't generally interested in ordering large quantities of toilet paper or invoicing travel budgets. As a result, between all the political and commercial activity, my notes were full of relentless, frustrating attempts to get adequate water pressure in the residence or new carpeting for the living room. That said, our love of Canada was obviously influenced by the fact that we were living a charmed life in a beautiful house with a first-rate staff at home and at the office.

All through the journals, too, I found myself wrestling to define, explain, and pinpoint all the differences I saw between the United States and Canada. It became partly a game, partly an obsession. Every day I learned something new about Canada and its people, from the pronunciation of "progress" and "schedule" to the usage of "college" and "holiday." Americans often like to tell Canadians that they're just like us. We think it's a compliment, a way to make them feel good. In fact, it's often taken as an insult. Saying "You're just like me" can come across as saying "You have no identity, no uniqueness, no individual character." Which, in the case of Canada, isn't true at all. Indeed, our differences start right there. The best thing you can say to an American is the worst thing you can say to a Canadian.

Nevertheless, the differences are usually so subtle and blurred that Americans rarely notice anything interesting or different north of the border. Nor do we often detect the hundreds of thousands of Canadians who work and live in our midst – in a way it's like the invasion of the body-snatchers – including Donald Sutherland, Dan Aykroyd, Neil Young, Jim Carrey, Joni Mitchell, James Cameron, Céline Dion, Morley Safer, Peter Jennings, Robert MacNeil, and William

Shatner, as well as 10 percent of the CEOs on the *Fortune* 500. (In fact, *The Economist* once declared that "Bill Clinton is a closet Canadian.") Certainly, compared to the French, the Italians, or the British, the majority of Canadians don't look or sound all that different. And we certainly have a lot in common, in values, policies, language, tourism, and family connections.

But if you've lived in both countries, you see a lot of differences. Canada has a different political system. It has a different geography. It has a different history. And it has a different culture – not radically different, perhaps, but different nonetheless. It would surprise most Americans to discover that the Canadians look at the world differently than we do. As Jake Warren, a former Canadian ambassador to the United States, once explained it to me, "When Americans wake up in the morning, they look east to Europe or west to Asia, maybe south from time to time. They never really look north. But when Canadians wake up in the morning, they may look east or west, but by God they always have one eye on what's going on to their south."

The border is a one-way mirror. Canadians are watching us on a regular basis. They're following our ups and downs, our successes and failures, our moments great and sad, sometimes cheering us on, sometimes shadow-boxing with us. When we look north, all we see is a reflection of ourselves.

In the immediate days and months after we left Canada, both Janet and I were struck by its instant and almost complete absence. After almost three years of eating, sleeping, and breathing Canada, we were cut off cold-turkey from a magical realm that, for a brief time, had been our whole life. "It's like it all never happened," Janet remarked. "It all seems like a wonderful dream," I replied. The whole world of activity, excitement, and fun with which we had been so completely engaged vanished from the media and the consciousness of those around us. And yet, despite that low profile, I now knew how much respect and leverage Canada actually has in Washington. American officials truly value what Canadians think, and as I witnessed with NAFTA, Bosnia, and Haiti, what Canada does can have a real impact on American policy. I also saw how much Canada's friendship with the United States earns it respect and leverage around the world too. That friendship should be cherished and strengthened, not taken for granted or frittered away on petty squabbles.

Certainly, for Janet and me, Canada is much less "the invisible world next door" than it used to be. We've kept in touch with many of our Canadian friends. We're often invited to Canadian events in Washington. And we're frequently in Toronto, Montreal, or Ottawa on business or just to see our friends. In Michigan we avidly follow what's happening on CBC-TV, and I even get *The Globe and Mail* every day at my office in Washington. But the reality remains that Canada seems very far away to most Americans, despite being so very close. We're ten times larger as a society; we're fundamentally self-absorbed and isolationist as a nation; and Canadians are generally so quiet and self-effacing.

If I learned anything from my stay in Canada, I learned that our two societies and nations have a great deal to learn from each other. Canadians, in my opinion, can use more of our optimism, entrepreneurship, and sense of unity. Even though Quebec City was founded more than a decade before the Pilgrims landed at Plymouth Rock, Canada is still a young and evolving country, in its issues, its attitudes, and its policies, compared to the United States. We were forged as a nation by 1776, after all, while Canada wasn't officially created until 1867 and it remained almost a ward of Great

Britain until after World War I. We Americans can use more of Canada's tolerance, compassion, restraint, and social justice. Beyond a shadow of a doubt, both Janet and I feel we are better Americans because of our days in Canada.

Finally, what shone throughout the journals – and I hope shines throughout this book – was the debt I owed to the work, support, and love of my wife, Janet. Because my son, Jay, was grown up and working in Washington, first with Senator John Glenn and then with the secretary of Education Richard Riley, Janet and I were free to share the joys and the burdens of the job, from the constant entertaining to the extensive traveling to the late-night meetings. So we were a team in Canada, and both the State Department and the Canadians benefited from her own experience and knowledge of politics and the White House. She was unofficially dubbed the "Ambassadrina" in recognition of her contribution.

~ ~

Always a hard worker, Janet never worked harder than in those final weeks of receptions, dinners, media interviews, last-minute guests, and packing up. By March 14th I was frantically trying to process every last letter, decision, and piece of paper across my desk at the office – including hundreds of personally signed notes to cabinet members, business leaders, fellow ambassadors, the media, and friends across the country – only interrupted by a farewell lunch at a local Chinese restaurant with my dear friend Eddie Goldenberg. My ambition was to leave an office that was cleaner and better organized than any other in my lifetime. I did, thanks to everyone in the office. Meanwhile, Janet was supervising the shippers at the house as to what was going to our house in Michigan, what to our apartment in Washington, what to the law firm, what to storage. By the time I got home for a "last supper" with Jim and Marian Walsh, the huge house was virtually empty, without a book on the shelf or a painting on the wall, little more than a few suitcases, a couple of boxes, and my journals.

The four of us ate by my "window on world" while watching another magnificent sunset over the river and the hills, a wonderful and fitting finale to our last evening in Canada. And after the Walshes left, Janet and I sat by the fire in the family room, ruminating about what wonderful people they both are and how much honor they do to the reputation of the United States foreign service. It was a little eerie and somewhat sad amid that emptiness. But there was also a sense of completion and satisfaction that we had been given such a wonderful opportunity, had made the most of it, and had handled our departure as well as we could.

That night we stayed in the President's Bedroom because every ambassador has to bring a bed (as well as sheets, towels, and spreads) and ours had already been sent home. I realized, with some embarrassment, that the mattress wasn't as good as ours. Too bad, Mr. President, I thought, if I had known, I would have bought you a new one. Worse, the next morning when I went to take a shower, I discovered that it was all screwed up and you couldn't get a decent spray. When I thought of all the VIPs who must have cursed it, I felt mortified, but no one ever said anything about it.

Then came our final official day in Canada. March 15th was a beautiful day, however tough emotionally. I was up at 6:30 taking pictures of the sunrise, then I showered, shaved, and finished packing. At ten o'clock Janet and I headed over to the office for coffee and doughnuts with the staff from all of our agencies and the foreign-service nationals from Ottawa. They gave us a lovely old print of the Parliament Buildings. Jim Walsh bade us a formal farewell; John Stewart, on behalf of our Canadian employees, thanked us for our special attention to them; and Yousuf Karsh presented both us and the embassy with the portrait he had taken in New York. Then I went back to my office for one last round of letter-signing and photographs. Finally, around 1:15, I hugged Joanne Holliday and Linda Grace, our two hard-working secretaries, and Jim Walsh walked me down to the front door where I posed with Vaughn Cameron and Jim's driver, Robin Smith, for our final photographs. Then Vaughn drove us home for the last time. There I walked around the empty rooms, lingered once more at the magnificent view of the river, and thought how truly blessed Janet and I had been to get this assignment and how much admiration and affection we had for this country.

I remember thinking how happy I was that I hadn't left Canada prematurely to run for the Senate or become DNC chair. I felt it was right that I had stayed to push Open Skies. It was in the stars that I should have remained for the referendum campaign and done my small part to help save the country. In my mind I thanked the people who had serendipitously guided me toward the job: thank you, David Peterson, thank you, Pamela Harriman, thank you, Tom Weston. And I thanked those who had given me the job: thank you, Bill Clinton and Al Gore, thank you, Warren Christopher, thank you Mack McLarty, thank you, Sandy Berger, thank you, Bruce Lindsey.

Then my mind raced across the countless men and women, Americans and Canadians alike, who had made the job so interesting and fun. And it settled, oddly enough, on a tall, distinguished-looking man, but dressed casually and wearing a baseball cap, who stopped me one day at Ottawa Airport and asked if I were Ambassador Blanchard. Yes, I said. Well, he said, my name is Harold Dick, and I'm just an average citizen here in Ottawa, but I want to thank you for the job you have done as ambassador. I've watched you on TV, he said, and you've been a real friend of Canada. Thank you, he said, and he just walked off. It was as tribute as great as the prime minister's toast. And so, standing in the empty house, I thought, I should thank you, Harold Dick, thank you very much.

Janet and I went downstairs, where all seven of the household staff were lined up as in a military inspection, and I gave each of them a letter of recommendation to whom it may concern. They gave Janet sandwiches and carrots for our drive to the States and presented us with a beautiful painting of people skating on the canal. Then, with everyone waving and yelling goodbye, I carried Janet out across the threshold – to no one's surprise because they knew us by now. We got in the Jeep and took one more look at the house and our Canadian family, who were still waving as we drove away. A wonderful part of our life had ended.

An hour later we came to the Canada-United States border crossing at the Thousand Islands bridge between Ontario and upstate New York. A lump came to my throat, and I could feel tears beginning to well up in my eyes. "We haven't lost a job," I said to comfort both Janet and myself. "We've gained a country."

ACKNOWLEDGMENTS

A personal memoir usually inspires a certain caution on the part of the reader since most writers tend to inflate their impact on the course of events. As John Kenneth Galbraith wrote recently, "There's always a danger as well as a pleasure in exaggerating one's own role in history; nothing, in consequence, is so rightly suspect."

Nevertheless, my work in Canada was so exciting and interesting I couldn't resist telling the story of our time there, even at the risk of appearing self-serving. But, first, a few disclaimers.

The words and thoughts expressed in this book are entirely my own. These were my observations about Canada and my feelings about the issues and events that occurred during my assignment in Ottawa.

In addition, I received a great deal of help on the job and our successes were the product of many individuals, not always referred to in the text. For example, Ambassador Raymond Chrétien and his wife, Kay, were very much part of the issue management and accomplishments during the years of 1994–96, as was Ambassador John de Chastelain and his wife, Marianne, during my first year in Canada in 1993.

The staff at our U.S. Embassy in Ottawa was fantastic and I couldn't have functioned without them. Our Canada Desk back in Washington, as well as our Bureau of Canadian and European Affairs, was always supportive and helpful, as were a host of other officials in Washington and at our six consulates in Canada. We had a team effort, which is the way U.S. Missions abroad are supposed to function.

Putting this book together was also a team effort, starting with the support of Janet and Jay Blanchard and extending to many friends on both sides of the border. These include my law partners at Verner, Liipfert, Bernhard, McPherson and Hand, in particular Harry McPherson, Larry Levinson, and Mike Roberts who were notable for their encouragement. Helpful as an adviser was Marty Lobel and my fellow directors at Nortel were also supportive. At the State Department, I would like to thank Deputy Assistant Secretary of State E. Anthony Wayne and Eric A. Kunsman, Director of Canadian Affairs, for their help in obtaining the necessary clearances for publication of this book. As stated above, the opinions and characterizations are those of the author and do not necessarily represent official positions of the United States government.

Logistically, I especially want to acknowledge my colleagues at EdperBrascan in Toronto, including Trevor Eyton, Jack Cockwell, and Bob Harding, and their assistants, Sue McGovern, Carol Parker, and Rita Wong, for their generous hospitality while I spent countless hours working on the book in their conference room high above the shiny blue waters of Lake Ontario.

Then there was the huge undertaking of organizing three years of journal notes. I wrote down my feelings and observations four or five times a week from 1993 through 1996 (partly inspired by Galbraith's *Ambassador's Journal*). A couple of thousand pages, as well as several hundred other documents, needed to be reviewed. For help in this effort I recruited Ron Graham, the best in the business. He was the editor of this book, and while the words are mine, both from my journals and extensive interviews, it was Ron Graham who helped me organize this effort. Simply put, I could not have done this book without him. Poor Ron even had to sit and listen to me ramble on and on for one whole month over a tape recorder. Together we worked very hard to tell my story.

And then there were the friends and colleagues who reviewed our work and made many helpful suggestions and corrections. They include, but are not limited to, Jim Walsh, David Weiss, Rosemary Freeman, Ron Thayer and Carolyn (Sparky) Hutting.

At the office my assistant, Kathy Burk, was most helpful, as was Joanne Holliday, my foreign service secretary for three years in Ottawa. At McClelland & Stewart in Toronto, Jonathan Webb's editorial assistance was also appreciated, as was Doug Gibson's encouragement and advice. In Michigan, I want to thank Sleeping Bear Press and its publisher, Brian Lewis, for their interest and support. I also want to acknowledge the support and encouragement I have received during my career from my family. My mother, Rosalie, instilled in her son a strong sense of public service. I carry her optimism with me wherever I go, including Canada.

Two final notes: I deeply appreciate the help and confidence both David Peterson and Avie Bennett placed in me in helping launch this project.

Lastly, I want to acknowledge the dedication of the members of the United States Foreign Service and their families, wherever they may be. Thank you for serving America and thank you for helping build a better world.

JAMES J. BLANCHARD
MICHIGAN, JUNE 1998

INDEX